ATTACK
AND
INTERCEPTOR
JETS

MICHAEL SHARPE

BARNES
&NOBLE
BOOKS
NEW YORK

This edition published by Barnes & Noble, Inc.,
by arrangement with Brown Packaging Books Ltd
1999 Barnes & Noble Books

M 10 9 8 7 6 5 4 3 2

ISBN: 0-7607-1258-1

Editorial and design by
Brown Packaging Books Ltd
Bradley's Close
74–77 White Lion Street
London N1 9PF

Design: Robert Mathias Publishing Workshop

Printed in Singapore

PICTURE CREDITS:
TRH Pictures

ARTWORK CREDITS
All artworks Aerospace Publishing except the following:
Bob Garwood: 73, 75, 193, 259, 296, 300, 309, 311

CONTENTS

Introduction

The first faltering steps into military jet technology were made some 70 years ago, in the golden era of canvas and wire aeroplanes and steam engines. As early as 1928, RAF officer Frank (later Sir Frank) Whittle patented the design of an engine based on a theory of propulsion that was destined to revolutionise global transportation. It would have taken a brave man, however, among the privileged few who witnessed the first run of Frank Whittle's crude jet engine, or the first flight of the Heinkel He 178, to predict the enormous impact that the jet engine would have on the aviation scene and on society as a whole.

The effect has been nothing less than revolutionary. Jet propulsion has enabled aircraft to fly to new heights and ever greater speeds. Transcontinental travel has become commonplace. Indeed, it is often said that the world itself has become a 'smaller place'. All of this can be attributed to the jet engine and the men whose faith, vision and tenacity

Above: The Me 262 was the first operational jet fighter. Its introduction into service earlier in World War II could have made a major impact on the outcome of the war.

Above: The MiG-15 was a major shock for the UN forces when it appeared in the skies over Korea.

created it. Although they were divided by nationality, politics and even war, the jet pioneers are united by a common military affiliation. In the case of Frank Whittle this proved as much of a hindrance as a benefit; for Ernst Heinkel, working in a country that prided itself on the practical application of technology, the opposite was true.

It would not be untrue to say that the single biggest motivating factor for the development of the jet engine was the desire to produce better, more capable and thus more lethal aircraft for military purposes. Whittle foresaw his engines powering transonic aircraft on transatlantic mail routes, but struggled with officialdom throughout the 1930s to generate anything approaching the enthusiasm his pioneering research merited. Only when the dark clouds of war hung over Europe was Whittle accorded the resources he needed. By 1941, Whittle was still struggling manfully with a small team that represented the entire Allied jet research programme. In Germany the jet propulsion programme had started later and yet had spawned the first jet aircraft. By comparison, in 1941 six separate teams – backed by substantial investment form the Third Reich – were employed in solving the inherent problems of the new technology.

When it became clear that Germany had stolen the lead in creating the first flying jet aircraft, it was perhaps inevitable that it would field the first jet aircraft in combat. In 1944, the Messerschmitt 262-A1 began operations and proved itself more than capable of catching the fastest and highest-flying aircraft the Allies could field. Suddenly the piston-engined aircraft was outmoded. The impact of the Me 262 on the air war over Europe was lessened to a degree by Hitler's insistence that many production aircraft should be equipped as fighter-bombers to attack advancing Allied forces (Me 262-1a), when they could have been far better employed in the interceptor role. Me 262 units were also forced to operate from bases in Germany that were subject to virtually constant attack from advancing Allied forces. Had the Me 262 entered service a year earlier, the air war over Europe would almost certainly have proved less decisive.

The Allies had nothing in the league of the Me 262. The Gloster Meteor F. Mk 1 began operational service in July 1944, but a poor rate of climb and modest range made it unsuitable for combat. The British Air Ministry had generously supplied the US with complete access to British research into jet technology, enabling the Americans to consolidate the Allied effort and throw behind it the might of their aircraft industry, but nevertheless when World War II ended the Germans were still far ahead. Germany was systematically stripped of her jet expertise by all the victorious powers, eager to lay their hands on this revolutionary new technology. Britain possessed similar expertise, but failed to exploit it, reduced her aircraft industry to a level of stagnation and thus lost the lead in jet technology. The influence of German research can be seen in the designs of American and Soviet aircraft for the next decade (the rocket that took men to the Moon has its ancestry in the V-2 rocket). Perhaps the most significant area of German research was in aerodynamics, particularly the swept wing. By incorporating this with jet propulsion, the gate was opened for a new generation of high-speed, supersonic aircraft.

MIG-15 VERSUS SABRE

If the summer of 1944 was the baptism of the military jet, then it earned its spurs in the Korean War. The United States Air Force (USAF) entered the war confident in the belief that it possessed the most advanced aircraft technology in the world, and the early actions of the war seemed to bear this fact out. Nothing prepared it for the profound shock of confronting Soviet-built MiG-15s in the skies over Korea. This agile, quick little fighter at once redressed the balance in air power over Korea and proved to the West that the Soviets had both the technology and industrial capacity to produce advanced jet aircraft. The appearance of the MiG-15 provoked a flurry of developments in the US. Foremost among these was the legendary North American F-84 Sabre. This aircraft, piloted by skilled and experienced pilots, did more than any other to win the air war in Korea. The war also highlighted some of the deficiencies of jet aircraft. Manoeuvrablity had been sacrificed for speed, take-off runs compared to piston-engined fighters were much longer (precluding jet operations from rough forward airstrips), and fuel consumption was prohibitively high for US squadrons forced to make long transit flights from southern bases to the combat area over the Yalu River.

During the early 1950s both the US and USSR, with their overseas commitments, sought to develop more capable strategic attack aircraft to spearhead the so-called nuclear deterrent. The late 1950s was the heyday of the strategic bomber: large, multi-engined aircraft designed to deliver nuclear or conventional weapons to targets across thousands of miles of ocean. Both the US and USSR fielded jet bombers early in the 1950s – the Boeing B-52 Stratofortress and the Tupolev Tu-16 'Badger' among them. Britain, because of her strategic position in Europe, concentrated on defence but was the only other nation to develop a strategic bomber force – the famous V-bombers. These aircraft are some of the most enduring military jets ever built. The B-52, for example, is expected to serve well into the next century, albeit in a revised role as a missile platform.

THE DEVELOPMENT OF THE INTERCEPTOR

To counter the threat of the new generation of strategic jet bombers, both East and West were forced to re-evaluate the role of the interceptor. In response, a new generation of fast-climbing, radar-equipped aircraft were created that matched in complexity the bombers they were designed to destroy. A new word was coined to describe the complex package of electronic aids that the task demanded – avionics. Coupled with improving infrared and radar-guided missiles, these aircraft were the forerunners of today's air-superiority fighters. The English Electric Lightning, Convair Delta Dagger and Lockheed Starfighter were all borne out of the basic need to intercept enemy bombers, and served continuously in this role until the 1980s. To lessen the workload on the pilot, many interceptors were crewed by both a pilot and a radar/weapons officer.

More than a mention must be made of France during this period of military jet development. While its involvement in Korea was only limited, the French aviation industry recovered quickly after the war and, spearheaded by the energetic Marcel Dassault, became a major competitor in the military aircraft industry. French mistrust of US foreign policy precluded the purchase of US aircraft, and as a result France rapidly advanced into the jet age. Readers will observe the wide range and diversity of aircraft produced by French manufacturers during the 1950s and early 1960s. These aircraft have enabled the air forces of many smaller nations to enter the jet age sooner than they could have hoped if forced to rely on indigenous development. The US, USSR, Britain and France produced the vast majority of military jets during the 1950s and early 1960s, and aircraft produced by these countries were exported widely and supplied *gratis* to friendly nations. To reflect this fact, I have chosen some of the lesser known variants of aircraft such as the de Havilland Vampire and Hawker Sea Hawk, or Dassault's enduring Mirage series in the plethora of national marking's in which they have flown.

Above: A trio of Lightning F.Mk 6 interceptors over the east coast of England. The Lightning was designed to counter the threat of long-range strategic bombers.

One of the most remarkable exceptions to the dominance of the four nations mentioned is Sweden. From the early 1950s this small, neutral nation developed some of the most advanced, cost effective and capable military jet fighter aircraft ever built, independent of the support of any other nation. However, in general the military aviation industry was monopolised by the major powers. Investment by both superpowers into research and development reached enormous levels in the early 1960s, with experimental aircraft such as the North American B-70 Valkyrie swallowing up huge amounts of capital. When America entered the Vietnam War in 1965, her armed forces possessed the most advanced aircraft in the world, covering a wide range of roles from transport to aerial reconnaissance. A good indication of the rapid advances that had been made by the US is to compare the Valkyrie with the Bell P-59A Airacomet, America's first jet aircraft produced barely 20 years previously.

Instances of air-to-air combat during the Vietnam War were few and far between. By far the greatest threat faced by American pilots were the surface-to-air missiles (SAMs) that many contemporary analysts believed would spell the end of the manned fighter aircraft. The US lost far more aircraft to Soviet-built SAMs than they did to North Vietnamese aircraft, and in response they rapidly developed dedicated electronic countermeasures (ECM) aircraft to counter the threat. The changing nature of air combat is perhaps best reflected in the long service of the F-4 Phantom II. Designed as a carrier-based fighter, it was developed into an attack aircraft, photo-reconnaissance aircraft, and finally as the F-4G 'Wild Weasel' ECM aircraft. Warfare again proved the greatest spur to military jet development, forcing the US to adapt its aircraft. For this conflict at least, though, the military jet played second fiddle to the most important aircraft available to US military commanders – the helicopter.

COMBAT EXPERIENCE

The late 1960s saw something of a lull in the arms race. This allowed the USSR, which had previously relied on strength in numbers over technical sophistication with regard to its aircraft, to produce more advanced types. The MiG-23, -25 and -27 represented a significant advance in Soviet combat capability, matched by the Tupolev Tu-22 'Backfire' series that endures to this day. Exports of Soviet aircraft to the Middle East gave nations such as Egypt, Libya and Iraq greater combat capability, as demonstrated during the 1967 Six-Day War and again in the 1973 Arab-Israeli War. In the end this proved insufficient to defeat the technically superior Israeli Air Force, flying French and US-built aircraft, but it did give the USSR valuable opportunities to evaluate its aircraft in combat. The late 1960s also heralded the arrival of a revolutionary new form of aircraft, the Vertical/Short TakeOff and Landing (V/STOL) Hawker Siddley Harrier, which to date has no real equal anywhere in the world.

Decreasing defence budgets and reduced order books forced many Western manufacturers to consolidate their efforts in the 1970s, the era that produced the majority of the current generation of military jet aircraft. Thus McDonnell teamed with Douglas and produced arguably the greatest fighter of the modern age, the F-15. In Europe an alliance of Britain, Italy and Germany developed the Tornado, and will produce the next generation of aircraft to replace it. A number of new manufacturers have emerged onto the scene, with many smaller nations such as Taiwan, Japan, Argentina and South Africa keen to break their reliance on imports and develop their indigenous aerospace industries. The end of the Cold War has changed strategic considerations and emphasised the need for rapidly deployable forces and multi-role combat aircraft to police international trouble spots. Stealth technology has emerged as the by-word of modern aviation, but as was demonstrated so forcefully during the 1991 Gulf War, the military jet continues to be the most potent and important symbol of military might.

Above: A fine view of the B-2 Spirit. Developed at enormous cost for a role that no longer exists, the B-2 is the most remarkable aircraft in service with any air force.

AIDC AT-3A Tzu Chung

In collaboration with Northrop, the Taiwanese Aero Industry Development Center developed a twin-fan military trainer for use by the Chinese Nationalist (Taiwanese) Air Force. Design of the aircraft began in 1975, and follows a conventional low-wing configuration with tricycle undercarriage, tandem seat cockpit, and twin turbojets mounted in nacelles either side of the fuselage. After design approval in 1978, the first prototypes were ordered in to production and the first of these made its maiden flight in September 1980. Evaluation led to a contract for 60 AT-3A Tzu Chung aircraft for the CNAF. In service the aircraft is operated in the advanced trainer role, and has won praise for its manoeuvrability. Weapons training can also be undertaken, with a wide variety of ordnance. Some 45 of the aircraft have been upgraded to AT-3B standard with radar and a HUD.

Country of origin:	Taiwan
Type:	two-seat advanced flying and weapons trainer
Powerplant:	two 1588kg (3500lb) Garrett TFE731-2-2L turbofans
Performance:	maximum speed at 11,000m (36,090ft) 904km/h (562mph); service ceiling 14,650m (48,065ft); range on internal fuel 2280km (1417 miles)
Weights:	empty 3855kg (8500lb); maximum take-off 7940kg (17,505lb)
Dimensions:	wingspan 10.46m (34ft 3.75in); length (including probe) 12.9m (42ft 4in); height 4.36m (14ft 3.75in); wing area 21.93sq m (236.05sq ft)
Armament:	provision for two 0.5in machine-guns in ventral pack; two wingtip rails for two AIM-9 Sidewinder air-to-air missiles; five other hardpoints with provision for up to 2720kg (5998lb) of stores, including air-to-surface missiles, cannon and machine-gun pods, rocket-launcher pods, bombs, and cluster bombs

AIDC Ching-Kuo IDF

The Ching-Kuo was developed in Taiwan to help that country overcome the considerable restrictions placed on foreign imports. The country had intended replacing its ageing fleet of F-104 Starfighters with the Northrop F-20 Tigershark, but this proved impossible when the US government placed an embargo on this and any other comparable advanced fighter. American expertise was therefore bought in from General Dynamics, Garrett, Westinghouse, Bendix/King and Lear who helped to finalise a design in 1985. The first prototype flew on May 28, 1989; from the outset, it was obvious that the production aircraft would bear many design characteristics familiar to the F-16 and F-18. The first aircraft was delivered to the Chinese Nationalist Air Force in 1994, although sales of the F-16 Fighting Falcon to Taiwan in 1992 reduced its production to a mere 130 aircraft.

Country of origin:	Taiwan
Type:	lightweight air-defence fighter with anti-ship capability
Powerplant:	two 4291kg (9460lb) ITEC (Garrett/AIDC) TFE1042-70 turbofans
Performance:	maximum speed at 10,975m (36,000ft) 1275km/h (792mph); service ceiling 16,760m (55,000ft)
Weights:	normal take-off weight 9072kg (20,000lb)
Dimensions:	wingspan 9.00m (29ft 6in) over missile rails; length 14.48m (47ft 6in)
Armament:	one 20mm General Electric M61A1 Vulcan rotary six-barrel cannon, six external pylons with provision for four Tien Chien 1 short range air-to-air missiles, or two Tien Chien 2 medium range air-to-air missiles, or four Tien Chien 1 and two Tien Chien 2, or three Hsiung Feng II anti-ship missiles and two Tien Chien 1 AAMs, or AGMs, or various combinations of rocket or cannon pods

AMX International AMX

The AMX International AMX is the product of a collaboration between the Italian companies of Aeritalia and Aermacchi, and the Brazilian EMBRAER company. It was born out of a requirement that the indigenous air forces of both countries had in the early 1980s for a small tactical fighter bomber, to replace Fiat G91s and F104Gs, and EMBRAER AT-26 Xavantes respectively. A Piaggio built Rolls-Royce tubofan was chosen as the powerplant for the compact and attractive little fighter. The first prototype flew in May 1984 and by 1990 the seven development aircraft had accumulated more than 2,500 hours. Aeritalia are responsible for approximately 50 percent of the work, including the major assemblies, with the other two partners completing all other sections. The aircraft entered service with the Aeronautica Italia Militare in April 1989.

Country of origin:	Italy and Brazil
Type:	single-seat multi-role combat aircraft
Powerplant:	One 5003kg (11,030lb) Fiat/Piaggio/Alfa Romeo (Rolls Royce) Spey Mk 807 turbofan
Performance:	maximum speed 1047km/h (651mph); service ceiling 13,000m (42,650ft); combat radius at low level 556km (345 miles)
Weights:	empty 6700kg (14,771lb); maximum take-off 13,000kg (28,660lb)
Dimensions:	wingspan 8.87m (29ft 1.5in); length 13.23m (43ft 5in); height 4.55m (14ft 11.25in); wing area 21sq m (226.04sq ft)
Armament:	one 20mm General Dynamics M61A1 cannon or two 30mm DEFA cannon (on Brazilian version); five exernal hardpoints with provision for up to 3800kg (8377lb) of stores; two wing tip rails for Sidewinder or similar air-to-air missiles

Aeritalia G91R/1A

The original G91 models were built by Fiat, who submitted the successful design to a NATO specification issued to European manufacturers in 1954. It was envisaged that the G91 would become standard equipment with member nations' air forces, but this aim was never realised. The program had an early setback when the first prototype was lost on the inaugural flight due to problems in the design of the vertical stabiliser. Despite this the aircraft was built in substantial numbers, equipping both the Italian Air Force and the Luftwaffe. First entering service in 1958, there are only a handful now left in service around the world. The G91 gained a reputation for being reliable and easy to fly. The manufacturers were quick to realise the suitability of the machine as a tactical reconnaissance aircraft, leading to the 'R' series.

Country of origin:	Italy
Type:	single-seat tactical reconnaissance aircraft
Powerplant:	one 2268kg (5000lb) Fiat built Bristol Siddeley Orpheus 803 turbojet
Performance:	maximum level speed at 1520m (5000ft) 1086km/h (675mph) or Mach 0.87; service ceiling 13100m (42,978ft); operational radius (standard fuel) 320km (200 miles)
Weights:	empty 3100kg (6835lb); maximum takeoff weight 5500kg (12,125lb)
Dimensions:	wingspan 8.56m (28ft 1in); length overall 10.30m (33ft 9.25in); height overall 4.00m (13ft 1.25in); wing area 16.42sq m (176.64sq ft)
Armament:	four 12.7mm machine guns; three 70mm Vinten cameras; four underwing pylons for two 227kg (500lb) bombs, tactical nuclear weapons, Nord 5103 air-to-air guided missiles, clusters of six 76mm (3in) air-to-air rockets, honeycomb packs of 31 air-to-ground folding fin rockets, machine gun pods containing one 12.7mm (0.5in) machine gun with 250 rounds

Aeritalia G91R/3

The R/3 was a further development of the GR1/B, and boasted the upgraded features of that aircraft. These included improved brakes, tubeless tyres, a strengthened main wing spar which allowed an increase in the maximum permitted underwing weapons load, and reinforced structure. The variant also featured internal navigational equipment changes. A doppler radar and Position and Homing indicator were fitted enabling the aircraft to operate independently of ground controllers. The R/3 was built to a West German specification and of a total of 344 aircraft completed, 270 were licence built by Messerschmitt (MBB), Heinkel (later VFW-Fokker), and Dornier. The Bristol Siddeley Orpheus was licence built by another European consortium. The R/3 was the first jet combat aircraft to be built in Germany since the war, and entered service with the German Air Force in 1962.

Country of origin:	Italy
Type:	single-seat tactical reconnaissance
Powerplant:	one 2268kg (5000lb) Fiat-built Bristol Siddeley Orpheus 803 turbojet
Performance:	maximum level speed at 1520m (5000ft) 1086km/h (675mph) or Mach 0.87; service ceiling 13100m (42,978ft); operational radius (standard fuel) 320 km (200 miles)
Weights:	empty 3100kg (6835lb); maximum takeoff weight 5500kg (12,125lb)
Dimensions:	wingspan 8.56m (28ft 1in); length overall 10.30m (33ft 9.25in); height overall 4.00m (13ft 1.25in); wing area 16.42sq m (176.64sq ft)
Armament:	two DEFA cannon (125 rpg); three 70mm Vinten cameras; four underwing pylons for two 227kg (500lb) bombs, tatctical nuclear weaons, Nord 5103 air-to-air guided missiles, clusters of six 76mm (3in) air-to-air rockets, honeycomb packs of 31 air-to-ground folding fin rockets, machine gun pods containing one 12.7mm (0.5in) machine gun with 250 rounds

Aeritalia G91R/4

The R/4 reconnaissance version was essentially a development of the R/3 aircraft, and featured improved navigational equipment and a reinforced structure to allow for an uprated weapons load. The American government had at first intended to supply 50 R/4s to Greece and Turkey as part of its Military Aid Plan, but in the end, the aircraft were diverted to the Federal German Air Force. The Portuguese Air Force received 40 aircraft from this source. In flight, the aircraft bears a notable resemblance to the North American F-86K Sabre. This G91R/4 wears the late-style Luftwaffe coding and the badge of Leichtenkampf-geschwader 43, based at Oldenburg in West Germany in 1970. Note the single barrel muzzle; R/3 and R/4 reconnaissance versions of the G91 carried only two fixed cannon.

Country of origin:	Italy
Type:	single-seat tactical reconnaissance
Powerplant:	one 2268kg (5000lb) Fiat-built Bristol Siddeley Orpheus 803 turbojet
Performance:	maximum level speed at 1520m (5000ft) 1086km/h (675mph) or Mach 0.87; service ceiling 13100m (42,978ft); operational radius (standard fuel) 320km (200 miles)
Weights:	empty 3100kg (6835lb); maximum takeoff weight 5500kg (12,125lb)
Dimensions:	wingspan 8.56m (28ft 1in); length overall 10.30m (33ft 9.25in); height overall 4.00m (13ft 1.25in); wing area 16.42sq m (176.64sq ft)
Armament:	two 12.7mm machine guns; three 70-mm Vinten cameras; four underwing pylons for two 227kg (500lb) bombs, tactical nuclear weapons, Nord 5103 air-to-air guided missiles, clusters of six 76mm (3in) air-to-air rockets, honeycomb packs of 31 air-to-ground folding fin rockets, machine gun pods containing one 12.7mm (0.5in) machine gun with 250 rounds

Aeritalia G91T/1

The G91T variants were developed in the late 1950s to provide advanced flying and weapons training at transonic speeds. From the outset it was intended to retain as much of the original G91 structure and equipment as possible. Externally, the aircraft can be distinguished by the two seat cockpit, which necessitated extending the fuselage by 1.36m. The aircraft could be rapidly converted to a combat role although avionics fit was slightly reduced; major users include Portugal and Germany, who took delivery of 66 of the T/3 models. The T/3 received updated flight equipment; 44 were built by Fiat (later amalgamated into Aeritalia) and 22 under licence by Dornier in Germany. Portugal was the last major user of the aircraft, which was replaced by the Aermacchi MB.339 after nearly 25 years' service in the Italian Air Force.

Country of origin:	Italy
Type:	twin-seat transonic trainer
Powerplant:	one 2268kg (5000lb) Fiat-built Bristol Siddeley Orpheus 803 turbojet
Performance:	maximum level speed at 1520m (5000ft) 1030km/h (640mph); service ceiling 12,200m (40,000ft); operational radius (standard fuel) 320km (200 miles)
Weights:	basic operating weight 3865kg (8520lb); maximum takeoff weight 6050kg (13,340lb)
Dimensions:	wingspan 8.56m (28ft 1in); length overall 11.67m (38ft 3.5in); height overall 4.45m (14ft 7.25in); wing area 16.42sq m (176.64sq ft)
Armament:	two 12.7mm (0.5in) machine guns; two underwing pylons for light bombs, missiles, or extra fuel tanks

Aeritalia G91T/3

The Fiat G91T/3 was a version of the T/1 produced for the Federal German Air Force. This aircraft was operated by Wattenschule 50. Keen to develop the G91 to its maximum possible potential, the Fiat designers proposed a new version of the T/1, known as the T/4. The reasoning behind this proposal was logical. In the early 1960s, the Italian Air Force had bought the European licence-built version of Lockheed's Starfighter, the F104G. To provide some measure of flight training on this difficult aircraft the company proposed fitting the T/1 airframe with the electronics from the Starfighter. It was an ambitious project but technically a feasible one. Nevertheless, it never progressed beyond the project stage. Note the high visibility paint for high conspicuousness during training missions.

Country of origin:	Italy
Type:	twin-seat transonic trainer
Powerplant:	one 2268kg (5000lb) Fiat-built Bristol Siddeley Orpheus 803 turbojet
Performance:	maximum level speed at 1520m (5000ft) 1030km/h (640mph); service ceiling 12200m (40,000ft); operational radius (standard fuel) 320km (200 miles)
Weights:	basic operating weight 3865kg (8520lb); maximum takeoff weight 6050kg (13,340lb)
Dimensions:	wingspan 8.56m (28ft 1in); length overall 11.67m (38ft 3.5in); height overall 4.45m (14ft 7.25in); wing area 16.42sq m (176.64sq ft)
Armament:	two 12.7mm (0.5in) machine guns; two underwing pylons for light bombs, missiles, or extra fuel tanks

Aermacchi M.B.326B

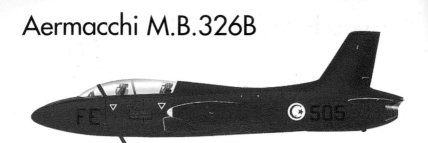

The 326B is one of the most important light attack and trainer aircraft to have emerged in the past four decades. The initial prototype flew in 1957; the basic airframe designed by Ermanno Bazzocchi of Aermacchi around a Rolls Royce Viper turbojet is conventional, with a well equipped tandem cockpit ahead of a slightly swept leading edge low/mid wing monoplane. The Aeronautica Militare Italia received the first of 85 M.B.326s in February of 1962. Vice free and predictable handling characteristics enabled the service to use the aircraft for all stages of flying training. In the training role, the M.B.326 has provided the AMI with a superb crossover trainer which provided countless pilots with jet experience prior to moving on to faster jets. Tunisia purchased eight armed trainer M.B.326s in 1965, which are painted in high-visibility orange.

Country of origin:	Italy
Type:	two-seat basic/advanced trainer
Powerplant:	one 1134kg (2500lb) Rolls Royce Viper 11 turbojet
Performance:	maximum speed 806km/h (501mph); standard range 1665km (1,035 miles)
Weights:	empty 2237kg (4930lb) maximum take-off 3765kg (8300lb)
Dimensions:	span over tip tanks 10.56m (34ft 8in); length 10.65m (34ft 11.25in); height 3.72m (12ft 2in); wing area 19sq m (204.5sq ft)
Armament:	two optional 7.7mm machine guns, six underwing pylons with provision for machine gun pods, rockets and/or bombs, or camera pods, up to a maximum of 907kg (2000lb)

Aermacchi M.B.326GB

The potential of the M.B.326 as a light ground attack aircraft was first realised in the 326A, which was equipped with underwing hardpoints for a variety of munitions including gun or rocket pods, bombs, and air-to-ground missiles. Although not required by the AMI, the ground attack variants have been supplied to numerous clients including Ghana (nine M.B.326Fs) and Tunisia (eight M.B.326Bs). In 1967 the first M.B.326G prototype was flown with the more powerful 1547kg (3,410lb) Rolls Royce Viper 20. Combined with localised strengthening of the airframe, this allowed a 100 per cent increase in the maximum permitted weapon load on earlier versions. Eight were supplied to the Argentine Navy, 17 to the air force of Zaire and 23 to Zambia. These aircraft are designated M.B.326GB.

Country of origin:	Italy
Type:	two-seat light attack aircraft
Powerplant:	one 1547kg (3410lb) Rolls Royce Viper 20 turbojet
Performance:	maximum speed 867km/h (539mph); standard range 1850km (1150 miles)
Weights:	empty 2685kg (5920lb) maximum take-off 4577kg (10,090lb)
Dimensions:	span over tip tanks 10.85m (35ft 7¼in); length 10.67m (35ft 0.25in); height 3.72 m (12ft 2in); wing area 19.35sq m (208.3sq ft)
Armament:	two optional 7.7mm (0.303in) machine guns; six underwing points for machine gun pods, rockets and/or bombs, or camera pods; maximum external load 1814 kg (4000 lb)

Aermacchi M.B.326K

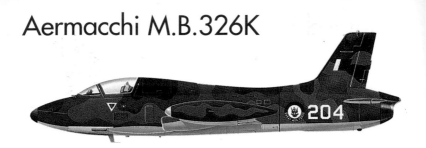

Having already proved the soundness of the basic 326 design and its usefulness as a weapons platform, it took Aermacchi a surprising length of time to finalise a design for a single-seat version. A primary goal of the design team was to provide the aircraft with more power, and the second prototype was equipped with the 1814kg (4000lb) Rolls Royce Viper 632-43 which became the standard fit on all production models. The installation of two electrically operated cannon in the lower forward fuselage in the MB.326K increased offensive capability of the aircraft, and maximum permitted weapons load was also increased. The space previously occupied by the rear cockpit now houses the cannon ammunition drums, the avionics suite, and an additional fuel tank. Export customers include South Africa, Dubai, Ghana, and Tunisia.

Country of origin:	Italy
Type:	single-seat close air support or tactical reconnaissance aircraft, and limited air-to-air interceptor
Powerplant:	one 1814kg (4000lb) Rolls Royce Viper 632-43 turbojet
Performance:	maximum speed at 1525m (5000ft) 890km/h (553mph); combat radius at low level with maximum armament 268km (167 miles)
Weights:	empty 3123kg (6885lb) maximum take-off 5895kg (13,000lb)
Dimensions:	span over tip tanks 10.85m (35ft 7.25in); length 10.67m (35ft 0.25in); height 3.72m (12ft 2in); wing area 19.35sq m (208.3sq ft)
Armament:	two 30mm DEFA 553 cannon with 125rpg, six underwing points with provision for machine gun pods, launchers for 37mm, 68mm, 100mm, 2.75in or 5in rockets, Matra 550 Magic air-to-air missiles, and/or bombs, or (on inboard pylon) four-camera reconnaissance pod; maximum external load 1814 kg (4000 lb)

Aermacchi M.B.339PAN

The Aermacchi M.B.339 has its ancestry firmly rooted in the early 326 class. Indeed, the aircraft was the result of a study contract received from the Aeronautica Militare Italia for a second-generation jet to succeed the venerable MB.326 and Fiat G91T during the 1980s. No fewer than nine separate design studies were undertaken, with different powerplant options. In February the AMI opted for the Viper-powered version. The forward fuselage was redesigned to provide the instructor in the rear seat with better all-round visibility. Significant avionics improvements include the installation of TACAN navigation computer blind landing instrumentation, IFF, VHF and UHF radio. Argentina, Peru, Dubai, Ghana, Malaysia and Nigeria are all export customers for this excellent trainer and close support aircraft.

Country of origin:	Italy
Type:	two-seat basic/advanced trainer and close air support aircraft
Powerplant:	one 1814kg (4000lb) Piaggio-built Rolls Royce Viper 632-43 turbojet
Performance:	maximum speed at 1525m (5000ft) 890km/h (553mph); combat radius at low level with maximum armament 268km (167 miles)
Weights:	empty 3123kg (6885lb) maximum take-off 5895kg (13,000lb)
Dimensions:	span over tip tanks 10.85m (35ft 7.25in); length 10.67m (35ft .025in); height 3.72 m (12ft 2in); wing area 19.35sq m (208.3sq ft)
Armament:	two 30mm DEFA 553 cannon with 125rpg, six underwing points with provision for machine gun pods, launchers for 37mm, 68mm, 100mm, 2.75in or 5in rockets, Matra 550 Magic air-to-air missiles, and/or bombs, or (on inboard pylon) four-camera reconnaissance pod; maximum external load 1814kg (4000lb)

Aermacchi M.B.339K

Adopting a similar route to the one taken with the M.B.326 trainer, the Aeromacchi company opted to develop a single-seat version of the popular and well received M.B.339. The similarities with the previous project did not end there. The extra space created by the adoption of a single-seat layout allowed designers to relocate the avionics suite from the nose, and to increase the overall fuel capacity by adding an extra tank. A wide range of options was offered to potential customers, including ECM jamming equipment and HUD. The company continued to show faith in the Piaggio-built Rolls Royce Viper, but when orders were not forthcoming (possibly because the prototype aircraft did not demonstrate a significant improvement in performance over the M.B.326K) it was decided to replace this with the uprated 2018kg (4450lb) Viper 680-43.

Country of origin:	Italy
Type:	fighter and ground attack lead-in trainer with operational capability
Powerplant:	one Piaggio-built 2018kg (4450lb) Viper 680-43
Performance:	maximum speed at 9150m (30,000ft) 815km/h (508mph); service ceiling 14,240m (46,700ft); combat radius at low level with maximum armament 371km (230 miles)
Weights:	empty 3310kg (7297lb) maximum take-off 6350kg (14,000lb)
Dimensions:	span over tip tanks 11.22m (36ft 10in); length 11.24m (36ft 1.5in); height 3.99m (13ft 1.25in); wing area 19.30sq m (207.74sq ft)
Armament:	two 30mm DEFA 553 cannon with 125rpg, six underwing points with provision for machine gun pods, launchers for 37mm, 68mm, 100mm, 2.75in or 5in rockets, two Sidewinder air-to-air missiles, two Maverick AGM-65 air-to-surface missiles, and/or bombs, maximum external load 1814kg (4000lb)

Aero L-29 Delfin

The Czech designed L-29 Delfin was selected in 1961 as the basic jet trainer of the USSR, in whose service the aircraft gained the NATO reporting name 'Maya'. Total production by Aero Vodochodny Narodni Podnik exceeded 3600. The L-29 is a simple, rugged aircraft that can be operated from grass, sand, or waterlogged airstrips. First entering service in 1963, the production lines remained in operation for the next 11 years. The Soviets took more than 2000 of the production total; deliveries were also made to almost every Communist Bloc air force. Many were exported to Soviet allies in the Middle East and Africa, where they are still in service. This aircraft wears the desert scheme of the Egyptian air force. The Egyptian aircraft can be configured for use in the attack role, and are fitted with equipment to suit.

Country of origin:	Czechoslovakia
Type:	two-seat basic and advanced trainer
Powerplant:	one 890kg (1960lb) Motorlet M 701 VC-150 turbojet
Performance:	maximum speed at 5000m (16,400ft) 655km/h (407mph); service ceiling 11,000m (36,100ft); standard range 640km (397 miles)
Weights:	empty 2280kg (5027lb); maximum take-off 3280kg (7231lb)
Dimensions:	wingspan 10.29m (33ft 8in); length 10.81m (35ft 5.5in); height 3.13m (10ft 3in); wing area 19.80sq m (213.1sq ft)

Aero L-39C Albatros

First entering service in 1974 with the Czech Air Force, the L-39 succeeded the L-29 as the standard jet trainer for the air forces of Czechoslovakia, the USSR, and East Germany. The aircraft continues in this role today in the air forces of many former Eastern Bloc countries. The prototype L-39 first flew in November 1968 and it was obvious from the trials that vastly improved performance over the L-29 had been achieved. This was due mainly to the adoption of the Ivchyenko I-25 turbofan engine, which produced nearly double the power of the L-29s Motorlet unit. Throughout the design process, emphasis was placed on ease of maintenance. An auxiliary power unit allows the aircraft to operate independently of ground facilities. The L-39C is the basic trainer variant. Many have been sold on the private market, and are a common sight at aviation meets.

Country of origin:	Czechoslovakia
Type:	two-seat basic and advanced trainer
Powerplant:	one 1720kg (3792lb) Ivchyenko AI-25TL turbofan
Performance:	maximum speed at 6000m (19,685ft) 780km/h (435mph); service ceiling 11,500m (37,730ft); standard range 1100km (683 miles)
Weights:	empty 3330kg (7341lb); maximum take-off 4700kg (10,632lb)
Dimensions:	wingspan 9.46m (31ft 0.5in); length 12.13m (39ft 9.5in); height 4.77m (15ft 7.75in); wing area 18.80sq m (202.36sq ft)

Aero L-39ZA Albatros

From the basic L-39 airframe Aero created four variants. By far the most numerous was the L-39C trainer model, but the success of this aircraft encouraged the Czech manufacturer to produce three subvariants. Part of the reason for the success was the the ease of maintenance afforded by the L-39s modular airframe, which can be readily broken down into three major subassemblies: wing, fuselage, and rear fuselage. To allow easy access to the engine, the rear fuselage can be removed in one piece. The L-39ZO is a single-seat version, featuring reinforced wings to facilitate the carriage of a variety of weapons on four underwing stations. Both Iraq and Libya have bought this aircraft and utilise it in the light attack role. More numerous is the L-39ZA, which retains the twin seat configuration of the trainer.

Country of origin:	Czechoslovakia
Type:	single-seat light ground attack aircraft (ZO)
Powerplant:	one 1720kg (3792lb) Ivchyenko AI-25TL turbofan
Performance:	maximum speed at 5000m (16,404ft) 630km/h (391mph); service ceiling 9000m (29,525ft); standard range 1750km (1087 miles)
Weights:	empty 3330kg (7341lb); maximum take-off 5270kg (11,618lb)
Dimensions:	wingspan 9.46m (31ft); length 12.32m (40ft 5in); height 4.72m (15ft 5.5in); wing area 18.80sq m (202.36 q ft)
Armament:	one 23-mm GSh-23L two barrel cannon with 150 rounds; four underwing pylons with provision for pods of 57 or 130mm rockets, gun pods, a single five camera pack, AA-2 Atoll air-to-air missiles, bombs up to 500kg (1102lb); maximum external load of 1100kg (2425lb)

Aerospatiale (Fouga) CM.170 Magister

One of the most successful and widely used trainer aircraft in the world, the Magister was conceived and designed by Castello and Mauboussin for Fouga in 1950. It was the first purpose built jet trainer in the world. Despite the unusual butterfly type tail, it proved a delight to fly. After prolonged testing, the Magister was put into production for the Armée de l'Air. Total production of this and the hooked navalised version (CM.75 Zephyr) was 437. Fouga was absorbed into the Potez company in 1958, which continued to produce a number of variants for international customers. In 1967, the Magister saw action during the Six-Day War with the Israeli Air Force. It was also previously the mount of the French national aerobatic team, the 'Patrouille de France'. The team now uses the Dassault/Dornier Alpha jet.

Country of origin:	France
Type:	two-seat trainer and light attack aircraft
Powerplant:	two 400kg (882lb) Turbomeca Marbore IIA turbojets
Performance:	maximum speed at 9150m (30,000ft) 715km/h (444mph); service ceiling 11,000m (36,090ft); range 925km (575 miles)
Weights:	empty equipped 2150kg (4740lb); maximum takeoff 3200kg (7055lb)
Dimensions:	over tip tanks 12.12m (39ft 10in); length 10.06m (33ft); height 2.80m (9ft 2in); wing area 17.30sq m (186.1sq ft)
Armament:	two 7.5mm (0.295in) or 7.62mm machine guns; rockets, bombs or Nord AS.11 missiles on underwing pylons

Antonov An-72 'Coaler-C'

The design of the An-72 'Coaler' is optimised for STOL capability, with a variety of high lift features to permit short field operation. The most noticeable of these is the positioning of the twin powerplants, at a position high up and well forward on the wing. When the inboard flaps are deployed, the engine exhaust is deflected over them producing greatly increased lift. The cabin design follows accepted convention, with a rear tailgate and broadly spaced main gear pods to optimise internal cargo space. The aircraft first flew on December 22, 1977, although it was first seen in the West at the Paris airshow of 1979. The aircraft has been adapted for a number of roles, including AEW. A development of the basic airframe known as the An-74 is designed for operations in the Antarctic, with de-icing equipment, improved avionics, and provision for fitting skis.

Country of origin:	USSR (Ukraine)
Type:	STOL transport
Powerplant:	two 6500kg (14,330lb) Zaporozhye/Lotarev D-36 turbofans
Performance:	maximum speed 705km/h (438mph) at 10,000m (32,810ft); service ceiling 11,800m (38,715ft); range 800km (497 miles) with maximum payload
Weights:	empty 19,050kg (41,997lb); maximum take-off weight 34,500kg (76,059lb)
Dimensions:	wingspan 31.89m (104ft 7.5in); length 28.07m (92ft 1in); height 8.65m (28ft 4.5in); wing area 98.62sq m (1,062sq ft)

Atlas Cheetah

Bearing a strong resemblance to the Israeli Kfir, the Atlas Cheetah is in fact the South African answer to an international arms embargo imposed on the country in 1977, which prevented the SAAF from importing a replacement for its ageing fleet of Mirage IIIs. The programme involved replacing nearly 50 percent of the airframe, and adding a host of improved features. Externally, a number of aerodynamic changes were made to the original airframe, the most obvious of which are the small inlet mounted canard foreplanes. The first aircraft was modified from a two-seat Mirage IIID2; production aircraft are modified from both single-seaters and twin seaters, the twin seaters possessing more advanced systems; all variants are configured to carry a host of indigenously produced weapons.

Country of origin:	South Africa
Type:	one/two-seat combat and training aircraft
Powerplant:	one 7200kg (15,873lb) SNECMA Atar 9K-50 turbojet
Performance:	maximum speed above 12,000m (39,370ft) 2337 km/h (1452mph); service ceiling 17,000m (55,775ft)
Weights:	not revealed
Dimensions:	wingspan 8.22m (26ft 11.5in); length 15.40m (50ft 6.5in); height 4.25m (13ft 11.5in); wing area 35sq m (376.75sq ft)
Armament:	two 30mm DEFA cannon, Armscor V3B and V3C Kukri air-to-air missiles, provision for external stores such as cluster bombs, laser designator pods, and rockets

Avro Canada CF-105 Arrow

The story of the Arrow bears a startling similarity to that of the BAC TSR.2. Both projects showed great promise during the early stages of development in the mid-1950s, and both were destroyed by the misguided decisions of politicians who were convinced that the days of the manned interceptor were numbered. The first stages of development of the Arrow, a two-seat all-weather interceptor, began in 1953, with planned entry into service as a replacement for the same company's CF-100 a decade later. Production of the first five prototypes began in April 1954. The design incorporated a huge high-set delta wing. The first flight of the aircraft was made on March 25, 1958, but a little under 10 months later, the whole project was cancelled. All the prototypes were destroyed in what must rank as one of the most short-sighted decisions made by any Canadian government.

Country of origin:	Canada
Type:	two-seat all-weather long range supersonic interceptor
Powerplant:	two 10,659kg (23,500lb) Pratt and Whitney J75-P-3 turbojets
Performance:	Mach 2.3 recorded during tests
Weights:	empty 22,244kg (49,040lb); average take-off during trials 25,855kg (57,000lb)
Dimensions:	wingspan 15.24m (50ft); length 23.72m (77ft 9.75in); height 6.48m (21ft 3in); wing area 113.8sq m (1,225sq ft)
Armament:	eight Sparrow air-to-air missiles in internal bay

Avro Vulcan B.Mk 2

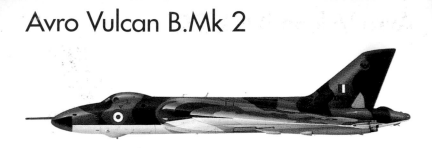

In the early 1950s, the Royal Air Force issued Specification B.14/46, which called for an aircraft that could deliver nuclear weapons from any of its bases in the world. The Avro Vulcan was thus designed ostensibly as a high level nuclear bomber. The first production aircraft were designated B. Mk 1 and entered service in this role in 1956 with the V-bomber force. The B.Mk 1 was joined in service in 1960 by the improved Vulcan B.Mk 2. These aircraft were furnished with inflight refuelling equipment. It was also intended that this variant would carry the Blue Steel or American Skybolt stand-off nuclear weapons, but, with the adoption of Polaris ,these plans never materialised. Existing Vulcan squadrons converted to the B.Mk 2A in 1962-64. This aircraft wears the bat emblem of No. 9 Squadron, and was later converted to B.Mk 2A standard.

Country of origin:	United Kingdom
Type:	long-range strategic bomber
Powerplant:	four 7711kg (17,000lb) Rolls-Royce Olympus 201 turbojets
Perfomance:	maximum speed at altitude 1038km/h (645mph); service ceiling 19,810m (65,000ft); range with normal bomb load 7403km (4600 miles)
Weights:	maximum takeoff weight 113,398kg (250,000lb)
Dimensions:	wingspan 33.83m (111 ft); length 30.45m (99ft 11in); height 8.28 m (27 ft 2in); wing area 368.26sq m (3964 sq ft)
Armament:	internal bay with provision for up to 21,454kg (47,198lb) of bombs

Avro Vulcan B.Mk 2A

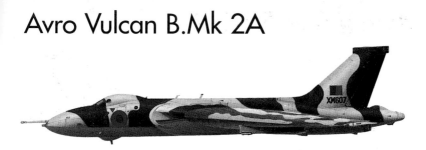

This Vulcan B.Mk. 2a of No.101 Squadron is depicted in the late low-visibility colour scheme. The low-visibility matt paint is paler than previous schemes, and Type B (two-colour) roundels and fin flash are also worn. The B.Mk 2A was optimised for low-level penetration missions, in response to the British government's decision to adopt Polaris missile submarines as the UK's primary nuclear deterrent. This meant adapting B.Mk 2 aircraft with more powerful Olympus Mk 301 engines, and subsequently fitting terrain-following radar in the nose and ARI 18228 passive radar warning in a front/rear facing fin-top installation. RAF Waddington was the home of the Vulcan, from where a number of long-distance raids against Port Stanley were launched during the 1982 Falklands conflict. The last Vulcan from a total purchase of 89 B.Mk 2As was delivered on January 14, 1965.

Country of origin:	United Kingdom
Type:	low-level strategic bomber
Powerplant:	four 9072kg (20,000lb) Olympus Mk.301 turbojets
Performance:	maximum speed 1038km/h (645mph) at high altitude; service ceiling 19,810m (65,000ft); range with normal bomb load about 7403km/h (4600 miles)
Weights:	maximum take-off 113,398kg (250,000lb)
Dimensions:	wingspan 33.83m (111ft); length 30.45m (99ft 11in); height 8.28m (27ft 2in); wing area 368.26sq m (3,964sq ft)
Armament:	internal weapon bay for up to 21,454kg (47,198lb) of bombs

BAC (English Electric) Canberra B.Mk 2

Before he left Westland aircraft, the company established by his family in 1915, W.E.W. Petter already had a scheme for a jet bomber. To meet specification B.3/45 he eventually planned a straightforward unswept aircraft with a broad wing for good behaviour at high altitude. Like the Mosquito the A.1 bomber was to be fast enough to escape interception. whilst carrying a 6000lb bomb load over a radius of 750 nautical miles. It was to have a radar sight for blind attacks in all conditions. The prototype, which flew for the first time on May 13, 1949 at the hands of Roland 'Bee' Beaumont, amazed everybody with its low-level manoeuvrability. Delays in the development of the bomb sight resulted in an initial order for a tactical day bomber, designated B.Mk 2. The first of these entered service with No. 101 Squadron on May 25, 1951.

Country of origin:	United Kingdom
Type:	two-seat interdictor aircraft
Powerplant:	two 2948kg (6500lb)`Rolls Royce Avon Mk 101 turbojets
Performance:	maximum speed at 12,192m (40,000ft) 917km/h (570mph); service ceiling 14,630m (48,000ft); range 4274km (2656 miles)
Weights:	empty not published approx 11,790kg (26,000lb); maximum take-off 24,925kg (54,950lb)
Dimensions:	wingspan 29.49m (63ft 11in); length 19.96m (65ft 6in); height 4.78m (15ft 8in); wing area 97.08sq m (1045sq ft)
Armament:	internal bomb bay with provision for up to 2727kg (6000lb) of bombs, plus an additional 909kg (2000lb) of underwing pylons

BAC (English Electric) Canberra PR.Mk 9

The Canberra jet bomber was designed originally by Teddy Petter for the English Electric company. The aircraft they subsequently produced served for over 40 years around the world in countless different variants. The PR. Mk 9 is an extensively modified high altitude reconnaissance version of the aircraft, with increased wing span, uprated Rolls Royce Avon engines, and redesigned cockpit. Development work was carried out by the Short company, one of the main subcontractors of English Electric. As an aid to high altitude reconnaissance flying, the 23 production aircraft were equipped with powered controls, increased internal fuel, and much modified avionics and EW equipment. The aircraft served with No.1 PRU, and Nos. 58 and 39 Squadrons until 1983, but five aircraft underwent a further modification to equip them for classified Elint and recce ops.

Country of origin:	United Kingdom
Type:	photo-reconnaissance aircraft
Powerplant:	two 4763kg (10,500lb) Rolls Royce Avon Mk 206 turbojets
Performance:	maximum speed about 650mph (1050km/h) at medium altitude; service ceiling 14,630m (48,000ft); range 5842km (3630 miles)
Weights:	empty not published approx 11,790kg (26,000lb); maximum take-off 24,925kg (54,950lb)
Dimensions:	wingspan 20.68m (67ft 10in); length 20.32m (66ft 8in); height 4.78m (15ft 8in); wing area 97.08sq m (1045sq ft)

BAC (English Electric) Lightning F.Mk 1A

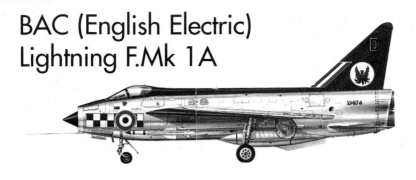

W.E.W. 'Teddy' Petter was again the driving force behind the aircraft that was for a period during the 1960s the most formidable interceptor in the world. The Lightning developed from a prototype built by English Electric, called the P.1, which first flew in August 1954. The P.1 was powered by two Bristol Siddeley Sapphire engines mounted 'under and over', and fed by a common inlet. P.1B was a completely redesigned version to meet the British government Specification F.23/49, with a two-shock intake. With Avon engines fitted, Mach 2 was attained in November 1958. Twenty preproduction aircraft were built before the first F.Mk 1 entered service in 1960. The F.Mk 1A had provision for flight refuelling and UHF radio. The Lightning was a complicated aircraft for its time, and maintenance time per flying hour was high.

Country of origin:	United Kingdom
Type:	single-seat all-weather interceptor
Powerplant:	two 6545kg (14,430lb) Rolls Royce Avon turbojets
Performance:	maximum speed at 10.970m (36,000ft) 2,414km/h (1,500mph); service ceiling 18,920m (60,000ft); range 1440km (895 miles)
Weights:	empty 12,700kg (28,000lb); maximum take-off 22,680kg (50,000lb)
Dimensions:	wingspan 10.6m (34ft 10in); length 16.25m (53ft 3in); height 5.95m (19ft 7in); wing area 35.31sq m (380.1sq ft)
Armament:	interchangeable packs of two all-attitude Red Top or stern chase Firestreak air-to-air missiles or two 30mm Aden guns, in forward part of belly tank

BAC (English Electric) Lightning F.Mk 6

The last single-seat fighter aircraft to see service with the Royal Air Force entered service in 1960. The history of the aircraft can be traced back to 1947, when the RAF issued a study contract to the English Electric company for a supersonic research aircraft, the P.1B. After nearly ten years of development work, during which time the company was amalgamated into the British Aircraft Corporation, the first Lightning F.1s were delivered. In service the aircraft proved to be as good as any all-weather interceptor then available, with a phenomenal top speed and rate of climb. However, it was hampered by poor duration. On the recommendation of BAC the RAF decided to modify the much improved F.3 to F.6 standard in 1965. The F.6 featured an extensively modified ventral tank and a cambered, kinked wing leading edge, to allow operations at greater weights.

Country of origin:	United Kingdom
Type:	supersonic all-weather interceptor, strike and reconnaissance aircraft
Powerplant:	two 7112kg (15,680lb) Rolls-Royce Avon 302 afterburning turbojets
Perfomance:	maximum speed 2415km/h (1500mph, Mach 2.3) at 12,190m (40,000ft); standard range 1287km (800miles); initial rate of climb 15,240m (50,000ft) per minute
Weights:	empty equipped 12,700kg (28,000lb); maximum take-off 22,680kg (50,000lb)
Dimensions:	wingspan 10.61m (34ft 10in); length 16.84 m (55ft 3in); height 5.97m (19ft 7in); wing area 35.31sq m (380.1 q ft)
Armament:	two 30mm Aden guns in ventral pack (120 rounds), two Fire Streak or Red Top air-to-air missiles, or five Vinten 360 70mm cameras, or night reconnaissance cameras and linescan equipment and underwing flares; underwing/overwing pylons for up to 144 rockets or six 454kg (1000lb) bombs

BAC TSR.2

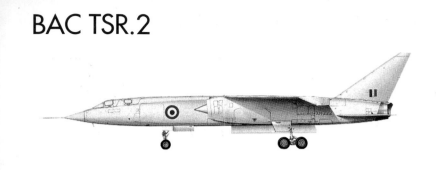

At the time, the cancellation of the TSR.2 programme was widely regarded within the aviation industry as the greatest disaster to befall the post-war British aviation industry. In retrospect it is clear that much of the pioneering research carried out by the project team was of great benefit during the development of Concorde. Conceived as a replacement for the English Electric Canberra, the aircraft was designed by a combined English Electric and Vickers Armstrong to an RAF requirement issued in 1957 for a high speed low level tactical strike and reconnaissance aircraft. In January 1959 it was decided to proceed with development. The aircraft that emerged represented a huge leap in airframe, avionics, engine, and equipment technology; XR219 first flew on September 27, 1964. Just four were built, although XR219 was the only example to fly.

Country of origin:	United Kingdom
Type:	two-seat strike/reconnaissance aircraft
Powerplant:	two 13884kg (30,610lb) thrust Bristol Siddeley Olympus 320 turbojets
Performance:	maximum speed at altitude 2390km/h (1485mph); maximum speed 1345km/h (836mph) at 61m (200ft); operating ceiling 16,460m (54,000ft); range at low level 1287km (800 miles)
Weights:	average mission take-off weight 36,287kg (80,000lb); maximum take-off weight 43,545kg (96,000lb)
Dimensions:	wingspan 11.28m (37ft); length 27.13m (89ft); height 7.32m (24ft); wing area 65.03sq m (700sq ft)
Armament:	(planned) up to 2722kg (6000lb) of conventional or nuclear weapons in an internal weapons bay; four underwing pylons for up to 1814kg (4000lb) of weapons

BAC (Vickers) VC-10 K.Mk 2

The RAF received 14 VC-10 C. Mk 1 aircraft, which were derived from the civil VC-10 and Super VC-10. The aircraft had the short fuselage of the VC.10 and many of the features of the 'Super' including uprated engines, a stronger structure, wet (integral tank) fin, extended leading edge, and increased gross weight. The RAF requirement also specified an Auxiliary Power Unit in the tail, a strengthened cabin floor and large cargo door for heavy freight. The aircraft cabin can be laid out for 150 rear facing seats, or mixed passenger/cargo, or all cargo use, or casevac use with provision for up to 78 litters. The 13 surviving aircraft were fitted with an inflight refuelling probe, and between 1990 and 1992 13 ex-commercial (BA and East African Airways aircraft) were rebuilt as tanker aircraft. The aircraft are designated VC-10 K.Mk 2 and Mk 3 respectively.

Country of origin:	United Kingdom
Type:	long-range transport and/or tanker aircraft
Powerplant:	four 9888kg (21,800lb) Rolls Royce Conway turbofans
Performance:	cruising speed at 30,000ft (9145m) 684km/h (425mph); service ceiling 12,800m (42,000ft); range with maximum payload 6276km (3900 miles)
Weights:	empty 66,224kg (146,000lb); maximum take-off 146,510kg (323,000lb)
Dimensions:	wingspan 44.55m (146ft 2in); length 48.36m (158ft 8in); height 12.04m (39ft 6in); wing area 272.38sq m (2,932sq ft)

BAe (HS) Harrier GR.Mk 3

The Gr.Mk 3 Harrier is essentially the same as the Gr.Mk 1, but with a retrofitted 9753kg (21,500lb) Rolls Royce Pegasus 103 turbofan. In operational service it was discovered that the Gr.Mk 1 used up a great deal of fuel in vertical take-off with full weapons load operations, so it was more common for the Harrier to be operated as a V/STOL aircraft. Standard equipment on the Gr.Mk 3 included inflight refuelling equipment, head-up display, and a laser range finder. From 1970 the aircraft equipped one RAF squadron in the UK and three in Germany. The final units to operate the Gr.Mk 3 were the Operational Conversion Unit and a flight stationed in Belize. After nearly 20 years' service, they have been replaced by the Gr.Mk 5 and Mk 7. Note the centreline Aden cannon fairing and semi-deployed airbrake. Matra rocket pods are also fitted.

Country of origin:	United Kingdom
Type:	V/STOL close support and reconnaissance aircraft
Powerplant:	one 9752kg (21,500lb) Rolls Royce Pegasus 103 vectored thrust turbofan
Performance:	maximum speed at low altitude over 1186km/h (737mph); service ceiling over 15,240m (50,000ft); range with one inflight refuelling 5,560 km (3,455 miles)
Weights:	basic operating empty 5579kg (12,300lb); maximum take-off 11,340kg (25,000lb)
Dimensions:	wingspan 7.7m (25ft 3in); length 13.87m (45ft 6in); height 3.45m (11ft 4in); wing area 18.68sq m (201.1sq ft)
Armament:	maximum of 2268kg (5000lb) of stores on underfuselage and underwing points; one 30mm Aden gun or similar gun, with 150 rounds, rockets, bombs

BAe/McDonnell Douglas Harrier GR.Mk 7

The most current version of the Harrier in front line service with the Royal Air Force is the GR.Mk 7. The collaboration of BAe and McDonnell Douglas resulted from a desire to improve the limited range/payload capability of the AV-8A operated by the US Marine Corps and Harrier GR.Mk 3. The resulting aircraft were tailored specifically to the needs of each service. The AV8-B Harrier is detailed elsewhere. The GR.Mk 5 differs in several ways from its predecessor. A wider wing made of composite materials permits the carriage of an extra 907kg (2000lb) of fuel, while revised wing control surfaces generate greater lift. In the cockpit, the GR.Mk 5 has a more complex avionics fit, with moving map display and IR sensor. Two extra wing pylons are fitted for Sidewinder missiles. The GR.Mk 5 made its service debut in November 1988, and was followed by the GR.Mk 7.

Country of origin:	United Kingdom/USA
Type:	V/STOL close-support aircraft
Powerplant:	one 9866kg (21,750lb) Rolls Royce Mk 105 Pegasus vectored-thrust turbofan
Performance:	maximum speed at sea level 1065km/h (661mph); service ceiling more than 15,240m (50,000ft); combat radius with 2722kg (6000lb bombload) 277km (172 miles)
Weights:	empty 7050kg (15,542lb); maximum take-off 14,061kg (31,000lb)
Dimensions:	wingspan 9.25m (30ft 4in); length 14.36m (47ft 1.5in); height 3.55m (11ft 7.75in); wing area 21.37sq m (230sq ft)
Armament:	two 25mm Aden cannon with 100 rpg; six external hardpoints with provision for up to 4082kg (9000lb) (Short take-off) or 3175kg (7000lb) (Vertical take-off) of stores, including AAMs, ASMs, freefall or guided bombs, cluster bombs, dispenser weapons, napalm tanks, rocket launchers and ECM pods

BAe/McDonnell Douglas AV-8B Harrier II

The AV-8B version of the Harrier was developed for the US Marine Corps, who had a requirement for a single-seat close support aircraft to supersede the AV-8A Harriers in service from the mid-1970s. The design resulted from a collaboration between the two companies, who had individually sought to improve on the Harrier design. The first of four full-scale development aircraft was flown on November 5, 1981. The design team made significant improvements by using carbon fibre in many of the major structural components, by introducing a range of lift augmenting devices, by redesigning the control surface, redesigning the cockpit/forward fuselage, and by adding two additional wing hard points. The aircraft entered service with the Marine Corps in January 1985. The Spanish navy operate a version of the AV-8A, designated AV-8G Matador.

Country of origin:	USA and UK
Type:	V/STOL close-support aircraft
Powerplant:	one 10,796kg (23,800lb) Rolls Royce F402-RR-408 Pegasus vectored thrust turbofan
Performance:	maximum speed at sea level 1065km/h (661mph); service ceiling more than 15,240m (50,000ft); combat radius with 2722kg (6000lb) bombload 277km (172 miles)
Weights:	empty 5936kg (13,086lb); maximum take-off 14,061kg (31,000lb)
Dimensions:	wingspan 9.25m (30ft 4in); length 14.12m (46ft 4in); height 3.55m (11ft 7.75in); wing area 21.37sq m (230sq ft)
Armament:	one 25mm GAU-12U cannon; six external hardpoints with provision for up to 7711kg (17,000lb) (Short take-off) or 3175kg (7000lb) (Vertical take-off) of stores, including AAMs, ASMs, freefall or guided bombs, cluster bombs, dispenser weapons, napalm tanks, rocket launchers and ECM pods

BAe Sea Harrier FRS.Mk 1

The Sea Harrier FRS.Mk 1 was ordered to equip the three Royal Navy 'through-deck cruisers' (a strange name dreamed up by defence staff for the Invincible class carriers) in fighter, anti-submarine and surface-attack roles, with Blue Fox radar and other weapons. Official policy during the time of the land-based Harrier's gestation was that all future Royal Navy combat aircraft must be helicopters, and this delayed development of its carrier borne equivalent until 1975. Installing the Blue Fox radar meant lengthening the nose, and the cockpit was raised to accommodate a more substantial avionics suite and to afford the pilot a better all-round view. Introduced into service shortly before the Falklands War, the aircraft proved an incalculably important asset during that conflict. The aircraft pictured is in Royal Navy colours.

Country of origin:	United Kingdom
Type:	shipborne multi-role combat aircraft
Powerplant:	one 9752kg (21,500lb) Rolls-Royce Pegasus Mk.104 vectored thrust turbofan
Performance:	maximum speed at sea level 1110km/h (690mph) with maximum AAM load; service ceiling 15,545m (51,000ft); Intercept radius 740km (460 miles) on high level mission with full combat reserve
Weights:	empty 5942kg (13,100lb); maximum take-off 11,884kg (26,200lb)
Dimensions:	wingspan 7.7m (25ft 3in); length 14.5m (47ft 7in); height 3.71m (12ft 2in); wing area 18.68sq m (201.1sq ft)
Armament:	two 30mm Aden cannon with 150 rounds, five external pylons with provision for AIM-9 Sidewinder or Matra Magic air-to-air missiles, and two Harpoon or Sea Eagle anti-shipping missiles, up to a total of 3629kg (8000lb)

BAe Sea Harrier FRS.Mk 2

In 1985, on orders from the Ministry of Defence and the Fleet Air Arm, British Aerospace began the development of an upgrade programme to modernise the fleet of FRS. Mk 1s. The primary aim of the program was to give the Sea Harrier the ability to engage multiple beyond-visual-range targets with the new AIM-120 AMRAAM medium-range air-to-air missile. The most obvious difference is to the shape of the forward fuselage, which accommodates the new Ferranti Blue Vixen pulse-Doppler track-while-scan radar. Further upgrades to the avionics include a MIL 1553B digital databus, redesigned HUD and dual head-down displays, Marconi Sky Guardian Radar Warning Receiver, and a secure data and voice link system. Two additional missile launch rails and the new Aden 25 cannon complete the package. Deliveries of the 33 converted aircraft commenced in April 1992.

Country of origin:	United Kingdom
Type:	shipborne multi-role combat aircraft
Powerplant:	one 9752kg (21,500lb) Rolls-Royce Pegasus Mk 106 vectored thrust turbofan
Performance:	maximum speed at sea level 1185km/h (736mph) at sea level with maximum AAM load; service ceiling 15,545m (51,000ft); intercept radius 185km (115 miles) on hi-hi-hi CAP with 90 minuted loiter on station
Weights:	empty 5942kg (13,100lb); maximum take-off 11,884kg (26,200lb)
Dimensions:	wingspan 7.7m (25ft 3in); length 14.17m (46ft 6in); height 3.71m (12ft 2in); wing area 18.68sq m (201.1sq ft)
Armament:	two 25mm Aden cannon with 150 rounds, five external pylons with provision for AIM-9 Sidewinder, AIM-120 AMRAAM, and two Harpoon or Sea Eagle anti-shipping missiles, up to a total of 3629kg (8000lb)

BAe (HS) Hawk T.Mk 1

The Hawk has been one of the truly outstanding successes of the British aerospace industry in the past three decades. Much of this success is due to the exceptional service life of the airframe, low maintenance requirements (the lowest per flight hour of any jet aircraft in the world), relatively inexpensive purchase price when originally offered for export, large optional payload, and its ability to operate in the medium range attack and air superiority role for a fraction of the cost of more powerful types. The Hawk was the only entirely new all-British military aircraft for 15 years in 1980. The first prototype flew in August 1974, and the first two operational aircraft were handed over in November 1976. Construction of the efficient Adour turbofan is modular, enabling easy maintenance. The basic RAF advanced trainer is designated the T.Mk 1.

Country of origin:	United Kingdom
Type:	two-seat basic and advanced jet trainer
Powerplant:	one 2359kg (5200lb) Rolls Royce/Turbomeca Adour Mk 151 turbofan
Performance:	maximum speed 1038km/h (645mph); service ceiling 15,240m (50,000ft); endurance 4 hours
Weights:	empty 3647kg (8040lb); maximum take-off 7750kg (17,085lb)
Dimensions:	wingspan 9.39m (30ft 9.75in); length 11.17m (36ft 7.75in); height 3.99m (13ft 1.75in); wing area 16.69sq m (179.64sq ft)
Armament:	underfuselage/wing hardpoints with provision for up to 2567kg (5660lb) of stores

BAe (HS) Hawk T.Mk 1A

As well as its fleet of T.Mk 1 trainer aircraft, the RAF also operates the aircraft for weapons instruction. Nos 1 and 2 Tactical Weapons Units, previously based at RAF Brawdy and RAF Chivenor, have now been incorporated into the Flying Training School at RAF Valley. The T.Mk1A has three pylons; the central one is normally occupied by a 30mm Aden cannon, the two underwing pylons can be fitted with a wide combination of weapons, including Matra rocket pods. The Hawk has in various formats been exported to more than 14 different countries, often as a dedicated attack aircraft. In 1985 construction began of the Hawk Mk 200, a single-seat version dedicated to the tactical attack role. This aircraft served with No. 1 Tactical Weapons Unit at Brawdy in Wales and is carrying a centreline drop tank and rocket pods for weapons training.

Country of origin:	United Kingdom
Type:	two-seat weapons training aircraft
Powerplant:	one 2359kg (5200lb) Rolls Royce/Turbomeca Adour Mk 151 turbofan
Performance:	maximum speed 1038km/h (645mph); service ceiling 15,240m (50,000ft); endurance 4 hours
Weights:	empty 3647kg (8040lb); maximum take-off 7750kg (17,085lb)
Dimensions:	wingspan 9.39m (30ft 9.75in); length 11.17m (36ft 7.75in); height 3.99m (13ft 1.75in); wing area 16.69sq m (179.64sq ft)
Armament:	underfuselage/wing hardpoints with provision for up to 2567kg (5660lb) of stores, wingtip mounted air-to-air missiles

BAe/McDonnell Douglas T-45A Goshawk

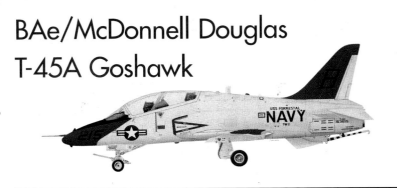

The Goshawk is a development of the highly successful BAe (HS) Hawk trainer for the US Navy. A joint McDonnell Douglas/BAe venture based Hawk emerged as the winner of a competition announced by the US Navy in the late 1970s for a carrier-equipped naval pilot trainer to replace the Rockwell T-2 Buckeye. The aircraft is significantly different from the Hawk, with strong twin-wheel nose gear, strengthened long-stroke main gear legs, an arrestor hook, and twin lateral airbrakes. Other changes include US Navy-style cockpit and avionics, and US Navy standard avionics. Emphasis was placed on the need for operational economy, and the Rolls-Royce/Turbomeca engine has been designed with this in mind. The aircraft, which are built by McDonnell in Missouri, entered service in 1990. Pictured is a T-45A Goshawk of Training Wing Two at Kingsville, Texas.

Country of origin:	USA
Type:	tandem-seat carrier-equipped naval pilot trainer
Powerplant:	one 2651kg (5845lb) Rolls Royce/Turbomeca F-405-RR-401 turbofan
Performance:	maximum speed at 2440m (8000ft) 997km/h (620mph); service ceiling 12,875m (42,250ft); range on internal fuel 1850km (1150 miles)
Weights:	empty 4263kg (9399lb); maximum take-off 5787kg (12,758lb)
Dimensions:	wingspan 9.39m (30ft 9.75in); length 11.97m (39ft 3.125in); height 4.27m (14ft); wing area 16.69sq m (179.6sq ft)

BAe (HS) Nimrod MR.Mk 2P

Hawker Siddeley began the design of the Nimrod in 1964, using the Comet 4C airliner as the basis for a new aircraft to replace the Avro Shackelton in the maritime patrol and anti-submarine warfare role with the Royal Air Force. The aircraft's basic fuselage was retained but an additional fuselage fairing covering almost the entire length of the lower fuselage was added to accommodate radar, weapons bay and various other systems. The aircraft began entering service in 1969, and were significantly updated to MR.Mk 2P standard from 1979 with improved avionics and weapons systems. Nimrods were very active during the Falklands War; inflight refuelling equipment was hastily added to a number of aircraft to allow them to operate from Ascension Island. The MR.Mk 2P is the version currently in service.

Country of origin:	United Kingdom
Type:	maritime patrol and anti-submarine warfare aircraft
Powerplant:	four 5507kg (12,140lb) Rolls Royce Spey Mk 250 turbofans
Performance:	maximum speed 925km/h (575mph); service ceiling 12,800m (42,000ft); range on internal fuel 9262km (5,755 miles)
Weights:	empty 39,010kg (86,000lb); maximum take-off 87,090kg (192,000lb)
Dimensions:	wingspan 35.0m (114ft 10in) excluding wingtip ESM pods; length 39.34m (129ft 1in); height 9.08m (29ft 9.5in); wing area 197.04sq m (2,121sq ft)
Armament:	internal bay with provision for 6123kg (13,500lb) of stores, including nine torpedoes and/or depth charges; underwing pylons for Harpoon anti-ship missiles or pairs of Sidewinder air-to-air missiles

BAe (BAC) 167 Strikemaster

The Strikemaster was originally developed from the Jet Provost trainer designed by Hunting. BAC absorbed Hunting in 1961, and refined the strike/attack BAC 145 into the more potent Strikemaster. With a more powerful Rolls-Royce Viper engine, the Strikemaster proved to be a great worldwide success. It had side by side ejector seats, and the ability to operate from the roughest airstrip whilst carrying an impressive load. The first customers were Saudi Arabia, South Yemen People's Republic, Sultanate of Oman (where the aircraft saw action against rebel forces), Kuwait, Singapore, Kenya, New Zealand and Ecuador. The aircraft has a considerably reinforced structure, making it extremely durable. Pictured is one of the Kuwaiti Air Force Mk. 83s equipped with a centreline drop tank and underwing rocket pods.

Country of origin:	United Kingdom
Type:	two seat light tactical aircraft and trainer
Engine:	one 1547kg (3410lb) Rolls Royce Viper
Performance:	maximum speed 774 km/h (481mph); service ceiling 13,410m (44,000ft); combat radius with 3300lb load 233km (145 miles)
Weights:	empty 2840kg (6270lb); maximum 5210kg (11,500lb)
Dimensions:	wingspan 11.23m (36ft 10in); length 10.27m (33ft 8.5in); height 3.34m (10ft 11.5in)
Armament:	two 7.62mm FN machine guns with 550rpg; four underwing hardpoints with provision for up to 1360kg (3000lb) of stores, including rockets, bombs and air-to-ground missiles, and drop tanks

Bell P-59A Airacomet

Development work on jet aircraft began rather later in America than in Europe, and with the considerable assistance of British expertise. In June 1941 the US government and General 'Hap' Arnold of the US Army Air Corps were told of Britain's development of the turbojet engine. On September 5, 1941 Bell Aircraft was requested to design a jet fighter and in October a Whittle turbojet. Complete engineering drawings and a team from Power Jets Ltd (Whittle's private company) arrived from Britain to hasten proceedings. Barely a year later, the Bell P-59A Airacomet was ready to fly, with Whittle engines built by General Electric. Development went extremely well, and 12 YP-59As were delivered for service trials in 1944. The P-59A was classed as a fighter trainer when it became clear that it would not make an effective front-line fighter. Total procurement amounted to 66.

Country of origin:	USA
Type:	single-seat jet fighter trainer
Powerplant:	two (907kg) 2,000lb General Electric J31-GE-3 turbojets
Performance:	maximum speed 671km/h (413mph); service ceiling 14,080m (46,200ft); maximum range with two 125 Imp gal drop tanks 837km (520 miles)
Weights:	empty 3610kg (7950lb); maximum take-off 6214kg (13,700lb)
Dimensions:	wingspan 13.87m (45ft 6in); length 11.63m (38ft 11.5in); height 3.66m (12ft); wing area 35.84sq m (385.8sq ft)

Bell P-59B Airacomet

Only 19 P-59Bs reached operational service, with the 412th FG who had been tasked with evaluating the P-59A from the end of 1944. The P-59B differed from its predecessor by way of the more powerful General Electric J31-GE-5 turbojets and greater fuel capacity. Service aircraft were fitted with a nose-mounted 37mm cannon, three 0.5in machine guns, and bomb racks under the wings, in common with the production P-59As. The technical expertise which the USAAF and the aircraft industry gained through the Airacomets served mainly to prepare the ground for the achievement of the first true jet fighter of the US Air Force, the P-80 Shooting Star. The P-80 began to arrive in service with the 412th FG at the end of 1945. This P-59B served with the USAF on drone control operations, and has an open cockpit in the nose to seat a drone operator.

Country of origin:	USA
Type:	single-seat jet fighter
Powerplant:	two 907kg (2000lb) General Electric J31-GE-5 turbojets
Performance:	maximum speed 658km/h (409mph); service ceiling 14,080m (46,200ft); maximum range 644km (400 miles)
Weights:	empty 3704kg (8165lb); maximum take-off 6214kg (13,700lb)
Dimensions:	wingspan 13.87m (45ft 6in); length 11.63m (38ft 1.5in); height 3.66m (12ft); wing area 35.84sq m (385.8sq ft)
Armament:	one 37mm M4 cannon and three 0.5in machine guns; underwing pylons for bombs and drop tanks

Blackburn Buccaneer S.2B

After the Defence White Paper of April 1957, which proclaimed manned combat aircraft obsolete, the only British aircraft which avoided cancellation was the Blackburn B.103. Development of this aircraft, the first to be designed specifically for carrier-borne strike operations at below radar level. The S.1 was marginal on power, but the greatly improved S.2 was a reliable and formidable aircraft. The first 84 were ordered by the Royal Navy, and after giving good service, most were transferred to the Royal Air Force from 1969. A program of substantial modification was carried out on the existing S.2 fleet, with a further 43 aircraft delivered from new. The primary difference with these aircraft, designated S.2B, was the provision to carry the Martel anti-radar missile. Some were equipped with a TIALD (Thermal Imaging And Laser Designation Pod) and deployed to the Gulf.

Country of origin:	United Kingdom
Type:	two-seat attack aircraft
Powerplant:	two 5105kg (11,255lb) Rolls Royce RB.168 Spey Mk 101 turbofans
Performance:	maximum speed at 61m (200ft) 1040km/h (646mph); service ceiling over 12,190m (40,000ft); combat range with typical weapons load 3701km (2300 miles)
Weights:	empty 13,608kg (30,000lb); maximum take-off 28,123kg (62,000lb)
Dimensions:	wingspan 13.41 (44ft); length 19.33m (63ft 5in); height 4.97m (16ft 3in); wing area 47.82sq m (514.7sq ft)
Armament:	four 454kg (1000lb) bombs, fuel tank, or reconnaissance pack on inside of rotary bomb door, four underwing pylons with provision for up to 5443kg (12,000lb) of bombs or missiles, including Harpoon and Sea Eagle anti-shipping missiles, and Martel anti-radar missiles

Boeing B-52D Stratofortress

The B-52 has been in continuous service with Strategic Air Command in one form or another since 1955, with service life for the current generation of B-52H aircraft likely to continue well into the next century. Development of this remarkable warhorse, which started life as a turboprop-powered project, began in 1945. The first prototype flew on October 2, 1951, and deliveries of 98 A, B, and C models began in June 1955. Boeing extensively revised the fore -control system for the tail-mounted armament of four 0.5in machine guns for the B-52D (Model 464-201-7). The company built 101 B-52Ds at its Seattle plant, before production was moved to Wichita where another 69 were completed. Deliveries of this version began in 1956. The aircraft had been designed to carry stand-off nuclear weapons but in 1964 a rebuilding programme began to allow it to carry 105 'iron bombs'.

Country of origin:	USA
Type:	long-range strategic bomber
Powerplant:	eight 4536kg (10,000lb) Pratt & Whitney J57 turbojets
Performance:	maximum speed at 7315m (24,000ft) 1014km/h (630mph): service ceiling 13,720m-16,765m (45,000ft-55,000ft); standard range with maximum load 9978km (6,200 miles)
Weights:	empty 77,200-87,100kg (171,000-193,000lb); loaded 204,120kg (450,000lb)
Dimensions:	wingspan 56.4m (185ft); length 48m (157ft 7in); height 14.75m (48ft 3in); wing area 371.60sq m (4,000sq ft)
Armament:	remotely controlled tail mounting with four 0.5in machine guns; normal internal bomb capacity 12,247kg (27,000lb) including all SAC special weapons; modified to take up to 31,750kg (70,000lb) of conventional bombs on internal and external pylons

Boeing B-52G Stratofortress

The B-52G introduced a host of significant improvements, including a wet wing that housed far more fuel, more powerful Pratt & Whitney J57-43W turbojets (as on the E and F models), a shortened fin of increased chord, and a remote controlled rear turret. The aircraft also benefited from the upgraded and much improved navigation and bombing systems introduced on the previous two variants. It was also fitted with Quail countermeasures vehicles and could carry a pair of North American AGM-28 Hound Dog missiles. First flown in October 1958, this model was delivered to SAC from the following February. A total of 193 B-52G models were built, the last in 1960. Some 173 of these were later converted to carry 12 Boeing AGM-86B Air Launched Cruise Missiles in addition to the eight AGM-69 SRAMS or other weapons carried in the internal bay.

Country of origin:	USA
Type:	long-range strategic bomber
Powerplant:	eight 6238kg (13,750lb) Pratt & Whitney J57-P-43W turbojets
Performance:	maximum speed at 7315m (24,000ft) 1014km/h (630mph): service ceiling 16,765m (55,000ft); standard range with maximum load 13,680km (8500 miles)
Weights:	empty 77,200-87,100kg (171,000-193,000lb); loaded 221,500kg (448,000lb)
Dimensions:	wingspan 56.4m (185ft); length 48m (157ft 7in); height 12.4m (40ft 8in); wing area 371.60sq m (4000sq ft)
Armament:	remotely controlled tail mounting with four 0.5in machine guns; normal internal bomb capacity 12,247kg (27,000lb) including all SAC special weapons; external pylons for two AGM-28B Hound Dog missiles

Boeing RB-47H Stratojet

Boeing began studies of jet bombers in 1943, but it was the discovery of the research that had been done into swept wings in Germany that spurred the Model 450. The design had passed through several stages, from the straight winged Model 424, through the swept wing Model 448 with fuselage mounted turbojets, until the final design was dubiously bought by the USAAF in October 1945. The bomber was at the peak of its career in the mid 1950s when it was probably the most important military aircraft in the West. Peak strength in SAC was reached in 1957, when about 1800 of all models were in service. Many hundreds were converted for a variety of specialist roles. Thirty-two were RB-47H models, completed in production for electronic reconnaissance missions, with the bomb bay converted to accommodate equipment and three EW officers.

Country of origin:	USA
Type:	strategic reconnaissance aircraft
Powerplant:	six 3,266kg (7200lb) General Electric J47-GE-25 turbojets
Performance:	maximum speed at 4970m (16,300ft) 975km/h (606mph); service ceiling 12,345m (40,500ft); range 6437km (4,000 miles)
Weights:	empty 36,630kg (80,756lb); maximum take-off 89,893kg (198,180lb)
Dimensions:	wingspan 35.36m (116ft); length 33.48m (109ft 10in); height 8.51m (27ft 11in); wing area 132.66sq m (1428 sq ft)
Armament:	two remotely controlled 20mm cannon in tail

Boeing KC-135E Stratotanker

The family of Boeing jet transports all stemmed from a privately-funded prototype, designated the Model 367-80, which first flew in July 1954. After evaluation the US Air Force decided to buy 29 developed versions to serve in the dual roles of tanker for Strategic Air Command, and logistic transport for Military Airlift Command. The first KC-135A left the assembly line at Renton, Washington in July 1956, with initial deliveries to the 93rd Air Refuelling Squadron the following June. Production of the aircraft totalled 724; when production ended in January 1965 it was decided to keep these aircraft operational until the next century, and a major overhaul programme was started in the mid-1970s. At the heart of this programme lay the task of reskinning the lower wing surfaces; by 1985 more than 500 aircraft had undergone this treatment.

Country of origin:	USA
Type:	inflight-refuelling tanker/cargo/transport aircraft
Powerplant:	four 8165kg (18,000lb) Pratt & Whitney TF33-P-5 turbofans
Performance:	cruising speed at 40,000ft 853km/h (530mph); range 4627km (2875 miles)
Weights:	maximum take-off 146,284kg (322,500lb); maximum fuel load 92,210kg (203,288lb)
Dimensions:	wingspan 39.88m (130ft 10in); length 41.53m (136ft 3in); height 12.7m (41ft 8in); wing area 226.03sq m (2,433sq ft)

Boeing RC-135V

Boeing's Model 717 (the military designation for the 707) has served in countless different roles, including reconnaissance, airborne early warning, electronic surveillance, VIP transport and avionics testing. Although derived from the 707, the RC-135V bears little physical relation to the civil aircraft. The R designation denotes a reconnaissance aircraft in USAF parlance; the RC-135V was the tenth of 12 variants, which have been tasked with electronic surveillance since the mid-1960s. The eight RC-135Vs were converted from RC-135C and one RC-135U aircraft. As well as the cheek antennae fairings and sidewards-looking airborne radar (SLAR) from these models, the modified aircraft were fitted with a distinctive thimble nose and a vast array of underfuselage blade aerials. These aircraft serve alongside RC-135Us with the 55th Strategic Reconnaissance Wing.

Country of origin:	USA
Type:	electronic reconnaissance aircraft
Powerplant:	four 8156kg (18,000lb) Pratt & Whitney TF33-P-9 turbojets
Performance:	maximum speed at 7620m (25,000ft) 991km/h (616mph); service ceiling 12,375m (40,600ft) range 4305km (2675 miles)
Weights:	empty 46,403kg (102,300lb) maximum take-off 124,965g (275,500lb)
Dimensions:	wingspan 39.88m (130ft 10in); length 41.53m (136ft 3in); height 12.7m (41ft 8in); wing area 226.03sq m (2,433sq ft)

Canadair CF-5 Freedom Fighter

When the Canadian government selected the Northrop F-5 for its air force, Canadair Ltd in Montreal was chosen to built the aircraft under licence in two versions, the CF-5A single-seat version and the CF-5D tandem seat aircraft. Canadair were able to incorporate a number of significant improvements to the design; the most important upgrade being uprated engines than the original US model. The potential range of the aircraft was also improved by fitting an inflight refuelling probe. Canadair have successfully exported the aircraft to a number of countries, including the Netherlands. In 1987 Bristol Aerospace received a contract to update 56 CF-5A/Ds for further use as lead-in trainers by the Canadian Air Force. This programme extended airframe life by 4,000 hours and, with other improvements, should allow the aircraft to remain in service well into the next century.

Country of origin:	USA and Canada
Type:	fighter and light attack aircraft
Powerplant:	two 1950kg (4300lb) Orenda (General Electric) J85-CAN-15 turbojets
Performance:	maximum speed at 10,970m (36,000ft) 1575km/h (978mph); service ceiling 15,500m (50,580ft); combat radius at maximum load 314km (195 miles)
Weights:	empty 3700kg (8157lb); maximum take-off 9249kg (20,390lb)
Dimensions:	wingspan 7.87m (25ft 10in); length 14.38m (47ft 2in); height 4.01m (13ft 2in); wing area 15.79sq m (170sq ft)
Armament:	two 20mm M39 cannon, underwing hardpoints with provision for two AIM-9 Sidewinder AAMs, gun and rocket pods, and bombs

Canadair CL-41G-5 Tebuan (CL-41 Tutor)

The Tutor has been the standard jet trainer of the Canadian Armed forces for over 30 years. In service the aircraft is known by the designation CT-114. The aircraft represented a significant step for the Canadian aerospace industry, as it was the first aircraft designed and built solely in that country. Early development was privately funded by the company because of a lack of interest from the Canadian government. Two prototypes were built powered by the built Pratt & Whitney JT12-A5 turbojet. Production examples were fitted with the indigenously built version of the General Electric CJ610, made in Canada as the J85-CAN-40. Production orders totalled some 190 aircraft, with 20 extensively modified CL-41G-5 Tebuan aircraft for Malaysia. The majority of the Canadian aircraft are based with No. 2 Flying Training School at Moose Jaw in Saskatchewan.

Country of origin:	Canada
Type:	two-seat jet trainer
Powerplant:	one 1338kg (2950lb) Orenda (General Electric) J85-CAN-40 turbojet
Performance:	maximum speed 797km/h (495mph); service ceiling 13,100m (43,000ft); standard range 1000km (621 miles)
Weights:	empty 2220kg (4895lb); maximum take-off 3532kg (7787lb)
Dimensions:	wingspan 11.13m (36ft 6in); length 9.75m (32ft); height 2.76m (9ft 1in); wing area 20.44sq m (220sq ft)
Armament:	six external hardpoints with provision for up to 1814kg (4000lb) of stores

Canadair Sabre Mk 4

Italy was one of nearly 20 countries which operated the North-American designed Sabre. Fiat licence-built 221 of the F-86K version for the Aeronautica Militare Italia. This aircraft, however, is a Sabre Mk 4 (F-86E), one of 430 built by the Canadair company with funds provided by the Mutual Defense Assistance Program to re-equip RAF fighter squadrons. The aircraft were later fitted with extended leading edges and passed on to Italy, who took 180; Yugoslavia, Greece and Turkey also took numbers. Unlike the Canadair-built Sabres Mk 5 and Mk 6, which were powered by a licence-built Orenda turbojet, the Mk 4 aircraft had the original General Electric engine. In all other respects the Mk 4 was the same as the F-86E, including the 'all-flying tail'. Note the prancing horse insignia on the tail, reminiscent of the badge used on a certain marque of Italian car!

Country of origin:	USA/Canada
Type:	single-seat fighter-bomber
Powerplant:	one 2358kg (5200lb) General Electric J47-GE-13 turbojet
Performance:	maximum speed at sea level 1091km/h (678mph); service ceiling 15,240m (50,000ft); range 1344km (835 miles)
Weights:	empty 5045kg (11,125lb); maximum loaded 9350kg (20,611lb)
Dimensions:	wingspan 11.30m (37ft 1in); length 11.43m (37ft 6in); height 4.47m (14ft 8.75in); wing area 27.76sq m (288sq ft)
Armament:	six 0.5in Colt-Browning M-3 with 267 rpg, underwing hardpoints for two tanks or two stores of 454kg (1000lb), plus eight rockets

Canadair Sabre Mk 6

Canadair continued their association with the Sabre through the Mk 5 (370 built) and the Mk 6 (655 built). The Mk 5 introduced a feature that was already in production by North American; the 6-3 leading edge, which extended the wing root leading edge by 6in and the tip l.e by 3in. This modification improved agility in high-speed combat. The South African Air Force, who flew F-86E and F aircraft with UN forces in the Korean War, purchased 34 of the Mk 6 version, with a 3300kg (7,275lb) Orenda engine. This aircraft is widely regarded as the finest dogfighter of the era, and remained in use with the SAAF until replaced by the Mirage F1CZ and F1AZ in the 1970s. The aircraft pictured served with No. 1 Squadron. Commonwealth Aircraft Corporation in Australia were also involved in Sabre production.

Country of origin:	USA/Canada
Type:	single-seat fighter-bomber
Powerplant:	one 3300kg (7275lb) Orenda 14 turbojet
Performance:	maximum speed at sea level 1091km/h (678mph); service ceiling 15,240m (50,000ft); range 1344km (835 miles)
Weights:	empty 5045kg (11,125lb); maximum loaded 9350kg (20,611lb)
Dimensions:	wingspan 11.30m (37ft 1in); length 11.43m (37ft 6in); height 4.47m (14ft 8.75in); wing area 27.76sq m (288sq ft)
Armament:	six 0.5in Colt-Browning M-3 with 267 rpg, underwing hardpoints for two tanks or two stores of 454kg (1000lb), plus eight rockets

CASA C-101EB-01 Aviojet (E.25 Mirlo)

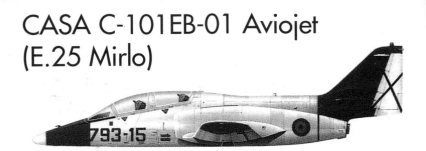

The C-101 was developed by the Spanish CASA company (Construcciones Aeronauticas SA) from the mid-1970s as a replacement for the Hispano HA.200 jet trainer in service with the Spanish Air Force (EdA). Assistance in the design was provided by Northrop and MBB, and many of the parts were sourced from foreign contractors, including the Dowty-built landing gear, Martin-Baker ejector seats, Garrett-AiResearch turbofan and Sperry flight control system. The first flight was made in June 1977. Production deliveries of the 92 aircraft supplied to the EdA began in 1980. From 1990 CASA upgraded the weapons system on the C-101 in the hope of encouraging export orders. These were forthcoming from Honduras (4 C-101BB), Chile (for a licence-built version designated T-36 and the upgraded C-101CC, which are designated A-36) and Jordan, who operate the C-101CC aircraft.

Country of origin:	Spain
Type:	two-seat advanced flying/weapons trainer
Powerplant:	one 1588kg (3500lb) Garrett AiResearch TFE731-2-2J turbofan
Performance:	maximum speed at 6095m (20,000ft) 806km/h (501mph); service ceiling 12,800m (42,000ft); endurance 7 hours
Weights:	empty 3470kg (7650lb); maximum take-off 4850kg (10,692lb)
Dimensions:	wingspan 10.6m (34ft 9.25in); length 12.5m (41ft); height 4.25m (13ft 11.25in); wing area 20sq m (215.3sq ft)
Armament:	one 30mm DEFA cannon; six external hardpoints with provision for up to 2000kg (4410lb) of stores, including rocket pods, missiles, bombs and drop tanks

Cessna A-37B Dragonfly

The 318E is a development of the Cessna Model T-37, one of the jet aircraft used during the 1950s and 1960s for pilot training in the US. In 1962 two T-37s were evaluated by the USAFs Special Warfare Centre for possible use in the counter-insurgency role. The aircraft were subsequently modified to accept engines that produced more than double the power of the original Continental J69-T-25s, permitting an increase in the possible weapons load. The war in South East Asia highlighted the need for such an aircraft and Cessna were requested in 1966 to convert 39 T-37s from the production line to a light strike role, equipped with eight underwing hardpoints, wing tip tanks, and powered by the more powerful engines. Delivery began in May 1967. The A-37B had a reinforced structure, increased maximum fuel capacity, and provision for inflight refuelling.

Country of origin:	USA
Type:	light attack and reconnaissance aircraft
Powerplant:	two 1293kg (2850lb) General Electric J85-GE-17A turbojets
Performance:	maximum speed at 4875m (16,000ft) 816km/h (507mph); service ceiling 12,730m (41,765ft); range with 1860kg (4100lb) load 740km (460 miles)
Weights:	empty 2817kg (6211lb); maximum take-off 6350kg (14,000lb)
Dimensions:	wingspan including tip tanks 10.93m(35ft 10.25in); length 8.62m (28ft 3in); height 2.7m (8ft 10.25in); wing area 17.09sq m (183.9sq ft)
Armament:	one 7.62mm GAU-2 Minigun six-barrel machine gun, eight underwing hardpoints with provision for more than 2268kg (5000lb) of stores, including bombs, rocket and gun pods, napalm tanks, and other equipment

Chance Vought F7U-1 Cutlass

The Cutlass was designed in 1946, when fighter aerodynamics had been thrown into considerable turmoil by wartime German research and emerging jet technology. The design incorporated a 38-degree swept wing carrying wide-span powered elevons, airbrakes, and full-span leading edge slats. Twin vertical tails were mounted at one-third span. These features were remarkably advanced for the time, as was the use of afterburning engines, an automatic stabilisation system, and controls with artificial feedback. Three prototype XF7U-1s were completed, and the first of these flew on September 29, 1949. After only 14 F7U-1s had been completed, the production run was halted and a number of major design revisions were made. Even so, the F7U-2 suffered severe engine difficulties and the final productions version, the F7U-3 and missile-armed -3M, had non-afterburning engines.

Country of origin:	USA
Type:	carrier-based fighter-bomber
Powerplant:	two 1905kg (4200lb) Westinghouse J34-32 turbojets
Performance:	maximum speed at sea level 1070km/h (665mph); service ceiling 12,500m (41,000ft); combat radius with maximum fuel 966km (600 miles)
Weights:	empty 5385kg (11,870lb); maximum take-off 7640kg (16,840lb)
Dimensions:	wingspan 11.78m (38ft 8in); length 12.07m (39ft 7in); height 3m (9ft 10in); wing area 46.08sq m (496sq ft)
Armament:	four 20mm M-2 cannon

Convair B-58A Hustler

The B-58 was an historic aircraft on many counts. It was the first supersonic bomber and the first to reach Mach 2. It was the first aircraft constructed mainly from a stainless steel honeycomb sandwich, the first to have a slim body and fat payload pod so that when the load was dropped, the aircraft became slimmer and lighter, the first to have stellar-inertial navigation, and the first weapon system to be procured as a single package from the prime contractor. The technical problems in realising the aircraft were daunting, yet the aircraft was developed with admirable speed and success. The first flight was made on November 11, 1956, and development continued for almost three years. The first production aircraft was delivered in September 1959, and the type entered service with the 43rd Bomber Wing of SAC in March 1960.

Coutry of origin:	USA
Type:	three-seat supersonic bomber
Powerplant:	four 7076kg (15,600lb) General Electric J79-5B turbojets
Performance:	maximum speed 2125km/h (1385mph); service ceiling 19,500m (64,000ft); range on internal fuel 8248km (5125 miles)
Weights:	empty 25,200kg (55,560lb); maximum take-off 73,930kg (163,000lb)
Dimensions:	wingspan 17.31m (56ft 10in); length 29.5m (96ft 9in); height 9.6m (31ft 5in); wing area 145.32sq m (1542sq ft)
Armament:	one 20mm T171 Vulcan rotary cannon in radar-aimed tail barbette, plus nuclear or conventional weapons in disposable underfuselage pod

Convair F-102 Delta Dagger

In 1948 Convair flew the world's first delta wing aircraft, the XF-92A, which was part of a programme intended to lead to a supersonic fighter. This was terminated, but the US Air Force later issued a specification for an extremely advanced all-weather interceptor to carry the Hughes MX-1179 electronic control system. This effectively made the carrier aircraft subordinate to its avionics, a radical concept in the early 1950s. The contract was contested between six airframe manufacturers, and awarded to Convair in September 1961. In the event the Hughes ECS system could not be delivered in time and was rescheduled for the F-106 program. Early flight trials of the F-102 prototype were disappointing, but once the design was right right, 875 were delivered. In the search mode the pilot flew with two control columns; the left hand being used to adjust the sweep angle and range of the radar.

Country of origin:	USA
Type:	supersonic all-weather single-seat fighter-interceptor
Powerplant:	one 7802kg (17,200lb) Pratt & Whitney J57-P-23 turbojet
Performance:	maximum speed at 10,970m (36,000ft) 1328km/h (825mph); service ceiling 16,460m (54,000ft); range 2172km (1350 miles)
Weights:	empty 8630kg (19,050lb); maximum take-off 14,288kg (31,500lb)
Dimensions:	wingspan 11.62m (38ft 1.5in); length 20.84m (68ft 4.5in); height 6.46m (21ft 2.5in); wing area 61.45sq m (661.5sq ft)
Armament:	two AIM-26/26A Falcon missiles, or one AIM-26/26A plus two AIM-4A Falcons, or one AIM-26/26A plus two AIM-4C/Ds, or six AIM-4As, or six AIM-4C/Ds, some aircraft fitted with 12 2.75in folding-fin rockets

Convair F-106 Delta Dart

The F-106 was originally designated F-102B to indicate the strong family connection with the earlier Delta Dagger. The aircraft is notable because of the fact that it was designed from the outset as an integral weapon system, in which each of the differing units (airframe, weapons, etc) would integrate as a compatible system. Central to this project was an electronic weapons control system. It had been hoped to realise this objective with the Delta Dagger, but delays in the program meant that the ECS was not ready until late in 1955, an unacceptable time scale to the USAF who planned to bring the F-102 into service that year. The F-106 program was delayed by engine problems, and flight tests proved disappointing. The Hughes designed MA-1 ECS was also not performing well. The aircraft eventually entered service in October 1959 and remained in service, in updated versions, until 1988.

Country of origin:	USA
Type:	light attack and reconnaissance aircraft
Powerplant:	two 1293kg (2850lb) General Electric J85-GE-17A turbojets
Performance:	maximum speed at 4875m (16,000ft) 816km/h (507mph); service ceiling 12,730m (41,765ft); range with 1860kg (4100lb) load 740km (460 miles)
Weights:	empty 2817kg (6211lb); maximum take-off 6350kg (14,000lb)
Dimensions:	wingspan including tip tanks 10.93m (35ft 10.25in); length 8.62m (28ft .4in); height 2.7m (8ft 1.33in); wing area 17.09sq m (183.9sq ft)
Armament:	one 7.62mm GAU-2 Minigun six-barrelled machine gun, eight underwing hardpoints with provision for more than 2268kg (5000lb) of stores, including bombs, rocket and gun pods, napalm tanks, and other equipment

Dassault/Dornier Alpha Jet A

Realisation that the Jaguar was too advanced and costly to be a standard basic trainer led the Armeé de l'Air to issue a requirement for a new trainer in 1967 (The jaguar was originally conceived in this role). The aircraft was also to be capable in the ground attack role. As it transpired the Luftwaffe had parallel need for such an aircraft, and on July 22, 1969 the two governments agreed to a common specification and agreed to adopt a common type of aircraft produced jointly by the two national industries. Following a design submission by Dassault/Dornier it was announced on July 24, 1970 that the Alpha Jet had been selected for production. Delivery of the first of 176 Alpha Jet A (Appui) light attack aircraft for the Federal German air force began in 1979. The A is distinguished by the pointed nose; that of the trainer is less acute.

Country of origin:	France and Germany
Type:	two-seat light strike and reconnaissance aircraft
Powerplant:	two 1350kg (2976lb) Turbomeca Larzac 04 turbofans
Performance:	maximum speed 927km/h (576mph); service ceiling 14,000m (45,930ft); comabat range on hi-lo-hi mission 583km (363 miles)
Weights:	empty 3515kg (7749lb); maximum take-off 8000kg (17,637lb)
Dimensions:	wingpsan 9.11m (29ft 10.75in); length 13.23m (43ft 5in); height 4.19m (13ft 9in); wing area 17.5sq m (188.37sq ft)
Armament:	one 27mm IWKA Mauser cannon, five fuselage harpoints with provision for up to 2500kg (5511lb) of stores

Dassault/Dornier Alpha Jet E

There are two basic forms of the Alpha Jet, the attack version previously discussed, and the two seat jet trainer initially produced for the Armeé de l'Air. Physically very similar to the attack version, the E (Ecole) replaced the Fouga Magister and Dassault Mystère as the basic and advanced jet trainers of the French Air Force. For all aircraft, the outer wings, tail unit, rear fuselage, landing gear doors and exhaust are manufactured in Germany; the forward and centre fuselage were manufactured in France, with other work contracted out to a Belgian company. The Alpha Jet made its first flight, at Istres, on October 26, 1973. A further development of the Ecole is Alpha Jet 3, fitted with state of the art cockpit controls and multiple cockpit displays for use in training aircrew with the navigation/attack systems of future aircraft.

Country of origin:	France and Germany
Type:	two-seat basic/advanced trainer aircraft
Powerplant:	two 1350kg (2976lb) Turbomeca Larzac 04 turbofans
Performance:	maximum speed 927km/h (576mph); service ceiling 14,000m (45,930ft); low level training mission 540km (335 miles)
Weights:	empty 3345kg (7374lb); normal take-off 5000kg (11,023 lb)
Dimensions:	wingpsan 9.11m (29ft 10.75in); length 11.75m (38ft 6.5in); height 4.19m (13ft 9in); wing area 17.5sq m (188.37sq ft)

Dassault M.D. 450 Ouragan

The Second World War effectively destroyed the French aircraft industry, and it had to be largely rebuilt from scratch while learning the new technology of jet propulsion. Most companies in the newly nationalised French aviation industry failed to see any of their designs built in any quantity, but the private firm of Dassault produced what is undoubtedly one of the most enduring and successful families of combat aircraft in the world. The whole line of Mirages, Etendards, Mystères, and Rafales stem from the simple, conventional, but highly effective Ouragan (Hurricane) of 1949. Powered by a licence built version of the British Rolls-Royce Nene turbojet, the first unarmed prototype was flown on February 28, 1949. Equipped with a pressurised cockpit and wingtip fuel tanks, the first of 150 production aircraft entered service in 1952.

Country of origin:	France
Type:	single-seat fighter/ground attack aircraft
Powerplant:	one 2300kg (5070lb) Hispano-Suiza Nene 104B turbojet
Performance:	maximum speed 940km/h (584mph); service ceiling 15,000m (49,210ft); range 1000km (620 miles)
Weights:	empty 4150kg (9150lb); maximum take-off 7600kg (17,416lb)
Dimensions:	wingspan over tip tanks 13.2m (43ft 2in); length 10.74m (35ft 3in); height 4.15m (13ft 7in); wing area 23.8sq m (256.18sq ft)
Armament:	four 20mm Hispano 404 cannon; underwing hardpoints for two 434kg (1000lb) bombs, or 16 105mm rockets, or eight rockets and two 458 litre (101 Imp gal) napalm tanks

Dassault Mystère IIC

Marcel Dassault's design philosophy was always to progress in easy steps. The first Mystère was merely an M.D 450 Ouragan with 30 degrees of sweep to the wings and tail. This aircraft, designated the Mystère I, first flew in February 1951. Over the course of the following two years, eight further prototypes were built and flown. The original aircraft was powered by the ubiquitous Rolls-Royce Nene, while the remainder were fitted with a licence-built (by Hispano Suiza) version of the Tay. Pre-production aircraft were fitted with the all-French Atar axial engine, the first use of any French gas turbine for military aircraft propulsion. In April 1953 the Armee de l'Air ordered 150 of the fighters; ultimately 180 were built, 156 for France and 24 for Israel (never delivered). Service career was short, but the aircraft is important as the first swept-wing fighter to go into production in Europe.

Country of origin:	France
Type:	single-seat fighter bomber
Powerplant:	one 3000kg (6600lb) SNECMA Atar 101D3 turbojet
Performance:	maximum speed 1060km/h (658mph); service ceiling 13,000m (42,650ft); range 1200km (745 miles)
Weights:	empty 5250kg (11,514lb); loaded 7450kg (16,442lb)
Dimensions:	wingspan 13.1m (42ft 9.75in); length 11.7m (38ft 6.25in); height 4.25m (13ft 11.75in)
Armament:	two 30mm Hispano 603 cannon with 150 rounds each

Dassault Mystère IVA

Although superficially similar to the II series aircraft, the IVA was in fact a completely new aircraft, with hardly a single structural part being common to both. The wing of the IV was thinner, more sharply swept, and much strengthened. The fuselage and tail were completely new and the pilot enjoyed powered controls. The US Air Force tested the prototype, which first flew as M.D 454-01 on September 28, 1952, and placed an off shore contract for 225 of the production aircraft in April 1953. The first 50 production aircraft had the Rolls Royce Tay engine, but the remainder each had a Hispano Suiza Verdon 350. Exports orders were won from Israel and India, in addition to the aircraft supplied to the Armée de l'Air. The French aircraft saw action during the Suez conflict in 1956; several variants have been built with radar and with a dual cockpit.

Country of origin:	France
Type:	single-seat fighter bomber
Powerplant:	one 2850kg (6,280lb) Hispano Suiza Tay 250A turbojet; or 3500kg (7716lb) Hispano Suiza Verdon 350 turbojet
Performance:	maximum speed 1120km/h (696mph); service ceiling 13,750m (45,000ft); range 1320km (820 miles)
Weights:	empty 5875kg (11,514lb); loaded 9500kg (20,950lb)
Dimensions:	wingspan 11.1m (36ft 5.75in); length 12.9m (42ft 2in); height 4.4m (14ft 5in)
Armament:	two 30mm DEFA 551cannon with 150 rounds, four underwing hardpoints with provision for up to 907kg (2000lb) of stores, including tanks, rockets, or bombs

Dassault Super Mystère B2

The Super Mystère developed from a Rolls-Royce Avon-engined version of the Mystère IV, known as the IVB. The Mystère IVB was a major leap forward, with tapered, milled and che-milled sheets, integral tanks, flush aerials, and a radar gunsight in the new nose.This aircraft proved to be a stepping stone to the bigger, heavier, and more powerful SMB.2, which introduced yet another new wing with 45 degrees of sweep and aerodynamics copied from the North American F-100 Super Sabre. The flattened nose also had more than a passing relationship to the American fighter. Although the first SMB.2 flew with the Rolls Royce Avon RA.7R, production examples were fitted with the Atar 101G. On its fourth flight, SMB.2-01, with Avon, easily exceeded Mach 1 in level flight, to make this the first supersonic aircraft to go into production, or in service.

Country of origin:	France
Type:	single-seat fighter bomber
Powerplant:	one 4460kg (9833lb) SNECMA Atar 101 G-2/-3 turbojet
Performance:	maximum speed at 12,000m (39,370ft) 1195km/h (743mph); service ceiling 17,000m (55,775ft); range 870km (540 miles)
Weights:	empty 6932kg (15,282lb); maximum take-off 10,000kg (22,046lb)
Dimensions:	wingspan 10.52m (34ft 6in); length 14.13m (46ft 4.25in); height 4.55m (14ft 11in); wing area 35sq m (376.75sq ft)
Armament:	two 30mm DEFA 551cannon, internal Matra launcher for 35 SNEB 68mm rockets, two underwing hardpoints with provision for up to 907kg (2000lb) of stores, including tanks, rockets, or bombs

75

Dassault Etendard IVP

The Dassault Etendard was designed to meet a NATO need for a light strike fighter capable of high subsonic speed and operation from unpaved forward strips. NATO specified that the engine should be the 4,850lb thrust Bristol Orpheus, and this aircraft took shape as the Etendard VI. However, it became clear at an early stage that this aircraft was woefully underpowered. The enigmatic M. Dassault decided to risk company money on developing a private venture aircraft with the Atar engine. The NATO competition was in fact won by the Fiat G91, but Dassault's private venture Etendard IV attracted the attention of the Aeronavale and went into production in two forms, the IVM strike aircraft and the IVP reconnaissance aircraft. Both aircraft were in service by 1962. The IVM became the standard strike aircraft of the carriers *Foch* and *Clemenceau*, distinguished by a folding refuelling probe.

Country of origin:	France
Type:	single-seat carrierborne strike/attack and interceptor aircraft
Powerplant:	one 4400kg (9700lb) SNECMA Atar 8B turbojet
Performance:	maximum speed 1180km/h (683mph) at low level; service ceiling 15,000m (49,215ft); maximum range 1700km (1056 miles)
Weights:	empty 5800kg (12,786lb); maximum take-off 12,000kg (26,455lb)
Dimensions:	wingspan 9.60m (31ft 6in); length 14.31m (46ft 11.2in); height 3.86m (12ft 8in); wing area 28.4sq m (305.7 q ft)
Armament:	two 30mm DEFA cannon with 150 rpg, five external hardpoints with provision for up to 1360 kg (3000lb) of stores, including nuclear weapons

Dassault Super Etendard

During the late 1960s it had been expected that the original Etendard force would be replaced in about 1971 by a specially developed carrier version of the Jaguar. This was rejected by the Aeronavale for political and financial reasons, and Dassault's proposal for an improved Etendard was chosen. The new aircraft has a substantially redesigned structure, a more efficient engine, inertial navigation system, and other upgraded avionics. The first prototype flew on October 3, 1975; deliveries to the Aeronavale began in June 1978. Fourteen Super Etendards were supplied to Argentina from November 1981; the five which had been delivered by the following spring were used to great effect against British shipping during the Falklands War. The aircraft in French service are due for replacement by Rafale in 2005, and an upgrade program is currently being carried out on the force.

Country of origin:	France
Type:	single-seat carrierborne strike/attack and interceptor aircraft
Powerplant:	one 5000kg (11,023lb) SNECMA Atar 8K-50 turbojet
Performance:	maximum speed 1180km/h (733mph) at low level; service ceiling 13,700m (44,950ft); combat radius 850km (528 miles) on hi-lo-hi mission with one Exocet and two external tanks
Weights:	empty 6500kg (14,330lb); maximum take-off 12,000kg (26,455lb)
Dimensions:	wingspan 9.60m (31ft 6in); length 14.31m (46ft 11.2in); height 3.86m (12ft 8in); wing area 28.4sq m (305.7sq ft)
Armament:	two 30mm DEFA 553 cannon with 125 rpg, five external hardpoints with provision for up to 2100kg (4630lb) of stores, including nuclear weapons, Exocet and (Argentina only) Martin Pescador air-to-surface missiles, Magic air-to-air missiles, bombs and rockets, refuelling and reconnaissance pods

Dassault Mirage IIIEA

The hugely successful Mirage program has brought incalculable prestige to the French aviation industry in the past four decades. The early prototype aircraft was conceived to meet an Armée de l'Air light interceptor specification of 1952. Once again Dassault found the powerplant insufficient and produced a larger, heavier, and more powerful aircraft, the Mirage III. On October 24, 1958 pre-production Mirage IIIA-01 became the first West European fighter to attain Mach 2 in level flight. The production version was designated the IIIC, a slightly developed version with either guns or a booster rocket for faster climb. Altogether 244 models were delivered to the Armée de l'Air, South Africa, and Israel. From this model emerged the longer and heavier IIIE for ground attack, with the Atar 9C turbojet and increased internal fuel. This variant first appeared on April 20, 1961.

Country of origin:	France
Type:	single-seat day visual fighter bomber
Powerplant:	one 6200kg (13,668lb) SNECMA Atar 9C turbojet
Performance:	maximum speed at sea level 1390km/h (883mph); service ceiling 17,000m (55,755ft); combat radius at low level with 907kg (2000lb) load 1200km (745 miles)
Weights:	empty 7050kg (15,540lb); loaded 13,500kg (27,760lb)
Dimensions:	wingspan 8.22m (26ft 11.875in); length 16.5m (56ft); height 4.50m (14ft 9in); wing area 35sq m (376.7sq ft)
Armament:	two 30mm DEFA 552A cannon with 125 rpg; three external pylons with provision for up to 3000kg (6612lb) of stores, including bombs, rockets, and gun pods

Dassault Mirage 5BA

A considerable number of variants have appeared as the Mirage continues its 40 year gestation. The Mirage 5 and 50 were the final development in the III series, and were largely intended for export. Three versions were built under licence in Belgium, as assault, reconnaissance, or trainer aircraft (hence the B designation). Fifteen of the Belgian 5BA aircraft, and five of the 5BD two-seat variants, underwent a major upgrade programme during the early 1990s to allow them to stay in service until 2005. Additions include a Ferranti HUD, laser range finder, updated navigation/attack avionics, fixed canard foreplanes and complete rewiring. The work was undertaken by Belgium's major aerospace company, SABCA. Many of these aircraft have been sold to Chile, who also operate new-build Mirage 50C, Mirage 50DC two-seat trainers and converted French 50F Mirages.

Country of origin:	France
Type:	single-seat day visual fighter bomber
Powerplant:	one 6200kg (13,668lb) SNECMA Atar 9C turbojet
Performance:	maximum speed 1912km/h (1188mph); service ceiling 17,000m (55,755ft); combat radius at low level with 907kg (2000lb) load 650km (404 miles)
Weights:	empty 6600kg (14,550lb); maximum take-off 13,700kg (30,203lb)
Dimensions:	wingspan 8.22m (26ft 11.6in); length 15.55m (51ft); height 4.50m (14ft 9in); wing area 35sq m (376.7 q ft)
Armament:	two 30mm DEFA 552A cannon with 125 rpg; seven external pylons with provision for up to 4000kg (8818lb) of stores, including bombs, rockets, and gun pods

Dassault Mirage 5BR

The 5BR is the Belgian licence-built version of the 5R (reconnaissance) Mirage variant. The 5R is broadly similar to the older IIIR from which it is derived, and conversion of the aircraft to an attack reconnaissance role proved equally straightforward. One notable difference is the chisel nose, which contains cameras instead of radar. The optional twin cannon pack is usually carried, and other options for armed reconnaissance included a reflector sight and low altitude bombing system. Most of the aircraft in Belgian service were retired during the mid-1990s. Other operators of the French built 5R are Abu Dhabi, Colombia, and Libya. Pictured is one of the aircraft operated by 42 Smaldeel of the Belgian air force at Florennes. Note the arrestor hook under the rear fuselage and the 1000 litre (220 Imp gal) centreline fuel tank.

Country of origin:	France
Type:	single-seat reconnaissance fighter with attack capability
Powerplant:	one 6200kg (13,668lb) SNECMA Atar 9C turbojet
Performance:	maximum speed 1912km/h (1188mph); service ceiling 17,000m (55,755ft); combat radius at low level with 907kg (2000lb) load 650km (404 miles)
Weights:	empty 6600kg (14,550lb); maximum take-off 13,700kg (30,203lb)
Dimensions:	wingspan 8.22m (26ft 11.6in); length 15.55m (51ft); height 4.50m (14ft 9in); wing area 35sq m (376.7sq ft)
Armament:	two 30mm DEFA 552A cannon with 125 rpg; external pylons with provision for up to 4000kg (8,818lb) of stores, including bombs, rockets, and gun pods

Dassault Mirage 5PA

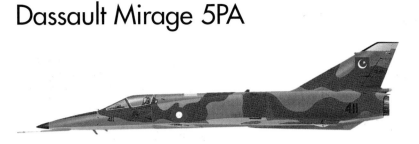

In 1966 the Israeli Air Force submitted a request to Dassault for a simplified version of the Mirage IIIE long range all-weather fighter bomber, optimised for the daytime clear weather ground attack role. This aircraft, designated the Mirage 5, first flew on May 19, 1967, but on General de Gaulle's orders they never reached their intended recipient. Instead the aircraft were supplied to other air forces, including that of Pakistan. The main physical differences between the III and 5 are the slimmer nose (because of relocation of the avionics suite to the space formerly occupied by the radar) and the addition of two additional underwing hardpoints. Because of the relocation of the avionics, an additional 470 litres (103 imp gal) of fuel can be carried in a tank to the rear of the cockpit. In the mid-1980s the Pakistani Mirage 5PA fleet were upgraded.

Country of origin:	France
Type:	single-seat day visual fighter bomber
Powerplant:	one 6200kg (13,668lb) SNECMA Atar 9C turbojet
Performance:	maximum speed 1912km/h (1188mph); service ceiling 17,000m (55,755ft); combat radius at low level with 907kg (2000lb) load 650km (404 miles)
Weights:	empty 6600kg (14,550lb); maximum take-off 13,700kg (30,203lb)
Dimensions:	wingspan 8.22m (26ft 11.6n); length 15.55m (51ft); height 4.50m (14ft 9in); wing area 35sq m (376.7sq ft)
Armament:	two 30mm DEFA 552A cannon with 125 rpg; seven external pylons with provision for up to 4000kg (8818lb) of stores, including bombs, rockets, and gun pods

Dassault Mirage 50C

Seen here in the colours of the Chilean Air Force, the Mirage 50 retains the same basic airframe as the Mirage III and 5, but is powered by a considerably more powerful version of the SNECMA 9-C turbojet. SNECMA began the programme to develop this engine, designated the 9K-50, in 1966 primarily for the next generation Mirage F.1 and G4 aircraft. Dassault soon realised the potentialities of fitting this engine into the standard delta-winged aircraft. The Mirage 50 was offered by Dassault with any of the considerable number of upgrades under development by the company since 1977, for instance single or dual cockpit, reconnaissance pack, enlarged nose to house radar, and a host of avionics options. Dassault marketed the aircraft quite aggressively, but the only countries to purchase were Chile (16 Mirage 50C) and Venezuela (6 Mirage 50EV and one DV).

Country of origin:	France
Type:	single-seat day multi-role fighter bomber
Powerplant:	one 7200kg (15,873lb) SNECMA Atar 9K-50 turbojet
Performance:	maximum speed at high altitude 2350km/h (1460mph); service ceiling 18,000m (59,055ft); combat radius at low level with 800kg (1764lb) load 685km (425 miles)
Weights:	empty 7150kg (15,763lb); maximum take-off 13,700kg (30,203lb)
Dimensions:	wingspan 8.22m (26ft 11.6in); length 15.55m (51ft); height 4.50m (14ft 9in); wing area 35sq m (376.7sq ft)
Armament:	two 30mm DEFA 552A cannon with 125 rpg; seven external pylons with provision for R.530 air-to-air missiles, AS.30 or A.30L missiles, rocket launcher pods, and various attack loads including 1000lb bombs

Dassault Mirage F1CK

The F1 once again demonstrates the willingness of the Dassault company to risk privately funded ventures. Recognising that the Mirage III family would eventually become redundant, the French government awarded Dassault a development contract for a successor, dubbed the F2. The aircraft was large with a conventional swept wing, breaking away from the classic Mirage form. Dassault privately funded a smaller version of the F2, called F1, sized to be powered by a single Atar engine. The Armée de l'Air subsequently chose to purchase this model. The aircraft marked a huge advance on the tailless delta form of previous models, with lower landing speeds and take-off runs. Other advances were made in the avionics suite and integral tankage for 45 per cent more fuel. Manoeuvrability was also substantially improved. Pictured is the F1CK, in service in Kuwait.

Country of origin:	France
Type:	single-seat multi-mission fighter attack aircraft
Powerplant:	one 7200kg (15,873lb) SNECMA Atar 9K-50 turbojet
Performance:	maximum speed at high altitude 2350km/h (1460mph); service ceiling 20,000m (65,615ft); range with maximum load 900km (560 miles)
Weights:	empty 7400kg (16,314lb); maximum take-off 15,200kg (33,510lb)
Dimensions:	wingspan 8.4m (27ft 6.75in); length 15m (49ft 2.25in); height 4.5m (14ft 9in); wing area 25sq m (269.11sq ft)
Armament:	two 30mm 553 DEFA cannon with 135 rpg, five external pylons with provision for up to 6300kg (13,889lb) of stores; Magic air-to-air missiles on wingtip rails, weapons include Matra Super 530 air-to-air missiles, conventional and laser guided bombs, rockets, AS.30L laser-guided air-to-surface missiles, AM.39 Exocet anti-ship missiles, ARMAT anti-radiation missiles, or Durandal, Belouga, or BAP anti-runway weapons

Dassault Mirage F1EQ5

Iraq's changing political allegiances since Saddam Hussein assumed control of the country are reflected in the widely varying aircraft types operated by the Iraqi Air Force. This was well demonstrated during the 1980 Iran/Iraq and 1991 Gulf wars. During the first conflict, France was the major supplier of Iraqi aircraft, having delivered no less than 89 Mirage F.1s. Included in this order was a batch of 29 F.1EQ5s with Agave radar for over-water operations and armed with Exocet anti-shipping missiles. These aircraft were delivered in October 1984 after much delay, and became operational in February the following year. At least 12 aircraft were equipped with SLAR (Sideways Looking Airborne Radar) and ground-data links for reconnaissance missions, alongside their normal fighter/bomber role. These aircraft operate alongside Soviet types, and were also used during the Gulf war.

Country of origin:	France
Type:	single-seat multi-mission fighter attack aircraft
Powerplant:	one 7200kg (15,873lb) SNECMA Atar 9K-50 turbojet
Performance:	maximum speed at high altitude 2350km/h (1460mph); service ceiling 20,000m (65,615ft); range with maximum load 900km (560 miles)
Weights:	empty 7400kg (16,314lb); maximum take-off 15,200kg (33,510lb)
Dimensions:	wingspan 9.32m (30ft 7in); length 15.3m (50ft 2.5in); height 4.5m (14ft 9in); wing area 25sq m (269.11sq ft)
Armament:	two 30mm 553 DEFA cannon with 135 rpg, five external pylons with provision for up to 6300kg (13,889lb) of stores; Magic air-to-air missiles on wingtip rails, weapons include Matra Super 530 air-to-air missiles, conventional and laser guided bombs, rockets, AS.30L laser-guided air-to-surface missiles, AM.39 Exocet anti-ship missiles, ARMAT anti-radiation missiles, or Durandal, Belouga, or BAP anti-runway weapons

Dassault Mirage 2000B

Because of the complexity of the third generation Mirage 2000 the French Air Force decided to pursue a programme of development for a two-seat trainer to run concurrently with the single-seat 2000C. The fifth Mirage 2000 prototype was flown in this format as the 2000B in October 1980. Production aircraft are distinguished by a slightly longer (7.5in) fuselage, and are not fitted with internal cannon. Internal fuel capacity is also reduced from 3980 to 3870 litres. The 2000B retains full operational capability in French service and first flew on October 7, 1983. Escadron de Chasse 1/2 'Cigognes' was the first French air force unit to become operational at Dijon on July 2, 1984. This aircraft has the famous 'stork' emblem of EC1/2 'Cigognes'. The aircraft has also been ordered by at least five countries in various formats to complement their single-seat fleets.

Country of origin:	France
Type:	dual-seat jet trainer with operational capability
Powerplant:	one 9700kg (21,834lb) SNECMA M53-P2 turbofan
Performance:	maximum speed at high altitude 2338km/h (1453mph); service ceiling 18,000m (59,055ft); range with two 1700 litre (374 Imp gal) drop tanks 1850km (1150miles)
Weights:	empty 7600kg (16,755lb); maximum take-off 17,000kg (37,480lb)
Dimensions:	wingspan 9.13m (29ft 11.5in); length 14.55m (47ft 9in); height 5.15m (16ft 10.75in); wing area 41sq m (441.3sq ft)
Armament:	seven external pylons with provision for R.530 air-to-air missiles, AS.30 or A.30L missiles, rocket launcher pods, and various attack loads including 1000lb bombs. For air defence weapon training the Cubic Corporation AIS (airborne instrumentation subsystem) pod, which resembles a Magic missile, may be carried

Dassault Mirage 2000C

Early research and experience had shown that the delta wing configuration carried some notable disadvantages, not least a lack of low speed manoeuvrability. With the development of fly-by-wire technology during the late 1960s and early 1970s, it was possible for airframe designers to overcome some of these problems, when coupled with advances in aerodynamics. The 2000C was designed by Dassault to be a single-seat interceptor to replace the F.1. The aircraft was adopted by the French government in December 1975 as the primary combat aircraft of the French air force, and was developed initially under contract as an interceptor and air superiority fighter. Deliveries to the Armée de l'Air began in July 1984; early production examples were fitted with the SNEMCA M53-5; aircraft built after that date have the more powerful M53-P2.

Country of origin:	France
Type:	single-seat air-superiority and attack fighter
Powerplant:	one 9700kg (21,834lb) SNECMA M53-P2 turbofan
Performance:	maximum speed at high altitude 2338km/h (1,453mph); service ceiling 18,000m (59,055ft); range with 1000kg (2,205lb) load 1,480km (920 miles)
Weights:	empty 7500kg (16,534lb); maximum take-off 17,000kg (37,480lb)
Dimensions:	wingspan 9.13m (29ft 11.5in); length 14.36m (47ft 1.25in); height 5.20m (17ft 0.75in); wing area 41sq m (441.3sq ft)
Armament:	two DEFA 554 cannon with 125rpg; nine external pylons with provision for up to 6300kg of stores, including R.530 air-to-air missiles, AS.30 or A.30L missiles, rocket launcher pods, and various attack loads including 1000lb bombs. For air defence weapon training the Cubic Corpn AIS (airborne instrumentation subsystem)

Dassault Mirage 2000H

In 1998 Dassault completed its contract to deliver 136 Mirage 2000C aircraft to the Armée de l'Air. Export contracts for the agile and capable 2000C have been justifiably plentiful; by 1990 the French company had received firm orders from Abu Dhabi, Egypt, Greece, India and Peru. The Indian aircraft pictured is one of 40 ordered in October 1982 which carry the designation 2000H. Final delivery was made in September 1984. The first of two Indian squadrons was formed at Gwalior AB on June 29, 1985, when the 2000H received the Indian name Vajra, meaning 'Thunder'. A follow-on order was signed in March 1986 for a further nine aircraft (six H and three TH). This aircraft is operated by No. 225 Squadron of the Indian Air Force and is pictured with drop tanks fitted. A two-seat low-level strike version is offered as the Mirage 2000N.

Country of origin:	France
Type:	single-seat air-superiority and attack fighter
Powerplant:	one 9700kg (21,834lb) SNECMA M53-P2 turbofan
Performance:	maximum speed at high altitude 2338km/h (1,453mph); service ceiling 18,000m (59,055ft); range with 1000kg (2205lb) load 1480km (920 miles)
Weights:	empty 7500kg (16,534lb); maximum take-off 17,000kg (37,480lb)
Dimensions:	wingspan 9.13m (29ft 11.5in); length 14.36m (47ft 1.25in); height 5.20m (17ft 0.75in); wing area 41sq m (441.3sq ft)
Armament:	two DEFA 554 cannon with 125rpg; nine external pylons with provision for up to 6300kg of stores, including R.530 air-to-air missiles, AS.30 or A.30L missiles, rocket launcher pods, and various attack loads including 1000lb bombs. For air defence weapon training the Cubic Corpn AIS (airborne instrumentation subsystem) pod, which resembles a Magic missile, may be carried

Dassault Rafale M

The Rafale has been designed and built to replace the Armée de l'Air's fleet of SEPECAT Jaguars, and to form part of the new French nuclear carrier force's air wing. Although both services considered the Eurofighter, they have opted instead for the Rafale, which is smaller and lighter than the multi-national aircraft. The Dassault company embarked on the project in early 1983, and the first flight took place on July 4, 1986. The airframe is largely constructed of composite materials, with a fly-by-wire control system. Early flight trials were particularly encouraging, with the aircraft achieving Mach 1.8 on only its second flight. Original production orders have been cut since the end of the Cold War. The three versions are the Rafale C single-seat operational aircraft for the Armée de l'Air, the Rafale B two seat multi-role aircraft, and the Rafale M navalised fighter (pictured).

Country of origin:	France
Type:	carrier based multi-role combat aircraft
Powerplant:	two 7450kg (16,424lb) SNECMA M88-2 turbofans
Performance:	maximum speed at high altitude 2130km/h (1324mph); combat radius air-to-air mission 1853km (1152 miles)
Weights:	empty equipped 9800kg (maximum take-off 19,500kg (42,990lb)
Dimensions:	wingspan 10.90m (35ft 9.175in); length 15.30m (50ft 2.5in); height 5.34m (17ft 6.25in); wing area 46sq m (495.1sq ft)
Armament:	one 30mm DEFA 791B cannon, 14 external hardpoints with provision for up to 6000kg (13,228lb) of stores, including air-to-air missiles, air-to-surface missiles, anti-ship missiles, guided and conventional bombs, rocket launchers, recce, Elint, and jammer pods

De Havilland Vampire NF.Mk 10

The RAF was remarkably slow to order jet night fighters, and the de Havilland company took the initiative to develop the D.H.113 NF. Mk 10 as a private venture. The aircraft was designed as a two-seater, and development was greatly speeded by the fact that the Vampire nacelle was similar in width to the nose of the Mosquito, so the crew compartment, AI Mk 10 radar and equipment of the NF versions could be transferred with the minimum of changes. Batches were delivered to the Egyptian air force before exports of arms to that country were banned in 1950. The RAF took over the contract and received 95 aircraft, which were first used by No 25 Squadron from West Malling in late 1951. The pilot and observer/radar operator sat close together in ordinary (non-ejecting) seats, which made emergency escape particularly hazardous.

Country of origin:	United Kingdom
Type:	two-seat night fighter
Powerplant:	one 1520kg (3350lb) de Havilland Goblin turbojet
Performance:	maximum speed 885km/h (549mph); service ceiling 12,200m (40,000ft); range 1255km (780 miles)
Weights:	empty 3172kg (6984lb); loaded 5148kg (11,350lb)
Dimensions:	wingspan 11.6m (38ft); length 10.55m (34ft 7in); height 2m (6ft 7in); wing area 24.32sq m (262sq ft)
Armament:	four 20mm Hispano cannon

De Havilland Vampire T.Mk 11

The success of the two-seat night-fighter version of the Vampire logically led Airspeed Ltd (a de Havilland subsidiary) to embark on the development of a trainer as a private venture. The nose radar was removed and full dual flight controls were added to the pressurised, if somewhat cramped cockpit, to produce the D.H. 115 Vampire T.Mk 11. The prototype was first flown in November 1950, and service deliveries began to the AFS at Weston Zoyland and Valley in early 1952. In 1956 the T.Mk 11 became the standard jet trainer of the Royal Air Force, and at one time was the most numerous of its aircraft, with over 530 delivered. The production run totalled 731, with export deliveries (as T.Mk 55s to 19 countries). Fifteen of the aircraft were still in service with the Swiss Air Force in 1990, although they have now been withdrawn.

Country of origin:	United Kingdom
Type:	two-seat basic trainer
Powerplant:	one 1589kg (3500lb) de Havilland Goblin 35 turbojet
Performance:	maximum speed 885km/h (549mph); service ceiling 12,200m (40,000ft); range on internal fuel 1370km (853 miles)
Weights:	empty 3347kg (7380lb); loaded (clean) 5060kg (11,150lb)
Dimensions:	wingspan 11.6m (38ft); length 10.55m (34ft 7in); height 1.86m (6ft 2in); wing area 24.32sq m (262sq ft)
Armament:	two 20mm Hispano cannon

De Havilland Vampire FB.Mk 6

Production of an improved fighter-bomber version of the Vampire began in 1948 with the FB.Mk 5. This aircraft featured a restressed wing clipped from 12.19m to 11.58m (40ft to 38ft), with wing pylons capable of carrying either two 227kg (500lb) bombs or eight rocket projectiles. The FB.Mk 6 was the result of efforts to improve the performance of the Vampire, with an uprated version of the Goblin turbojet that afforded a marked increase in maximum speed. The FB.Mk 6 was not ordered by the RAF, but attracted much attention from overseas customers. At the time Switzerland was seeking a low-cost replacement for its fleet of Messerschmitt Bf 109s. The low cost and impressive performance of the Vampire persuaded the Swiss government to purchase 75 FB.Mk 6s. A licence was later granted to build the aircraft, and 100 were subsequently completed for the Swiss Air Force.

Country of origin:	United Kingdom/Switzerland
Type:	single-seat fighter-bomber
Powerplant:	one 1498kg (3300lb) de Havilland Goblin 35 turbojet
Performance:	maximum speed 883km/h (548mph); service ceiling 13,410m (44,000ft); range with drop tanks 2253km (1400 miles)
Weights:	empty 3266kg (7200lb); loaded with drop tanks 5600kg (12,290lb)
Dimensions:	wingspan 11.6m (38ft); length 9.37m (30ft 9in); height 2.69m (8ft 10in); wing area 24.32sq m (262sq ft)
Armament:	four 20mm Hispano cannon with 150 rounds, wing pylons capable of carrying either two 227kg (500lb) bombs or 60lb rocket projectiles

De Havilland Venom NF.Mk 2A

The two-seat radar-equipped night fighter version of the Venom was originally developed as a private venture, and flown without the equipment for combat use. Early flight trials during 1950 indicated that it handled well, although hampered by a poor rate of roll. Like the two-seat Vampire there was no provision for emergency escape (a fact that proved less than popular with aircrew) but in 1952 the type began production at Chester. The NF.Mk 2 differed from the FB.Mk 1 in having a widened fuselage to accommodate pilot and observer, and an extended nose for the radar equipment. The Mk 2A was a redesignation of the Mk 2 following incorporation of a clear view canopy and modifications made to the tail unit. A version of the Mk 2 supplied to the Royal Swedish Air Force was designated as the NF.Mk 51. Total production for the Mk 2 was 60.

Country of origin:	United Kingdom
Type:	two-seat night fighter
Powerplant:	one 2245kg (4950lb) de Havilland Ghost 104 turbojet
Performance:	maximum speed 1013km/h (630mph); service ceiling 15,000m (49,200ft); range 1610km (1000 miles)
Weights:	empty 4000kg (8800lb); loaded 7166kg (15,800lb)
Dimensions:	wingspan 12.70m (41ft 8in); length 11.17m (36ft 8in); height 1.98m (6ft 6in); wing area 24.32sq m (262sq ft)
Armament:	four 20mm Hispano cannon

De Havilland Venom FB.Mk 4

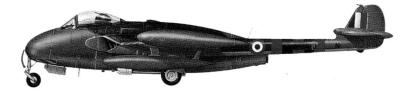

The design of the Venom can be traced to the Vampire Mk 8, which the company fitted with a more powerful Ghost engine in place of the Goblin, in the hope of wringing more performance from the same basic design. Other changes included a thinner wing of greater area fitted with a 355 litre (78 Imp gal) tank on each tip with a revised fuel system to match, spring-tab controls and extended boundary-layer deflectors on the fuselage – forward of the inlets. Despite the availability of swept-wing technology de Havilland persisted with conventional aerodynamics, and in one stroke removed any chance the Venom had of competing with its best foreign rivals. From initial deliveries of the FB.Mk 1 in December 1951, de Havilland continued to develop the troubled aircraft. The FB.Mk 4 was a great improvement, with powered controls, more efficient tail surfaces, and an ejector seat.

Country of origin:	United Kingdom
Type:	single-seat fighter bomber
Powerplant:	one 2336kg (5150lb) de Havilland Ghost 105 turbojet
Performance:	maximum speed 1030km/h (640mph); service ceiling 14,630m (48,000ft); range with drop tanks 1730km (1075 miles)
Weights:	empty 4174kg (9202lb); maximum loaded 6945kg (15,310lb)
Dimensions:	wingspan (over tip tanks) 12.7m (41ft 8in); length 9.71m (31ft 10in); height 1.88m (6ft 2in); wing area 25.99sq m (279.75sq ft)
Armament:	four 20mm Hispano cannon with 150 rounds, two wing pylons capable of carrying either two 454kg (1000lb) bombs or two drop tanks; or eight 27.2kg (60lb) rocket projectiles carried on centre-section launchers

De Havilland (EFW) Venom FB.Mk 1

Switzerland have been one of the most enthusiastic of de Havilland's export customers. The FB.Mk 1 was adopted in 1952 as a successor to the Vampire, and de Havilland supplied a small number of FB.Mks under the designation FB.Mk 50. The FB.Mk 1 was subsequently built under licence by the EFW consortium (Federal Aircraft Factory at Emmen, Flug-und Fahrzeugwerke at Altenrhein and Pilatus at Stans). Some 100 aircraft were completed followed by another 150 to Venom FB.Mk 4 standard, with Fiat- and Sulzer-built engines. These aircraft had long service careers and the final aircraft were not retired until 1983, albeit with substantially altered systems and structures. The example pictured was one of the first batch of 100. In 1979 it was operated by 10 Fliegerstaffel with a completely redesigned nose to accommodate radio equipment, and a reconnaissance pod under the wing.

Country of origin:	United Kingdom/Switzerland
Type:	single-seat tactical reconnaissance with secondary attack capability
Powerplant:	one 2200kg (4850lb) de Havilland Ghost 103 turbojet
Performance:	maximum speed 1030km/h (640mph); service ceiling 13,720m (45,000ft); range with drop tanks 1730km (1075 miles)
Weights:	empty 3674kg (8100lb); maximum loaded 6945kg (15,310lb)
Dimensions:	wingspan (over tip tanks) 12.7m (41ft 8in); length 9.71m (31ft 10in); height 1.88m (6ft 2in); wing area 25.99sq m (279.75sq ft)
Armament:	four 20mm Hispano cannon with 150 rounds, two wing pylons capable of carrying either two 454kg (1000lb) bombs, or two drop tanks, or reconnaissance pods; or eight 27.2kg (60lb) rocket projectiles carried on centre-section launchers

De Havilland Sea Vixen FAW Mk 2

The Sea Vixen, like many of the aircraft operated by the Royal Navy, was originally designed to a Royal Air Force requirement for a land-based all weather interceptor, first issued in 1946. The aircraft lost the competition to the Gloster Javelin. Fortunately for de Havilland the Royal Navy had a similar requirement for a carrier based aircraft, and after successful trials from the deck of HMS *Albion* an initial order was placed in January 1955. The first 92 aircraft to be completed by the de Havilland factory at Christchurch were designated FAW. Mk 1s and featured a hinged and pointed radome, powerfolding wings and hydraulically steerable nosewheel. The later FAW Mk.2 had increased fuel capacity and provision for four Red Top missiles in place of the Firestreaks carried by the Mk 1. Most were brought up to Mk 2 standard by 1964 and remained in service until 1971.

Country of origin:	United Kingdom
Type:	two-seat all-weather strike fighter
Powerplant:	two 5094kg (11,230lb) Rolls-Royce Avon 208 turbojets
Perfomance:	maximum speed 1110km/h (690mph) at 20,000ft at sea level; climb to 3050m (10,000ft) in 1 min 30 secs; service ceiling 21,790m (48,000ft); range about 600 miles (FAW 1) and 800 miles (FAW 2)
Weight:	empty weight about 22,000lb; maximum take-off 18,858kg (41,575lb)
Dimensions:	wingspan 15.54m (51ft); length 17.02 m (55ft 7in); height 3.28 m (10ft 9in); wing area 60.20sq m (648sq ft)
Armament:	on four inboard wing pylons; four Firestreak air-to-air missiles (FAW 1) or four Red Top air-to-air missiles (FAW 2); on outer pylons 1000 lb bombs, Bullpup air-to-surface missiles or equivalent stores; as built, but not used, provision for 28 folding fin aircraft rockets in two flip-out boxes beneath cockpit floor

Douglas A3 Skywarrior

The A3 Skywarrior was realised by a team led by legendary Douglas designer Ed Heinemann at El Segundo. It is notable as the first carrier based strategic nuclear bomber, designed to be operated from the deck of the Forrestal class of carriers that came into service in 1948. Both the outer wings and tail were designed to fold hydraulically and thus minimise the space occupied by the aircraft on deck. An advanced blind-bombing radar was carried in the nose, although delivery from Westinghouse was seriously delayed. The first of the two prototypes flew on October 28, 1952 powered by two Westinghouse engines, but the failure of this program meant that the Pratt & Whitney J57-P-6 powered that production A3D-1. Deliveries began in March 1956 to the US Navy's VH-1 attack squadron. Later variants saw much service in Vietnam as Elint, and ECM platforms.

Country of origin:	USA
Type:	carrier-based strategic bomber
Powerplant:	two 5635kg (12,400lb) Pratt & Whitney turbojets
Performance:	maximum speed 982km/h (610mph); service ceiling 13,110m (43,000ft); range with maximum fuel 3220km (2000 miles)
Weights:	empty 17,875kg (39,409lb); maximum take-off 37,195kg (82,000lb)
Dimensions:	wing span 22.1m (72ft 6in); length 23.3m (76ft 4in); height 7.16m (23ft 6in); wing area 75.43sq m (812sq ft)
Armament:	two remotely controlled 20mm cannon in tail turret, plus provision for 5443kg (12,000lb) of conventional or nuclear weapons in internal bomb bay

Douglas B-66 Destroyer

The B-66 Destroyer was produced by Douglas at Long Beach to meet the needs of the US Air Force, whose involvement in the Korean War had highlighted an urgent need for a high-performance tactical bomber. Air Force chiefs planned to speed the availability of such an aircraft by procuring a modified version of the A-3D then in service with the US Navy. What began as a minimal modification of the A-3, however, turned into a totally different aircraft. Though it looked similar, hardly a single airframe part or item of equipment was common and the B-66 proved difficult to maintain and expensive. The arrestor gear, folding wing and tail mechanisms, and strengthened gear were all junked, in favour of crew ejector seats, multiple camera installation and precision bombing and navigation radar. Many were built as Elint and ECM aircraft and saw action over South East Asia.

Country of origin:	USA
Type:	all-day/night reconnaissance and bombing aircraft
Powerplant:	two 4627kg (10,200lb) Allison J71-A-11 turbojets
Performance:	maximum speed 1015km/h (631mph); service ceiling 11,855m (38,900ft); combat radius 1489km (925 miles)
Weights:	empty 19,720kg (43,476lb); maximum take-off 37,648kg (83,000lb)
Dimensions:	wing span 22.1m (72ft 6in); length 22.9m (75ft 2in); height 7.19m (23ft 7in); wing area 72.46sq m (780sq ft)
Armament:	two remotely controlled 20mm cannon in tail turret, plus provision for 5443kg (12,000lb) of conventional or nuclear weapons in internal bomb bay

Douglas F4D-1 Skyray

Details of German research into delta wings generated great interest in the US Navy, prompting senior officers to request a design submission from Douglas based on the theories. This was finalised as a variation on a pure delta wing configuration in 1948, and Douglas were awarded a contract to build two prototypes in December of that year. The first aircraft made its maiden flight in January 1951 with an Allison turbojet, although continual engine problems during the development programme led to the selection of a Pratt & Whitney unit for production aircraft. The design was a cantilever mid-wing monoplane controlled by trailing edge elevons serving collectively as elevators or differentially as ailerons. The cockpit was situated well forward of the wing and afforded the pilot excellent all-round visibility.

Country of origin:	USA
Type:	single-seat carrier-based fighter
Powerplant:	one 4626kg (10,200lb) Pratt & Whitney J57-P-8A turbojet
Performance:	maximum speed at 10,975m (36,000ft) 1162km/h (695mph); service ceiling above 16,765m (55,000ft); range 1931km (1,200 miles)
Weights:	empty 7268kg (16,024lb); maximum take-off 11,340kg (25,000lb)
Dimensions:	wingspan 10.21m (33ft 6in); length 13.93m (45ft 8.25in); height 3.96m (13ft); wing area 51.75sq m (557sq ft)
Armament:	four 20mm cannon; six underwing hardpoints with provision for up to 1814kg (4000lb) of stores, including AIM-9C Sidewinder air-to-air missiles, bombs, rockets, or drop tanks

Eurofighter EF-2000 Typhoon

The agreement to develop the Eurofighter was signed in May 1988 between the UK, West Germany, and Italy. Spain joined in November of that year. The aircraft was designed ostensibly for the air-to-air role, with secondary air-to-surface capability. With the canard design and fly by wire control system it is hoped the aircraft will be supremely manoeuvrable in the air. Other advanced features include extensive use of composite materials for airframe construction and an advanced sensor and avionics suite. Flight testing is well underway, but the program has been consistently delayed by political and financial wrangling. The first aircraft should enter production in 2005. However, the Eurofighter is entering a highly competitive market, and with a unit price of £60 million plus, export orders may be hard won.

Country of origin:	Germany, Italy, Spain, and United Kingdom
Type:	multi-role fighter
Powerplant:	two 9185kg (20,250lb) Eurojet EJ200 turbofans
Performance:	maximum speed at 11,000m (36,090ft) 2125km/h (1,321mph); combat radius about 463 and 556km
Weights:	empty 9750kg (21,495lb); maximum take-off 21,000kg (46,297lb)
Dimensions:	wingspan 10.50m (34ft 5.5in); length 14.50m (47ft 4in); height 4.0m (13ft 1.5in); wing area 52.4sq m (564.05sq ft)
Armament:	one 27mm Mauser cannon; thirteen fuselage hardpoints for a wide variety of stores including ASRAAM, FMRAAM missile programs; also air-to-surface missiles, anti-radar missiles, guided and unguided bombs

FMA IA 27 Pulquí

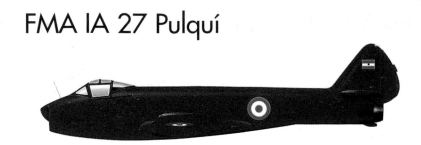

The Pulquí (Arrow) was designed by Emile Dewoitine, who had established his own aircraft company in France in 1920. The aircraft achieved two firsts, being not only the first single-seat fighter to be designed in Argentina but also the first turbojet powered aircraft to be built by her fledgling aviation industry. The aircraft followed a conventional low wing cantilever monoplane design, constructed of metal, and powered by the Rolls-Royce Derwent turbojet. The aircraft first flew on August 9, 1947, but flight trials proved disappointing in every aspect. The project was subsequently abandoned. Enlisting the assistance of former Focke-Wulf designer Kurt Tank, the Argentine government sought to rekindle the project with the Pulquí II, but a protracted development period and the withdrawal of Dr Tank meant that it too was abandoned in 1960.

Country of origin:	Argentina
Type:	single-seat fighter
Powerplant:	one 2268kg (5000lb) Rolls Royce Nene 2 turbojet
Performance:	maximum speed at 5000m (16,405ft) 1050km/h (652mph); service ceiling 15,000m (49,210ft); endurance 2 hours 12 minutes
Weights:	empty 3600kg (7937lb); maximum take-off 5550kg (12,236lb)
Dimensions:	wingspan 10.60m (34ft 9.25in); length 11.68m (38ft 3.75in); height 3.50m (11ft 5.75in); wing area 25.10sq m (270.18sq ft)
Armament:	four 20mm cannon

FMA IA 63 Pampa

The physical resemblance between the Pampa and the Dassault/Dornier stems from the close association between Argentinian manufacturer FMA and Dornier on the project. Design work began in 1979 to provide a jet trainer to replace the Morane-Saulnier MS.760 Paris in service with the Argentine Air Force. Wings and tailplanes for the prototype were based on a unswept version of the Alpha Jet wing. Other features were designed for simplified maintenance and cheap operation, such as the aircraft's single-engined configuration and reduced avionics suite. Rough airstrip operations are possible. The first prototype, which is depicted here with its Paris Air Show registration, flew on October 6, 1984. The first of 100 aircraft ordered for the Argentine Air Force was delivered to IV Brigada Aärea in April 1988.

Country of origin:	United Kingdom
Type:	two-seat advanced pilot trainer with combat capability
Powerplant:	one 1588kg (3500lb) Garrett TFE731-2-2N turbofan
Performance:	maximum speed 750km/h (466mph); service ceiling 12,900m (42,325ft); combat radius on hi-lo-hi mission with 1000kg (2205lb) load 360km (223 miles)
Weights:	empty 2821kg (6219lb); maximum take-off 5000kg (11,023lb)
Dimensions:	wingspan 9.69m (31ft 9.25in); length (excluding probe) 10.93m (35ft 10.25in); height 4.29m (14ft 1in); wing area 15.63sq m (168.2sq ft)
Armament:	provision for a 30mm DEFA cannon and four underwing pylons for up to 1160kg (2557lb) of stores

Fairchild Republic A-10A Thunderbolt II

The Fairchild Republic A-10A grew out of the US Air Force's A-X program, begun in 1967, to produce a highly battleproof, heavily armed close air support aircraft to replace the A-1 Skyraider. In December 1970 three companies were chosen to build prototypes for evaluation and Fairchild's YA-10A emerged as the winner in January 1973. Six pre-production aircraft were submitted for evaluation, resulting in a production contract for 52A-10As in December 1974. Some 727 have been procured by the USAF. The A-10A is dominated by the huge GAU-8/A cannon, but the range of weaponry that it can carry is truly devastating. This was proved effectively during actions against Iraqi armour during the 1991 Gulf War, although critics have questioned whether its slow speed would make it more vulnerable against a more formidable enemy.

Country of origin:	USA
Type:	single-seat close support aircraft
Powerplant:	two 4112kg (9065lb) General Electric TF34-GE-100 turbofans
Performance:	maximum speed at sea level 706km/h (439mph); combar radius 402km (250 miles) for a 2-hour loiter with 18 Mk82 bombs plus 750 rounds cannon ammunition Weights: empty 11,321kg (24,959lb); maximum take-off 22,680kg (50,000lb)
Dimensions:	wingspan 17.53m (57ft 6in); length 16.26m (53ft 4in); height 4.47m (14ft 8in); wing area 47.01sq m (506sq ft)
Armament:	one 30mm GAU-8/A rotary cannon with capacity for 1350 rounds of ammunition, eleven hardpointts with provision for up to 7528kg (16,000lb) of disposable stores; weapons include conventional bombs, incendiary bombs, Rockeye cluster bombs, AGM-65 Maverick air-to-surface missiles, laser and optronically guided bombs and SUU-23 20mm cannon pods

Fiesler Fi 103 Reichenburg IV

This aircraft bears interesting comparison to the better known and more widely produced Fi 103, from which the V-1 flying bomb was developed. Long before that offensive commenced, the German high command were considering using piloted missiles to make precision attacks on high priority targets. With the war situation deteriorating, Hitler gave the go-ahead for such a project in March 1944, and the unmanned Fi 103 was adopted as the weapon best suited for use. By placing a cockpit and conventional flying controls in the body of the weapon the designers were able to produce a controllable machine. The operational version was designated Fi 103R-IV and although 175 were produced none were ever used operationally. Flying this machine would have been an unenviable task for even the most skilled pilot. Once aimed at its target, he/she was expected to bale out.

Country of origin:	Germany
Type:	piloted missile
Powerplant:	one 350kg (772lb) thrust Argus 109-014 pulse jet
Performance:	maximum speed approximately 650km/h (404mph)
Dimensions:	wingspan 5.72m (18ft 9.25in); length 8.00m (26ft 3in)
Armament:	one 852kg (1874lb) warhead

Fuji T-1A

Once the Japanese aircraft industry had been cleared to begin production again in 1953, the government awarded a number of substantial contracts to Fuji with the aim of producing indigenous jet-powered aircraft to replace American-supplied piston-engined T-6 Texans. The company had already constructed a small turbojet engine to power just such an aircraft, but the first T1F1 was powered by an imported Bristol Siddeley Orpheus engine. The design leant heavily on the North American F-86 Sabre. Designated T-1A by the JASDF, the Orpheus powered aircraft began to enter service in 1961 and by July of the following year 40 had been delivered. The company also produced a T1-B version, powered, or rather underpowered, by the Japan Jet Engine Co. J3-3. This engine delivered only two-thirds of the thrust of the Bristol engine.

Country of origin:	Japan
Type:	two-seat intermediate jet trainer
Powerplant:	one 1814kg (4000lb) Rolls-Royce (Bristol Siddeley) Orpheus Mk 805 turbojet
Performance:	maximum speed 925km/h (575mph) at high altitude; service ceiling 14,400m (47,250ft); range 1860km (1156 miles) at high altitude with drop tanks
Weights:	empty 2420kg (5335lb); maximum take-off 5000kg (11,023lb)
Dimensions:	wingpsan 10.49m (34ft 5in); length 12.12m (39ft 9.2in); height 4.08m (13ft 4.6in); wing area 22.22sq m (239.2sq ft)
Armament:	optional 0.5in Browning M53-2 gun in nose; two underwing pylons with provision for up to 680kg (1500lb) of stores, including bombs, Sidewinder air-to-air missiles, or gun pods; usually only tanks carried

General Dynamics F-16A

The F-16 is undoubtedly one of the most important fighter aircraft of this century. It started fairly inauspiciously as a technology demonstrator to see to what degree it would be possible to build a useful fighter that was significantly smaller and cheaper than the F-15 Eagle. The US Air Force termed this the Lightweight Fighter programme and it was not initially intended to lead to a production aircraft. Contracts for two prototypes each of the General Dynamics 401 and Northrop P.530 were awarded in April 1972. Interest in the concept from a number of America's NATO allies led to a total revision of the LWF program; it was subsequently announced that the US Air Force would buy 650 of the successful Air Combat Fighter design. In December 1974 the General Dynamics design was announced as the winner. The first production F-16A was flown on August 7, 1978.

Country of origin:	USA
Type:	single-seat air combat and ground attack fighter
Powerplant:	either one 10,800kg (23,770lb) Pratt & Whitney F100-PW-200 or one 13,150kg (28,984lb) General Electric F110-GE-100 turbofan
Performance:	maximum speed 2142km/h (1320mph); service ceiling above 15,240m (50,000ft); operational radius 925km (525 miles)
Weights:	empty 7070kg (15,586lb); maximum take-off 16,057kg (35,400lb)
Dimensions:	wingspan 9.45m (31ft); length 15.09m (49ft 6in); height 5.09m (16ft 8in); wing area 27.87sq m (300sq ft)
Armament:	one General Electric M61A1 20mm multi-barrelled cannon, wingtip missile stations; seven external hardpoints with provision for up to 9276kg (20,450lb) of stores, including air-to-air missiles, air-to-surface missiles, ECM pods, reconnaissance or rocket pods, conventional or laser guided bombs, or fuel tanks

General Dynamics F-16B

The F-16B is a two-seat trainer version of General Dynamics' highly successful Fighting Falcon, and shares a physically similar airframe. The second cockpit occupies the area taken up by a fuel tank in the single-seat F-16A. Two of the eight pre-production aircraft were ordered as two-seaters, with the first one flying in August 1977. The USAF has ordered approximately 204 of the two-seat version, and most foreign customers have opted to purchase both types in conjunction. The USAF fleet of F-16A/Bs have undergone a mid-life Multi-national Staged Improvement Program to ensure their effectiveness as combat aircraft into the next century. A further two-seat variant designated the F-16D has been produced, which incorporates the avionics and systems improvements that have been retrofitted to the MSIP F-16A/B aircraft.

Country of origin:	USA
Type:	single-seat air combat and ground attack fighter
Powerplant:	either one 10,800kg (23,770lb) Pratt & Whitney F100-PW-200 or one 13,150kg (28,984lb) General Electric F110-GE-100 turbofan
Performance:	maximum speed 2142km/h (1320mph); service ceiling above 15,240m (50,000ft); operational radius 925km (525 miles)
Weights:	empty 7070kg (15,586lb); maximum take-off 16,057kg (35,400lb)
Dimensions:	wingspan 9.45m (31ft); length 15.09m (49ft 6in); height 5.09m (16ft 8in); wing area 27.87sq m (300sq ft)
Armament:	one General Electric M61A1 20mm multi-barrelled cannon, wingtip missile stations; seven external hardpoints with provision for up to 9276kg (20,450lb) of stores, including air-to-air missiles (AIM-9 Sidewinder and AIM-120 AMRAAM), air-to-surface missiles, ECM pods, reconnaissance or rocket pods, conventional or laser guided bombs, or fuel tanks

General Dynamics F-111

The variable geometry F-111 suffered a difficult gestation, earning it the unwelcome nickname Aardvark. Developed to meet a bold Department of Defense edict that a common type of fighter should be developed to meet all future tactical needs of the US armed forces, the F-111 seemed at the outset both a success and a great failure. Public disagreements over who should get the contract were further clouded by problems in the development of almost every one of the aircraft's systems. Eventually the first of 117 aircraft, designated F-111As, were delivered into service in 1967. A carrier borne long-range interceptor variant of the F-111 for the US Navy foundered after only nine had been built. The Royal Australian Air Force bought the F-111C with increased span and stronger undercarriage but this was the only export success for the aircraft.

Country of origin:	USA
Type:	two-seat multi-purpose attack aircraft
Powerplant:	two 11,385kg (25,100lb) Pratt & Whitney TF-30-P100
Performance:	maximum speed at optimum altitude 2655km/h (1650mph); service ceiling above 17,985m (59,000ft); range with internal fuel 4707km (2925 miles)
Weights:	empty 21,398kg (47,175lb); maximum take-off 45,359kg (100,000lb)
Dimensions:	wingspan unswept 19.20m (63ft); swept 9.74m (32ft 11.5in); length 22.40m (73ft 6in); height 5.22m (17ft 1.5in); wing area 48.77sq m (525sq ft) unswept
Armament:	one 20mm multi-barrelled M61A-1 cannon and one 340kg (750lb) B43 bomb, or two B43 bombs in internal bay, eight underwing hardpoints with provision for 14,290kg (31,000lb) of stores, inner four pivot to keep stores in alignment as wings sweep

Gloster Meteor F.Mk 8

The Gloster Meteor was designed by George Carter to Air Ministry Specification F.9/40. It was the first Allied jet combat design, and the only one to see service during World War II. Trials were carried out with various basic engine types, the Rolls-Royce W.2B, the de Havilland developed Halford H.1, and the Metrovick F.2 among them. The first 20 production aircraft were powered by modified W.2B/23C Welland turbojets. The Meteor entered service with No. 616 Squadron on July 12, 1944, and saw action against V-1 flying bombs. The F.Mk 8 was the most prolific variant, with a lengthened fuselage, redesigned tail, and additional 432-litre (95 Imp gal) fuel tank, and a bubble canopy. Later F.Mk 8s also had bigger engine inlets. The aircraft also boasted a gyro-stabilised gunsight and one the first Martin Baker ejection seats. The first of 1,183 F.Mk 8s was flown on October 12, 1948.

Country of origin:	United Kingdom
Type:	single-seat fighter
Powerplant:	two 1,587kg (3,600lb) Rolls Royce Derwent 8 turbojets
Performance:	maximum speed at 10,000m (33,000ft) 962km/h (598mph); service ceiling 13,106m (43,000ft); range 1580km (980 miles)
Weights:	empty 4820kg (10,626lb); loaded 8664kg (19,100lb)
Dimensions:	wingspan 11.32m (37ft 2in); length 13.58m (44ft 7in); height 3.96m (13ft)
Armament:	four 20mm Hispano cannon, foreign F.8s often modified to carry two iron bombs, eight rockets, or other offensive stores

Gloster Meteor PR.Mk 10

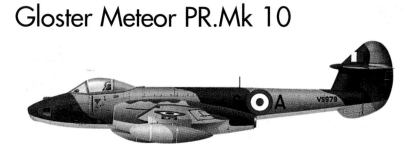

The PR.Mk 10 was a specialised photo-reconnaissance version of the Meteor, which followed the FR.Mk 9 into production in 1950. The Mk 10 was something of a hybrid, with the longer wings of early Mk III models, the tail unit of the Mk IV, and the longer fuselage of the Mk 9 carrying a camera nose. Unlike the previous model the Mk.10 had no armament, and could operate at higher altitude. It also carried vertical cameras, and effectively replaced the Spitfire PR.XIX for strategic reconnaissance at high altitude. The first PR.Mk 10 made its initial flight on March 22, 1950. The Mk 10 entered service with the Royal Air Force with 541 Squadron in January 1951. A total of 58 were produced, along with 126 of the Mk 9s. These were the only two photo-reconnaissance versions built. Note the centreline fuel tank introduced on the F.Mk 8.

Country of origin:	United Kingdom
Type:	single-seat photo-reconnaissance aircraft
Powerplant:	two 1587kg (3600lb) Rolls-Royce Derwent 8 turbojets
Performance:	maximum speed at 10,000m (33,000ft) 962km/h (598mph); service ceiling 13,106m (43,000ft); range 1580km (980 miles)
Weights:	empty 4895kg (10,970lb); loaded 6946kg (19,100lb)
Dimensions:	wingspan 13.1m (43ft); length 13.54m (44ft 3in); height 3.96m (13ft)

Gloster Meteor NF.Mk 11

The N.F Meteor series were tandem-seat night fighters. Development work began in 1949, and was carried out by Armstrong Whitworth. It was decided to use the cockpit section of the T.Mk 7 Meteor trainer for the prototype. The T.Mk 7 was originally developed by Gloster as a private venture but subsequently was bought by both the Royal Navy and Royal Air Force. The forward fuselage was extended to accommodate SCR-720 AI Mk 10 radar, which was mated to an F.Mk 8 rear fuselage and tail unit. The wing was similar to that used on the F.Mk 1 but redesigned to house the four 20mm cannon displaced from the nose. This aircraft was the basis of the first Meteor night fighter, designated N.F.11, which appeared in prototype form on May 31, 1950. One still flies with Jet Heritage Ltd in the United Kingdom. Like many other two-seaters it ended its life as a target tug.

Country of origin:	United Kingdom
Type:	twin-seat night fighter
Powerplant:	Two 1587kg (3,600lb) Rolls-Royce Derwent 8 turbojets
Performance:	maximum speed at 10,000m (33,000ft) 931km/h (579mph); service ceiling 12,192m (40,000ft); range 1580km (980 miles)
Weights:	empty 5400kg (11,900lb); loaded 9979kg (22,000lb)
Dimensions:	wingspan 13.1m (43ft); length 14.78m (48ft 6in); height 4.22m (13ft 10in)
Armament:	four 20mm Hispano cannon

Gloster Meteor NF.Mk 13

The scope of the career of the first British jet fighter is revealed by a few figures. Between 1942 and 1954, 3545 Meteors in 11 basic versions left the assembly lines to serve with the air forces of no less than 12 nations; these were joined by another 330 constructed under licence in the Netherlands by Fokker. The countries that used the Meteor were Argentina, the Netherlands, Belgium, France, Denmark, Egypt, Brazil, Syria, Israel and Sweden. The NF.Mk 13 variant was first flown on December 23, 1952, and has the large greenhouse style canopy seen on the NF.Mk 11. The NF.Mk 13 was built in very small numbers and was specially designed for tropical operation. It first flew in December 1952, and equipped only two squadrons stationed in the Middle East. This aircraft is one of six supplied to Egypt during June-August 1955 and used during the Suez crisis.

Country of origin:	United Kingdom
Type:	two-seat night fighter
Powerplant:	Two 1,587kg (3,600lb) Rolls-Royce Derwent 8 turbojets
Performance:	maximum speed at 10,000m (33,000ft) 931km/h (579mph); service ceiling 12,192m (40,000ft); range 1,580km (980 miles)
Weights:	empty 5400kg (11,900lb); loaded 9979kg (22,000lb)
Dimensions:	wingspan 13.1m (43ft); length 14.78m (48ft 6in); height 4.22m (13ft 10in)
Armament:	four 20mm Hispano cannon

Gloster Meteor NF.Mk 14

Last in the series of Meteor night fighters. The variant may be identified by the revised clear-view canopy and extended nosecone. Less obvious are some minor aerodynamic and equipment changes. These included American-built APS-21 radar and fin-leading edge fairings first used on the NF.Mk 12. Slight improvement was made to the top speed. In all 100 of the Mk 14s were completed, bringing the total for the NF. series to 335, before the final delivery was made in May 1954. Many were later converted to navigation trainers, designated NF(T)Mk 14. This aircraft wears the colours of No. 85 (fighter) Squadron, based at West Malling and Church Fenton in the mid-1950s. The last operational sortie by an RAF Meteor was flown in an NF.Mk 14 of No. 60 Squadron at Tengpah, Singapore in September 1961.

Country of origin:	United Kingdom
Type:	twin-seat night fighter
Powerplant:	two 1587kg (3600lb) Rolls-Royce Derwent 8 turbojets
Performance:	maximum speed at 10,000m (33,000ft) 940km/h (585mph); service ceiling 12,192m (40,000ft); range 1580km (980 miles)
Weights:	empty 5400kg (11,900lb); loaded 9300kg (20,500lb)
Dimensions:	wingspan 13.1m (43ft); length 15.23m (49ft 11.5in); height 4.22m (13ft 10in)
Armament:	four 20mm Hispano cannon

Gloster Meteor U.Mk 16

As the Meteor was gradually superseded by more modern types a new lease of life was given to old airframes through conversion programmes. Major conversions were included the NF(T).14 navigation trainer and the remotely piloted U.14, U.16, and U.17 and the target tug TT.20. The remotely piloted aircraft were designed to provide the three services with a realistic airborne target for gunnery and missile testing. A remote controlled system was designed the aircraft, which were converted from single-seat fighters. Most were painted in high-visibility paint schemes to aid detection, and were sometimes fitted with cameras to record missile impacts. This aircraft is a U.Mk 16, converted from an F.Mk 8 airframe. A version designated U.Mk 21 was used at the Woomera missile ranges in Australia. These aircraft were based on the F.Mk 8 airframe.

Country of origin:	United Kingdom
Type:	remotely piloted target aircraft
Powerplant:	two 1587kg (3600lb) Rolls-Royce Derwent 8 turbojets
Performance:	maximum speed at 10,000m (33,000ft) 962km/h (598mph); service ceiling 13,106m (43,000ft); range 1580km (980 miles)
Weights:	empty 4820kg (10,626lb); loaded 8664kg (19,100lb)
Dimensions:	wingspan 11.32m (37ft 2in); length 13.58m (44ft 7in); height 3.96m (13ft)

Grumman A-6 Intruder

Selected from 11 competing designs in December 1957, the Intruder was specifically planned for first pass blind attack on point surface targets at night or in any weather conditions. The aircraft was designed to be subsonic and is powered by two straight turbojets. In the original design the efflux was routed through tilting jetpips to enhance STOL capabilities. Despite its considerable gross weight the Intruder has excellent slow flying qualities with full span slats and flaps. The crew are afforded a good all round view by the broad canopy. The navigator controls one of the most sophisticated avionics suites on any current aircraft. The Intruder first came into service with the US Navy in February 1963; during the Vietnam War the A-6A was worked round-the-clock on precision bombing missions that no other aircraft was capable of undertaking until the introduction of the F-111.

Country of origin:	USA
Type:	two-seat carrierborne and landbased all-weather strike aircraft
Powerplant:	two 4218kg (9300lb) Pratt & Whitney J52-P-8A turbojets
Performance:	maximum speed at sea level 1043km/h (648mph); service ceiling 14,480m (47,500ft); range with full weapon load 1627km (1011 miles)
Weights:	empty 12,132kg (26,746lb); maximum take-off 26,581kg (58,600lb) for carrier launch or 27,397kg (60,400lb) for field take-off
Dimensions:	wingspan 16.15m (53ft); length 16.69; height 4.93m (16ft 2in); wing area 49.13sq m (528.9sq ft)
Armament:	five external hardpoints with provision for up to 8165kg (18,000lb) of stores, including nuclear weapons, conventional and guided bombs, air-to-surface missiles, and drop tanks

Grumman EA-6 Prowler

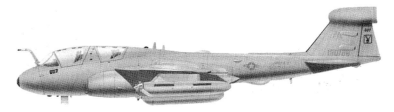

The US Navy rarely undertakes a strike mission without the protection offered by the EA-6 ECM. This aircraft was developed from the successful A-6 Intruder family, although it is substantially different in almost every respect. The large cockpit provides seating for the pilot and three electronic warfare officers, who control the most sophisticated and advanced ECM equipment ever fitted to a tactical aircraft. At the heart of this system is the ALQ-99 tactical jamming system, which is capable of dealing with multiple hostile electronic signals across a broad range of frequencies. The aircraft first entered service in 1972 with VAQ-132. Despite its proven capabilities, the Prowler was only produced in small numbers. In the mid-1990s the US Navy updated many aircraft to ADVCAP (Advanced Capability Standard).

Country of origin:	USA
Type:	electronic countermeasures platform
Powerplant:	two 5080kg (11,200lb) Pratt & Whitney J52-P-408 turbojets
Performance:	maximum speed at sea level 982km/h (610mph); service ceiling 11,580m (38,000ft); combat range with full external fuel 1769km (1099 miles)
Weights:	empty 14,588kg (32,162lb); maximum take-off 29,484kg (65,000lb)
Dimensions:	wingspan 16.15m (53ft); length 18.24m (59ft 10in); height 4.95m (16ft 3in); wing area 49.13sq m (528.9sq ft)
Armament:	none on early models, retrofitted with external hardpoints for four or six AGM-88 HARM air-to-surface anti-radar missiles

Grumman (General Dynamics) EF-111A Raven

During the Vietnam conflict the biggest threat to US aircraft proved to be ground-based radar-guided missiles, supplied by the USSR to NVA forces. This highlighted the need for effective ECM aircraft to provide jamming coverage for attacking forces, and in 1974 the USAF awarded study contracts to Grumman and General Dynamics for the development of a suitable conversion of the F-111A strike aircraft. Grumman's proposal was accepted, and the aircraft they produced entered service after protracted development of the electronics system in 1981. The most recognisable feature of the EF-111 is the fin-tip pod that houses the jamming system's receiver and antenna. Located in the weapons bay is the proven ALQ-99 tactical jamming system, and this is supplemented by ECM dispenser, radar countermeasures receiver, self-protection and terminal threat warning systems.

Country of origin:	USA
Type:	two-seat ECM tactical jamming aircraft
Powerplant:	two 8391kg (18,500lb) Pratt & Whitney TF-30-P3 turbofans
Performance:	maximum speed at optimum altitude 2272km/h (1,412mph); service ceiling above 13,715m (45,000ft); range with internal fuel 1495km (929 miles)
Weights:	empty 25,072kg (55,275lb); maximum take-off 40,346kg (88,948lb)
Dimensions:	wingspan unswept 19.20m (63ft); swept 9.74m (32ft 11.5in); length 23.16m (76ft); height 6.10m (20ft); wing area 48.77sq m (525sq ft) unswept

Grumman F-14A Tomcat

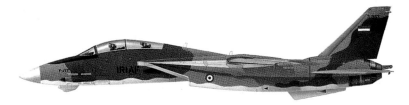

The F-14 was developed largely because of the failure of the F-111B fleet fighter programme, yet has not enjoyed a trouble free service life itself. Continuing problems with the engines have led to escalating maintenance costs (one of the reasons for the development of the cheaper F-18) and a relatively high accident rate. Despite these problems the Tomcat is widely regarded as the finest interceptor flying anywhere in the world. Development of the F-14A was hampered by the loss of the first prototype in December 1970. The aircraft entered service less than two years later with VF-125, before embarking for the first operational tour with VF-1 and VF-2 on USS *Enterprise* in September 1974. The F-14 succeeded the F-4 as the premier fleet defence fighter. A total of 478 F-14As were supplied to the US Navy. Eighty aircraft were exported to Iran from 1976.

Country of origin:	USA
Type:	two-seat carrierborne fleet defence fighter
Powerplant:	two 9480kg (20,900lb) Pratt & Whitney TF30-P-412A turbofans
Performance:	maximum speed at high altitude 2517km/h (1564mph); service ceiling 17,070m (56,000ft); range about 3220km (2000 miles)
Weights:	empty 18,191kg (40,104lb); maximum take-off 33,724kg (74,349lb)
Dimensions:	wingspan 19.55m (64ft 1.5in) unswept; 11.65m (38ft 2.5in) swept; length 19.10m (62ft 8in); height 4.88m (16ft); wing area 52.49sq m (565sq ft)
Armament:	one 20mm M61A1 Vulcan rotary cannon with 675 rounds; external pylons for a combination of AIM-7 Sparrow medium range air-to-air missiles, AIM-9 medium range air-to-air missiles, and AIM-54 Phoenix long range air-to-air missiles

Grumman F-14D Tomcat

In 1973 the US Navy was forced to curtail development of the first F-14B project, powered by twin 12,741kg (28,090lb) Pratt & Whitney F401-P400 turbofans. The result of the cancellation was that all production F-14As were fitted with the TF30, which had only ever been designed as an interim engine. In 1984 it was decided to develop an interim improved version of the F-14 with General Electric F110-GE-400, designated the F-14A (Plus). Thirty-two aircraft were converted and later designated F-14B. The F-14D project suffered a seemingly endless round of cancellations and reinstatements prior to the funding of 37 new-build aircraft and 18 rebuilds from F-14As. The F-14D benefits from an improved version of the powerful APG-70 radar, the APG-71, redesign of the cockpit instrumentation, improved defensive suite and tactical jamming system.

Country of origin:	USA
Type:	two-seat carrierborne fleet defence fighter
Powerplant:	two 12,247kg (27,000lb) General Electric F110-GE-400 turbofans
Performance:	maximum speed at high altitude 1988km/h (1241mph); service ceiling 16,150m (53,000ft); range about 1994km (1239 miles) with full weapon load
Weights:	empty 18,951kg (41,780lb); maximum take-off 33,724kg (74,349lb)
Dimensions:	wingspan 19.55m (64ft 1.5in) unswept; 11.65m (38ft 2.5in) swept; length 19.10m (62ft 8in); height 4.88m (16ft); wing area 52.49sq m (565sq ft)
Armament:	one 20mm M61A1 Vulcan rotary cannon with 675 rounds; external pylons for a combination of AIM-7 Sparrow medium range air-to-air missiles, AIM-9 medium range air-to-air missiles, and AIM-54A/B/C Phoenix long range air-to-air missiles

Handley-Page Victor K.Mk 2

The Victor was the third and last of the V-bombers to go into service with RAF Bomber Command in 1955-58. The design of the aircraft, with the distinctive crescent-shaped wing for maximum cruising speed represented a superb technical achievement. Development time was long and by the time the Victor had entered service it could be intercepted by fighters or shot down by missiles. The number ordered was correspondingly small and the cost was high. Survivors of the 50 B.Mk 1 and B.Mk 1H Victors built were converted by Handley Page to K.Mk 1 two-point and K.Mk 1H three-point tanker standard between 1965 and 1967. Thirty-four improved Victor B.Mk 2s, with increased power and redesigned airframe were supplied to the RAF, but their vulnerability led to the conversion of 27 aircraft to K.Mk 2 tanker standard in 1973-74.

Country of origin:	UK
Type:	four-seat air-refuelling tanker
Powerplant:	four 9344kg (20,600lb) Rolls-Royce Conway Mk 201 turbofans
Performance:	maximum speed at 12,190m (40,000ft) 1030km/h (640mph); maximum cruising height 18,290m (60,000ft); range with internal fuel 7,400km (4,600 miles)
Weights:	empty 41,277kg (91,000lb); maximum take-off 105,687kg (233,000lb)
Dimensions:	wingspan 36.58m (120ft); length 35.05m (114ft 11in); height 9.2m (30ft 1.5in); wing area 223.52sq m (2,406sq ft)

Hawker Hunter F.Mk 1

Without question the most successful post-war British fighter aircraft, the Hunter has a grace and elegance that complements its effectiveness as a warplane. It is fondly remembered by a generation of pilots who delighted in its superb handling characteristics. The first production F.Mk 1 entered service in July 1954; the aircraft was produced in dozens of different guises, and enjoyed a service career across the globe that spanned 40 years. The F.Mk 1 was easily supersonic in a shallow dive and packed a devastating punch with four 30mm Aden cannon in a quick-release pack winched up as a unit. One early problem on this otherwise vice-free aircraft was the tendency for the Avon 100 engine to stop when the guns were fired! On September 7, 1953, the one-off Mk 3 raised the world speed record to 727.6mph off the Sussex coast, piloted by Squadron Leader Neville Duke.

Country of origin:	United Kingdom
Type:	single-seat fighter
Powerplant:	one 2925kg (6500lb) Rolls-Royce Avon 100 turbojet
Performance:	maximum speed at sea level 1144km/h (710mph); service ceiling 15,240m (50,000ft); range on internal fuel 689km (490 miles)
Weights:	empty 5501kg (12,128lb); loaded 7347kg (16,200lb)
Dimensions:	wingspan 10.26m (33ft 8in); length 13.98m (45ft 10.5in); height 4.02m (13ft 2in); wing area 32.42sq m (349sq ft)
Armament:	four 30mm Aden cannon; underwing pylons with provision for two 1000lb bombs and 24 3in rockets

Hawker Hunter T.Mk 8M

In 1953 Hawker began to develop a dual seat trainer version of the Hunter. In July 1955, the prototype P.1101 was flown; production aircraft were designated T.Mk 7 and began entering service with the Royal Air Force in 1958. From this a sub-series was derived for naval use-the T.Mk 8. Naval trainer versions can be distinguished by the arrestor hook under the rear fuselage. Common to all trainer versions was the enlarged cockpit with side-by-side seating and dual controls, and an enlarged dorsal fairing. Production total for the T.Mk 8 was 41. Both the Defence Evaluation and Research Agency and the Empire Test Pilot's School still operate the aircraft. Two-seat trainer aircraft were supplied under a variety of designations to Denmark, Peru, India, Jordan, Lebanon, Kuwait, Switzerland, Iraq, Chile, Singapore, Abu Dhabi, Qatar and Kenya.

Country of origin:	United Kingdom
Type:	dual-seat advanced trainer
Powerplant:	one 3428kg (8000lb) Rolls-Royce Avon 122 turbojet
Performance:	maximum speed at sea level 1117km/h (694mph); service ceiling 14,325m (47,000ft); range on internal fuel 689km (429 miles)
Weights:	empty 6406kg (14,122lb); loaded 7802kg (17,200lb)
Dimensions:	wingspan 10.26m (33ft 8in); length 14.89m (48ft 10in); height 4.02m (13ft 2in); wing area 32.42sq m (349sq ft)
Armament:	two 30mm Aden cannon with 150 rounds

Hunting (Percival) P.84 Jet Provost

In the early 1950s the RAF were continuing to train pilots for fast jet operations on the piston engined Percival Provost. This situation was less than ideal; Hunting recognised the likelihood of an RAF requirement for a basic jet trainer and developed the Jet Provost as a private venture in response. The prototype retained the wings and tail unit of the piston engined P.56 Provost, mated to a new fuselage housing the turbine engine and landing gear. The T.Mk 1 first flew on June 16, 1953, and subsequently was built in large numbers for the RAF. The Jet Provost remained in service in three basic versions. The last version, the T.Mk 5, introduced a pressurised cabin, lengthened nose to house avionics equipment, and strengthened wings with increased internal fuel capacity. This was the RAF's basic trainer until 1989, when it was replaced by the Short Tucano.

Country of origin:	United Kingdom
Type:	two-seat basic trainer
Powerplant:	one 1134kg (2500lb) Bristol Siddeley Viper Mk 202 turbojet
Performance:	maximum speed at 7620m (25,000ft) 708km/h (440mph); service ceiling 11,185m (36,700ft); maximum range with tip tanks 1448km (900 miles)
Weights:	maximum take-off with tip tanks 4173kg (9200lb)
Dimensions:	wingspan 10.77m (35ft 4in); length 10.36m (34ft); height 3.10m (10ft 2in); wing area 19.85 q m (213.7sq ft)

Hawker P.1127

In the 1950s the realisation that the thrust/weight ratio of the gas turbine made possible a new class of high speed jets with VTOL capability led to a rash of unconventional prototypes and research machines. With the exception of the far less capable Yakovlev Yak-38 'Forger' only one has led to a useful combat aircraft. This was the P.1127, designed by a team led by Hawker chief designer Sir Sidney Camm around the unique Bristol BS.53, which had been designed specifically to provide jet-lift to vertical lift-off fixed wing aircraft. The engine was tested on a bizarre rig accurately nicknamed 'The Flying Bedstead'. The first of seven prototype P.1127 made its initial hovering flight on October 21, 1960. Vertical take-off was achieved by vectoring the thrust from the engine down through four adjustable nozzles, which could then be swivelled to make the transition to level flight.

Country of origin:	United Kingdom
Type:	experimental V/STOL aircraft
Powerplant:	(typical; many installations used during trials of the six prototypes) one 8618kg (19,000lb) Rolls-Royce Pegasus vectoring thrust turbojet
Performance:	Mach 1.2 (in dive)
Weights:	n/a
Dimensions:	n/a

Hawker Sea Hawk FB.Mk 3

The Sea Hawk was legendary Hawker designer Sir Sidney Camm's first jet fighter. The first flight of the initial prototype took place on September 2, 1947. The Royal Navy ordered 151 of the navalised version fitted with carrier equipment and with the wing span increased by 0.9m (2ft 6 in). Hawker Siddeley built only 35 of these F.1s; all subsequent design and production was handled by Armstrong Whitworth of Coventry. The F.2 featured powered ailerons, and the FB.3 was fitted with underwing racks to permit the carriage of two bombs or mines. The FB.Mk 3 also had a strengthened main wing spar to accommodate the increased weapon load. In total 116 of the FB.Mk 3s were delivered to the Royal Navy. Many were later converted to FB.Mk 5 standard by fitting a more powerful 2449kg (5400lb) Rolls-Royce Nene 103.

Country of origin:	United Kingdom
Type:	single-seat carrier-based fighter-bomber
Powerplant:	one 2268kg (5000lb) Rolls-Royce Nene turbojet
Performance:	maximum speed at sea level 958km/h (599mph); or 939km/h (587mph) at height; service ceiling 13,560m (44,500ft); standard range 1191km (740 miles)
Weights:	empty 9720lb; maximum take-off 7355kg (16,200lb)
Dimensions:	wingspan 11.89m (39ft); length 12.09m (39ft 8in); height 2.64m (8ft 8in); wing area 25.83sq m (278sq ft)
Armament:	four 20mm Hispano cannon in nose, underwing hardpoints for two 227kg (500lb) bombs

Hawker Sea Hawk FB.Mk 3

After a successful series of piston-engined aircraft produced during World War II, Hawker turned its attention to jet aircraft. After much privately-funded development work on the P.1040 prototype the type was selected by the Royal Navy for quantity production in January 1949. These F.Mk 1 aircraft were built by Hawker at Kingston, although this was shifted to Armstrong Whitworth after only 30 had been completed because of the pressures of Hunter production. The final variant in the first order for 151 Fleet Air Arm machines was the FB.Mk 3 fighter-bomber, of which 116 were built, with strengthened wings for two 227kg (500lb) bombs or mines. The FB.Mk 3 first entered service in July 1954, and although they were soon replaced by the FB.Mk 6, a few saw service in the 1956 Suez campaign. The aircraft pictured wears the colour scheme of the 'Red Devils' Aerobatic Team.

Country of origin:	United Kingdom
Type:	single-seat carrier based fighter-bomber
Powerplant:	one 2270kg (5000lb) Rolls-Royce Nene 101 turbojet
Performance:	maximum speed at sea level 969km/h (602mph); service ceiling 13,565m (44,500ft); combat radius (clean) 370km (230 miles)
Weights:	empty 4409kg (9720lb); maximum take-off 7348kg (16,200lb)
Dimensions:	wingspan 11.89m (39ft); length 12.09m (39ft 8in); height 2.64m (8ft 8in); wing area 25.83sq m (278sq ft)
Armament:	four 20mm Hispano cannon with 200 rpg; plus underwing hardpoints with provision for two 227kg (500lb) bombs

Hawker Sea Hawk FGA.Mk 6

Although the design of the bifurcated jet pipe caused some concern among defence staff when the prototype P.1040 was first unveiled, Sidney Camm's Sea Hawk has a well earned reputation as a reliable, good handling fighter. The final production version of the Sea Hawk was designated FG.Mk 6, equipped with the more powerful Rolls-Royce Nene 103 but otherwise similar to the F.Mk.4. Earlier versions of the Sea Hawk saw action with the Fleet Air Arm during the Suez crisis. Hawker actually built only 35 F.1 Sea Hawks. The remainder were constructed by Armstrong Whitworth who built all 87 of the FGA Mk 6 version. The aircraft remained in service with the FAA until 1960. In 1959 the Indian Navy ordered 24 aircraft similar to the Mk 6. Some were new-build and the rest were refurbished ex-RN Mk 6s.

Country of origin:	United Kingdom
Type:	single-seat carrier based fighter-bomber
Powerplant:	one 2449kg (5400lb) Rolls-Royce Nene 103 turbojet
Performance:	maximum speed at sea level 969km/h (602mph); service ceiling 13,565m (44,500ft); combat radius (clean) 370km (230 miles)
Weights:	empty 4409kg (9720lb); maximum take-off 7348kg (16,200lb)
Dimensions:	wingspan 11.89m (39ft); length 12.09m (39ft 8in); height 2.64m (8ft 8in); wing area 25.83sq m (278sq ft)
Armament:	four 20mm Hispano cannon; plus underwing hardpoints with provision for four 227kg (500lb) bombs, or two 227kg (500lb) bombs and 20 three-inch or 16 five-inch rockets

Hawker Sea Hawk Mk 50

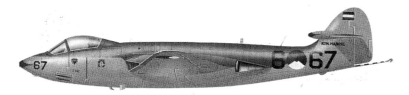

The qualities of the Sea Hawk were early on recognised by a number of foreign naval air services leading to the production of export versions. The Mk 50 was an export version of the Sea Hawk F.Mk 6 for the Royal Netherlands Navy. Some 22 were delivered between 1956-7 and they remained in service until the end of 1964, serving on board the carrier *Karel Doorman*. The Sea Hawk also went for export to India, which was the last remaining operator of the type. This aircraft is a Mk 50 of No. 860 Squadron, Royal Netherlands Navy, distinguished by the broad blade aerial on top of the fuselage. Note the squadron's emblem on the forward fuselage. The unit operated the Sea Hawk during its entire service with the RNN. The Dutch aircraft had provision for Sidewinder 1A air-to-air guided missiles.

Country of origin:	United Kingdom
Type:	single-seat carrier based fighter-bomber
Powerplant:	one 2449kg (5400lb) Rolls-Royce Nene 103 turbojet
Performance:	maximum speed at sea level 969km/h (602mph); service ceiling 13,565m (44,500ft); combat radius (clean) 370km (230 miles)
Weights:	empty 4409kg (9720lb); maximum take-off 7348kg (16,200lb)
Dimensions:	wingspan 11.89m (39ft); length 12.09m (39ft 8in); height 2.64m (8ft 8in); wing area 25.83sq m (278sq ft)
Armament:	four 20mm Hispano cannon; plus underwing hardpoints with provision for four 227kg (500lb) bombs, or two 227kg (500lb) bombs and 20 three-inch or 16 five-inch rockets

Hawker Sea Hawk Mk 100

The other major export versions of the Sea Hawk were the Mk 100, 34 of which were supplied to the West German Kriegsmarine, and the Mk 101 night fighter. The Mk 100 was simply an export version of the FGA.Mk 6, but the Mk 101 featured an enlarged fin and rudder, and was equipped with Ekco 34 search radar in a pod underneath the right wing. Thirty-four Mk 101s were supplied. Operated from shore bases, these were replaced by Lockheed F-104G Starfighters in the mid-1960s. Some of these aircraft were subsequently sold to the Indian Navy, serving aboard INS *Vikrant* until they were replaced by the Sea Harrier FRS.Mk 51 in 1983. The order was fulfilled in 1958 and all aircraft was based at Schleswig for Baltic air defence, as Germany had no aircraft carriers. Germany replaced the Sea Hawk with the Lockheed F-104G Starfighter in the mid-1960s.

Country of origin:	United Kingdom
Type:	single-seat carrier based fighter-bomber
Powerplant:	one 2449kg (5400lb) Rolls-Royce Nene 103 turbojet
Performance:	maximum speed at sea level 969km/h (602mph); service ceiling 13,565m (44,500ft); combat radius (clean) 370km (230 miles)
Weights:	empty 4409kg (9720lb); maximum take-off 7348kg (16,200lb)
Dimensions:	wingspan 11.89m (39ft); length 12.09m (39ft 8in); height 3.04m (9ft 9.5in); wing area 25.83sq m (278sq ft)
Armament:	four 20mm Hispano cannon; plus underwing hardpoints with provision for four 227kg (500lb) bombs, or two 227kg (500lb) bombs and 20 three-inch or 16 five-inch rockets

Hawker Siddeley Gnat T.Mk 1

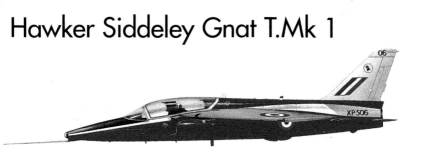

British designer W.E.W. 'Teddy' Petter planned the Gnat to reverse the trend towards larger and more complex combat aircraft, considering a simple lightweight fighter would offer equal performance at a much lower cost. Folland Aircraft proceeded to fund a private venture prototype known as the Midge and eventually gained an order for a development batch of six, the first of which flew in May 1956. India signed a licence agreement in September 1956 and built 213 at Hindustan Aircraft Ltd at Bangalore. With the knowledge that the RAF was seeking to replace its de Havilland Vampire trainer aircraft Folland funded a further private venture to incorporate a dual seat cockpit. A new wing was designed, the fuselage lengthened, and the control surfaces revised. This aircraft entered service as the Gnat T.Mk 1, which served as the RAF's advanced jet trainer.

Country of origin:	United Kingdom
Type:	two-seat advanced trainer
Powerplant:	one 1919kg (4230lb) Bristol Siddeley Orpheus turbojet
Performance:	maximum speed at 9450m (31,000ft) 1024km/h (636mph); service ceiling 14,630m (48,000ft); range with two 300 litre (66 Imp gal) tanks 1852km (1151 miles)
Weights:	empty 2331kg (5140lb); maximum take-off 3915kg (8630lb)
Dimensions:	wingspan 7.32m (24ft); length 9.68m (31ft 9in); height 2.93m (9ft 7.5in); wing area 16.26sq m (175 q ft)

Heinkel He 162 Salamander

Popularly known as the 'Volksjager' (People's Fighter), the He 162 was designed and produced by the war-torn German aviation industry in only six months. With experienced aircrew, fuel, and materials in desperately short supply this strikes as an incredible achievement. On September 8, 1944 the Riechsluftfahrtsministerium issued a specification calling for a 750km/h (466mph) fighter to be regarded as a piece of consumer goods and to be ready by January 1, 1945. Huge numbers of workers were seconded to the project and a rapid training programme for the Hitler Youth was mounted, using mainly glider aircraft. Heinkel, which had built the world's first turbojet aircraft, the He 178, won the design competition with a tiny wooden machine with an engine perched on top. The first prototype flew on December 6, 1944, and deliveries began in January 1945.

Country of origin:	Germany
Type:	single-seat jet interceptor
Powerplant:	one 800kg (1764lb) BMW 003A-1 turbojet
Performance:	maximum speed at 6000m (19,685ft) 840km/h (522mph); service ceiling 12,040m (39,500ft); endurance 57 minutes at 10,970m (35,990ft)
Weights:	empty 2050kg (4250lb); maximum take-off 2695kg (5941lb)
Dimensions:	wingspan 7.20m (23ft 7.5in); length 9.05m (29ft 8.25in); height 2.55m (8ft 4.25in); wing area 11.20sq m (120.56sq ft)
Armament:	two 20mm MG151/20 cannon

Heinkel He 178

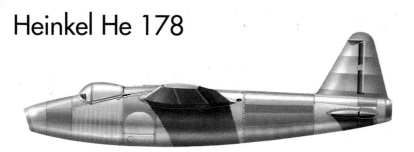

Developed as a private venture in conjunction with the He 176 rocket powered aircraft, the He 178 was powered by Heinkel's HeS 3b turbojet. The aircraft was only ever intended as an experimental test bed, although it made its mark in the history books when on August 27, 1939, Flugkapitan Erich Warsitz lifted off for the first time in a jet-powered aircraft and circled the factory airfield at Rostock-Marienehe. Although officials from the RLM came to inspect the aircraft in October, little official interest was shown and the project was discontinued in favour of the larger He 280. It should be noted though, that the He 178 flew nearly two years before the Gloster E.28/39, despite Britain's early lead in jet technology. Note the fabric-covered tail and high-set wing. The undercarriage retracted into the fuselage just forward of the leading edge.

Country of origin:	Germany
Type:	single-seat experimental jet
Powerplant:	one 454kg (1000lb) He S 3b turbojet
Performance:	n/a
Weights:	n/a
Dimensions:	n/a

Heinkel He 280

When work on the He 178 was discontinued in the winter of 1939, Heinkel redirected their energies into the twin-engined He 280 project. The aircraft was far more advanced, and designed to be powered by pairs of the more powerful HeS 8 and HeS 30. Development problems with both meant that the first prototype airframe was unpowered, the aircraft being towed to release height by a He 111 for its inaugural test flight on September 22, 1940. By March of the next year the HeS 8 engines were ready for installation, and the aircraft took off under its own power on April 2. With only 500kg (1102lb) of thrust available pilot Fritz Schäfer found that performance was hardly sparkling; by early 1943 this had risen to a little over 600kg. Even with BMW 109-003 engines fitted, the aircraft failed to impress and never entered full-scale production, losing out to the Messerschmitt Me 262.

Country of origin:	Germany
Type:	single-seat experimental jet
Powerplant:	two 600kg (1323lb) Henkel HeS 8A turbojets
Performance:	maximum speed at 6458kg (19,685ft) 800km/h (497mph)
Weights:	loaded 4340kg (9550lb)
Dimensions:	wingspan 12m (39ft 4in); length 10.4m (34ft 1in)

Horton Ho IX V2

As early as the 1920s Reimar and Walter Horten were extolling the merits of tailless aircraft which they believed possessed superior flying characteristics. They began an experimental series in 1931, which culminated in the Ho IX V2 (The prototype Ho X was never completed). Their Ho IX V2 bears more than a passing similarity to the incredible Northrop B2 Spirit, and was the first jet-powered Horten aircraft. Designed as a fighter, the first flight of the unpowered V1 prototype was completed during 1944. A second prototype powered by two 900kg (1984lb) turbojets was built, but after barely two hours of flight tests it was lost after an engine flameout. Production had been planned on a large scale at the Gotha factory. However, only one aircraft had been completed before US forces captured the workshops, and all of the vital research documents.

Country of origin:	Germany
Type:	single-seat experimental flying wing jet fighter
Powerplant:	two 900kg (1984lb) BMW 003 turbojets
Performance:	about 800km/h (500mph) at 6100m (20,000ft)
Weights:	about 9080kg (20,000lb)
Dimensions:	wingspan 16m (52ft 6in)
Armament:	(proposed) four 30mm MK 108 cannon for day fighter; provision for up to 908kg (2000lb) of bombs as fighter-bomber

IAI Kfir C1

During the 1950s, Israel was forced to rely almost solely on France for procurement of combat aircraft. The original Mirage IIIC actually owes much of its inception to the close ties between Dassault and Israel. During the Six Day War of 5-10 June 1967 this aircraft performed magnificently, yet Dassault was ordered by an irate General de Gaulle that he could not deliver the improved Mirage 5 attack aircraft which had been developed for Israel and already paid for. Israeli Aircraft Industries were thus directed to concentrate their energies on making Israel more self-sufficient in combat aircraft, and to devise an improved version of the Mirage III. The company adapted the airframe to take a General Electric J79 turbojet, under a programme dubbed Black Curtain. Some of these aircraft participated in the 1973 Yom Kippur War.

Country of origin:	Israel
Type:	single-seat interceptor
Powerplant:	one 8119kg (17,900lb) General Electric J79-J1E turbojet
Performance:	maximum speed above 11,000m (36,090ft) 2445km/h (1,520mph); service ceiling 17,680m (58,000ft); combat radius as interceptor 346km (215 miles)
Weights:	empty 7285kg (16,090lb); maximum take-off 16,200kg (35,715lb)
Dimensions:	wingspan 8.22m (26ft 11.5in); length 15.65m (51ft 4.25in); height 4.55m (14ft 11.25in); wing area 34.80sq m (374.60sq ft)
Armament:	one IAI (DEFA) 30mm cannon; nine external hardpoints with provision for up to 5775kg (12,732lb) of stores; for interception duties AIM-9 Sidewinder air-to-air missiles, or indigenously produced AAMs such as the Shafrir or Python

IAI Kfir C1

The Kfir (Lion Cub) represented a significant improvement over the Mirage III on which it was based. The installation of the J79 engine necessitated redesign of the fuselage and addition of a ram-cooling inlet ahead of the fin. The shorter engine resulted in a shorter rear fuselage, but the nose was lengthened to take a comprehensive avionics suite. Only 27 of the Kfir C1 model were built, and they equipped two squadrons of the Israeli Defence Force before replacement by the improved C2. The aircraft could be used in both ground attack and interceptor roles, and was a major achievement for IAI. All except two were leased to the US Navy and Marine Corps for 'aggressor' training after upgrading to C2 standard. The aircraft was also offered for export. The aircraft pictured served with USN Squadron VF-43 at NAS Oceana, Virginia between 1985-1988, under the designation F-21A.

Country of origin:	Israel
Type:	single-seat interceptor/ground attack aircraft
Powerplant:	one 8119kg (17,900lb) General Electric J79-J1E turbojet
Performance:	maximum speed above 11,000m (36,090ft) 2445km/h (1520mph); service ceiling 17,680m (58,000ft); combat radius as interceptor 346km (215 miles)
Weights:	empty 7285kg (16,090lb); maximum take-off 16,200kg (35,715lb)
Dimensions:	wingspan 8.22m (26ft 11.5in); length 15.65m (51ft 4.25in); height 4.55m (14ft 11.25in); wing area 34.80sq m (374.60sq ft)
Armament:	one IAI (DEFA) 30mm cannon; nine external hardpoints with provision for up to 5775kg (12,732lb) of stores; including conventional and guided bombs, cluster bombs, rockets, napalm tanks, air-to-ground missiles and air-to-air missiles

IAI Kfir C2

The C2 was the major production version of the Kfir, and was first publicly
demonstrated on July 20, 1976. Improvements included the adoption of small
removable swept canard foreplanes on the inlet trunks to improve flying
characteristics, a small strake on each side of the nose, and extended chord
(breadth) outer wings to improve take-off, landing and general combat
performance. Later aircraft in the run of 185 (including TC2 trainer aircraft) were
fitted with an improved radar system. Between 1983-85 most C2s were upgraded
to C7 standard, with improved engine thrust and avionics, and two additional
external stores pylons. None remain in service with the IDF. The aircraft was also
supplied to Colombia. This aircraft was based at Hatzerim in the Negev desert,
and wears standard IDF/AF camouflage.

Country of origin:	Israel
Type:	single-seat interceptor/ground attack aircraft
Powerplant:	one 8119kg (17,900lb) General Electric J79-J1E turbojet
Performance:	maximum speed above 11,000m (36,090ft) 2445km/h (1,520mph); service ceiling 17,680m (58,000ft); combat radius as interceptor 346km (215 miles)
Weights:	empty 7285kg (16,090lb); maximum take-off 16,200kg (35,715lb)
Dimensions:	wingspan 8.22m (26ft 11½in); length 15.65m (51ft 4n); height 4.55m (14ft 11¼in); wing area 34.80 sq m (374.60 sq ft)
Armament:	one IAI (DEFA) 30mm cannon; nine external hardpoints with provision for up to 5775kg (12,732lb) of stores; for ground attack duties a wide range of stores, including conventional and guided bombs, cluster bombs, rockets, napalm tanks, air-to-ground missiles

Ilyushin Il-28 'Beagle'

First appearing in prototype form as early as 1948, the Il-28 afforded Eastern Bloc armed forces the same degree of flexibility and duration of service as the Canberra did for Britain. The prototype was powered by two Soviet-built turbojets developed directly from the Rolls-Royce Nene, supplied by the British government in a fit of contrition. The unswept wing is set high and well back on the fuselage, to reduce the moment caused by fuel tanks located in the rear fuselage and the aft gunners compartment. The gunner also acts as the radio operator, with the navigator housed in the glazed nose section. After a public fly-past during the 1950 May Day parade, Soviet units began to equip with the Il-28 in some numbers. The aircraft served with all Warsaw Pact light bomber units between 1955-70. A trainer version (Il-28U) was also produced.

Country of origin:	USSR
Type:	three seat bomber and ground attack/dual control trainer/torpedo carrier
Powerplant:	two 2700kg (5952kg) Klimov VK-1 turbojets
Performance:	maximum speed 902 km/h (560mph); service ceiling 12,300m (40,355ft); range 2180km (1355 miles); with bomb load 1100km (684 miles)
Weights:	empty 12890kg (28,418lb); maximum take-off 21,200kg (46,738lb)
Dimensions:	wingspan 21.45sq m (70ft 4.5in); length 17.65m (57ft 10.75in); height 6.70m (21ft 11.8in); wing area 60.80sq m (654.47sq ft)
Armament:	two 23mm NR-23 fixed cannon in nose, two 23mm NR-23 trainable cannon in tail turret; internal bomb capacity of up to 1000kg (2205lb), maximum bomb capacity 3000kg (6614lb); torpedo version had provision for two 400mm light torpedoes

Ilyushin Il-28 'Beagle'

Nearly 10,000 of the Ilyushin Il-28 were produced in standard VK-1 form with the Nene derived engine. Three main variants were adapted from the basic airframe, and retain the same configuration. The Il-28T naval torpedo bomber was used for many years for operations over the Baltic by the Soviet Navy. The Il-28U 'Mascot' dual control trainer is instantly recognisable by the distinctive stepped cockpit. The Il-28R, although popularly believed to be a tactical reconnaissance variant, was in fact distinguished only by having tip-tanks to increase fuel payload. Although no longer in service with any of the former Soviet states, the Il-28 is still operated by a number of ex-Soviet allies and with the Chinese People's Liberation Army air force. China also licence-built the aircraft, although the one pictured is one of 500 supplied by the USSR.

Country of origin:	USSR
Type:	three-seat bomber and ground attack/dual control trainer/torpedo carrier
Powerplant:	two 2700kg (5952kg) Klimov VK-1 turbojets
Performance:	maximum speed 902 km/h (560mph); service ceiling 12,300m (40,355ft); range 2180km (1355 miles); with bomb load 1100km (684 miles)
Weights:	empty 12890kg (28,418lb); maximum take-off 21,200kg (46,738lb)
Dimensions:	wingspan 21.45sq m (70ft 4.5in); length 17.65m (57ft 10.75in); height 6.70m (21ft 11.8in); wing area 60.80sq m (654.47sq ft)
Armament:	two 23mm NR-23 fixed cannon in nose, two 23mm NR-23 trainable cannon in tail turret; internal bomb capacity of up to 1000kg (2205lb), maximum bomb capacity 3000kg (6614lb); torpedo version had provision for two 400mm light torpedoes

Ilyushin Il-76MD 'Candid-B'

The Il-76 'Candid' (NATO reporting name) was first seen in the West at the 1971 Paris Air Salon. The design was prepared to meet a basic need in the Soviet Union for a really capable freighter, which, while carrying large indivisible loads, with a high cruising speed and intercontinental range, could operate from relatively poor and partially prepared airstrips. Aeroflot was the first operator, who used it on Siberian routes. The Il-76T 'Candid A' was delivered to the Soviet air force for evaluation in 1974, and featured a rear gun turret. Within two years deliveries of the Il-76M 'Candid-B' began. The Il-76MD pictured features a host of improvements, including an increased fuel capacity which in turn provides an increase in range. The MD is unarmed, has more powerful engines, and can carry a heavier payload. India are among the foreign clients, operating a fleet of 24.

Country of origin:	USSR (now CIS)
Type:	heavy freight transport
Powerplant:	four 12,000kg (26,455lb) Soloviev D-30KP-1 turbofans
Performance:	maximum speed at 11,000m (36,090ft) 850km/h (528mph); maximum cruising altitude 12,000m (39,370ft); range with 40,000kg (88,185lb) payload 5000km (3107 miles)
Weights:	empty about 75,000kg (165,347lb); maximum take-off 170,000kg (374,786lb)
Dimensions:	wingspan 50.50m (165ft 8.2in); length 46.59m (152ft 10.25in); height 14.76m (48ft 5in); wing area 300sq m (3229.28sq ft)
Armament:	provision for two 23mm cannon in tail

Kawasaki C-1

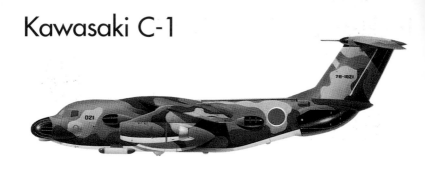

The C-1 was designed specifically to replace the redoubtable Curtiss C-46 Commando transport aircraft in service with the Japanese Air Self Defence Force. The first two prototypes were built during 1968 by Kawasaki Heavy Industries from a design submitted by the Nihon Aeroplane Manufacturing Company. The first flight was made in November 1970; flight testing and evaluation led to a production order for 11 in 1972. The C-1 follows conventional military transport design with a high set wing configuration to maximise cabin volume, podded main landing gear and a rear loading ramp. Limited maximum payload curtailed plans to develop variants, with the exception of the sole C-1Kai ECM trainer pictured. This aircraft differs from standard models by distinctive radomes on the nose and tail, an ALQ-5 ECM system, and antennae beneath the fuselage.

Country of origin:	Japan
Type:	ECM trainer aircraft
Powerplant:	two 6577kg (14,500lb) Mitsubishi (Pratt & Whitney) JT8-M-9 turbofans
Performance:	maximum speed at 7620m (25,000ft) 806km/h (501mph); service ceiling 11,580m (38,000ft); range 1300km (808 miles) with 7900kg (17,417lb) payload
Weights:	empty 23320kg (51,412lb); maximum take-off 45,000kg (99,208lb)
Dimensions:	wingspan 30.60m (100ft 4.75in); length 30.5m (100ft 4in); height 10.0m (32ft 9.3in); wing area 102.50sq m (1297.09sq ft)

Lockheed C-141B StarLifter

Designed and developed in the early 1960s to a USAF Military Airlift Command requirement, the StarLifter is still the most numerous of MACs strategic transport aircraft. It had been intended that the C-117 would supplant the older aircraft in service but budget restrictions have led to a reduction in the order. The aircraft entered service in April 1965, and the last aircraft was delivered in February 1968. All 270 surviving C-141As were converted to C-141B standard by stretching the fuselage by 7.11m (23ft 4in) in a programme that began in 1976. The aircraft has seen service in during the Vietnam War, during the US invasion of Grenada, and most recently in the 1991 Gulf War. The aircraft pictured has a 'Europe One' camouflage scheme, although many have now been repainted with an overall grey scheme.

Country of origin:	USA
Type:	heavy strategic transport
Powerplant:	four 9526kg (21,000lb) Pratt & Whitney TF33-7 turbofans
Performance:	maximum speed 912km/h (567mph); range with maximum payload 4723km (2935 miles)
Weights:	empty 67,186kg (148,120lb); maximum take-off 155,582kg (343,000lb)
Dimensions:	wingspan 48.74m (159ft 11in); length 51.29m (168ft 3.5in); height 11.96m (39ft 3in); wing area 299.88sq m (3,228sq ft)

Lockheed C-5A Galaxy

For a time during the early 1970s the giant C-5 Galaxy reigned as the world's largest aircraft, although it has now been overtaken by the Antonov An-124 Ruslan 'Condor'. Despite its huge size the Galaxy can operate from rough airstrips. To this end it has a high flotation landing gear with 28 wheels. During the development programme extreme difficulties were encountered with the aerodynamics and structural weight. As the result, the unit cost escalated and eventually production had to be cut to a total of 81, equipping four MAC squadrons. The aircraft can carry complete missile systems and M1 Abrams tanks to potential trouble spots around the globe, and has proved an invaluable asset to the US armed forces in this role. In 1982 the C-5B, was authorised. This included the modifications evolved in the C-5A – uprated engines, extended life wing and better avionics.

Country of origin:	USA
Type:	heavy strategic transport
Powerplant:	(C5A) four 18,642kg (41,000lb) General Electric TF39-1turbofans
Performance:	maximum speed 919km/h (571mph); service ceiling at 272,910kg (615,000lb) 10,360m (34,000ft); range with maximum payload 100,228kg (220,967lb) 6033km (3749 miles)
Weights:	empty 147,528kg (325,244lb); maximum take-off 348,810kg (769,000lb)
Dimensions:	wingspan 67.88m (222ft 8.5in); length 75.54m (247ft 10in); height 19.85m (65ft 1.5in); wing area 575.98sq m (6,200sq ft)

Lockheed K. Mk 1 TriStar

Since March 1986, the Royal Air Force has operated a converted version of the Lockheed Tristar jetliner from Brize Norton in Oxfordshire as its primary tanker aircraft. Six of the 500 series aircraft were acquired from British Airways, and adapted by Marshall of Cambridge for inflight refuelling operations. This involved installing tanks in the cargo holds to give an extra 45,359kg (100,000lb) of fuel, and twin Hose and Drum Units in the rear fuselage. Four of the aircraft retained a commercial type cabin configuration to allow passengers to be carried. These are designated K.Mk 1. The two other aircraft were fitted with a large cargo door on the port side to allow the carriage of freight. These are designated KC.Mk 1. Three more were acquired from Pan-American in 1984/85 and converted to K.Mk 2 tanker/passenger aircraft, with a slightly reduced internal fuel capacity.

Country of origin:	UK/US
Type:	long-range strategic transport and inflight refuelling tanker
Powerplant:	three 22,680kg (50,000lb) Rolls-Royce RB.211-524B turbofans
Performance:	maximum cruising speed 964km/h (599mph) at 10,670m (35,000ft); service ceiling 13,105m (43,000ft); range on internal fuel with maximum payload 7783km (4836 miles)
Weights:	empty 110,163kg (242,684lb); maximum take-off 244,944kg (540,000lb)
Dimensions:	wingspan 50.09m (164ft 4in); length 50.05m (164ft 2.5in); height 16.87m (55ft 4in); wing area 329.96sq m (3541sq ft)

Lockheed P-80A Shooting Star

The P-80A was the first production model of the Shooting Star. The lettered prefix was later changed from 'P' (Pursuit) to 'F' (Fighter) due to changes in the American designation system in 1947. The aircraft pictured 44-85226 'Betsy Jean' is adorned with the vertical coloured stripes of the commander of the 412th Fighter Group. This type of national insignia and the PN buzz-code was used until 1947, when the USAF became an independent service. In June 1947, Colonel Alfred Boyd flew a modified P-80R to a new world speed record of 1003.8 km/h (623.8mph) at Muroc Dry Lake, California. The aircraft was also subject to a great deal of experimentation, with various armament and propulsion packages tried at various points throughout its service life. Many aircraft ended their days as unmanned target drones.

Country of origin:	USA
Type:	single-seat fighter bomber
Powerplant:	one 1746kg (3850lb) Allison J33-GE-11 turbojet
Performance:	maximum speed at sea level 966km/h (594mph); service ceiling 14,265m (46,800ft); range 1328km (825 miles)
Weights:	empty 3819kg (8420lb); maximum take-off 7646kg (16,856lb)
Dimensions:	wingspan 11.81m (38ft 9in); length 10.49m (34ft 5in); height 3.43m (11ft 3in); wing area 22.07sq m (237.6sq ft)
Armament:	six 0.5in machine guns, plus two 454kg (1000lb) bombs and eight rockets

Lockheed F-80C-5 Shooting Star

The Lockheed P-80 was designed in less than 180 days around the British Halford H.1 (Goblin) engine, by a Lockheed team led by Clarence L. 'Kelly' Johnson. The aircraft first flew in January 1944 and P-80s were flying under combat conditions in Italy a year later. By the time of the Korean War, the aircraft were considered somewhat obsolete, but nonetheless undertook the brunt of the initial flying, flying 15,000 sorties in the first four months and shooting down the first MiG-15 on November 8, 1950 in what is thought to have been the first jet combat. The F-80 C-5 was the final production version, with more powerful engines. Later production versions of the F-80 C had the 2449kg (5400lb) J33-A-35 turbojet. Total production of the Shooting Star was 1718; many were converted to other duties after front-line retirement.

Country of origin:	USA
Type:	single-seat fighter bomber
Powerplant:	one 2449kg (5400lb) Allison J33-A-35 turbojet
Performance:	maximum speed at sea level 966km/h (594mph); service ceiling 14,265m (46,800ft); range 1328km (825 miles)
Weights:	empty 3819kg (8420lb); maximum take-off 7646kg (16,856lb)
Dimensions:	wingspan 11.81m (38ft 9in); length 10.49m (34ft 5in); height 3.43m (11ft 3in); wing area 22.07sq m (237.6sq ft)
Armament:	six 0.5in machine guns, plus two 454kg (1000lb) bombs and eight rockets

Lockheed T-33A

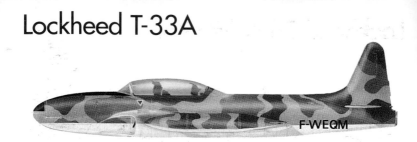

F-WEQM

Longest serving of all Shooting Star variants was the T-33 trainer conversion, produced by lengthening a standard F-80C airframe by more than a metre to accommodate a second seat beneath a single canopy. The first conversion, designated TF-80C, flew on March 22, 1948. The aircraft was adopted as the standard jet trainer of the US Air Force, and found a ready market overseas. Many were supplied to US allies under the Military Assistance Program. Production by Lockheed continued until August 1959, by which time a total of 5691 had been built. The aircraft has been adapted for many other roles; the QT-33 target drone perhaps the most important of these conversions. A version for service with smaller air forces had armament revision making it suitable for weapons training and counter-insurgency.

Country of origin:	USA
Type:	two-seat jet trainer
Powerplant:	one 2449kg (5400lb) Allison J33-A-35 turbojet
Performance:	maximum speed at 7,620m (25,000ft) 879km/h (546mph); service ceiling 14,630m (48,000ft); endurance 3 hours 7 minutes
Weights:	empty 3667kg (8084lb); maximum take-off 6551kg (14,442lb)
Dimensions:	wingspan 11.85m (38ft 10.5in); length 11.51m (37ft 10in); height 3.56m (11ft 8in); wing area 21.81sq m (234.8sq ft)
Armament:	two 0.5mm machine guns; wide variety of ordnance in COIN role

Lockheed T-1A SeaStar

The final variant in the F-80/T-33/F-94 family was the T2V-1 SeaStar jet trainer, an advanced version of the T-33A two-seat trainer aircraft. The navalised version of this aircraft was designated the TV-2, and featured arrestor gear for carrier landings. The T2V-1 (later T1-A) was a further refinement, with humped cockpit, leading and trailing edge flaps, boundary layer control and a 2769kg (6100lb) Allison turbojet. Nearly 700 T2-V aircraft were produced for the US Navy and it served for a considerable time as their standard trainer aircraft. The aircraft pictured served with the US Navy Test Pilot School in Maryland during the 1960s, until replaced by the Northrop T-38 Talon. The red/white colour scheme has been standard for US Navy trainers since the 1950s. Some SeaStars have been converted for use as avionics test beds.

Country of origin:	USA
Type:	two-seat jet trainer
Powerplant:	one 2769kg (6100lb) Allison J33-A-35 turbojet
Performance:	maximum speed at 7,620m (25,000ft) 879km/h (546mph); service ceiling 14,630m (48,000ft); endurance 3 hours 7 minutes
Weights:	empty 3667kg (8084lb); maximum take-off 6551kg (14,442lb)
Dimensions:	wingspan 11.85m (38ft 10.5in); length 11.51m (37ft 10in); height 3.56m (11ft 8in); wing area 21.81sq m (234.8sq ft)

Lockheed F-94A Starfire

Retaining many of the features of the F-80 and T-33 aircraft from which it was developed, the tandem-seat Starfire was conceived in 1949 as a radar-equipped all-weather interceptor. Two prototypes were produced by converting existing T-33 airframes. Changes included the installation of a 2724kg (6000lb) Allison J33-A-33 afterburning turbojet, remodelling the nose to accommodate radar, and revised accommodation for the pilot and radar operator. The first flight took place on July 1, 1949, and production of 110 similar F-94As began the same year. The first deliveries, to the 319th All Weather Fighter Squadron began in June 1950. Two improved variants were produced, the F-94B with a blind landing system and raised tip tanks, and the F-94C, with redesigned wing and fin, longer fuselage, more powerful engine, and 24 Mighty Mouse unguided air-to-air rockets in the nose.

Country of origin:	USA
Type:	tandem-seat all-weather interceptor
Powerplant:	one 2724kg (6000lb) Allison J33-A-33 turbojet
Performance:	maximum speed at 30,000ft 933km/h (580mph); service ceiling 14,630m (48,000ft); range 1850km/h (1150 miles)
Weights:	empty 5030kg (11,090lb); maximum take-off 7125kg (15,710lb)
Dimensions:	wingspan not including tip tanks 11.85m (38ft 10.5in); length 12.2m (40ft 1in); height 3.89m (12ft 8in); wing area 22.13sq m (238sq ft)
Armament:	four 0.5in machine guns

Lockheed F-104G Starfighter

The F-104G was a complete redesign of the Starfighter to meet the needs of the Luftwaffe for a tactical nuclear strike and reconnaissance aircraft. This aircraft was developed especially for export to client countries and was first flown in prototype form in June 1960. By comparison with the F-104D the 'F' had a substantially strengthened fuselage, and boasted Nasarr multi-mode radar, inertial navigation system, manoeuvring flaps and other improvements.
Ninety-six were supplied to the Luftwaffe who deployed them in a number of different roles. The aircraft pictured carries the MBB Kormoran anti-ship missile and was operated by the Marine Hieger. Some 184 RF-104Gs, which is a tactical reconnaissance version of the Starfighter were constructed. Italy and Germany were among the last major operators of the aircraft.

Country of origin:	USA
Type:	single-seat multi-mission strike fighter
Powerplant:	one 7076kg (15,600lb) General Electric J79-GE-11A turbojet
Performance:	maximum speed at 15,240m (50,000ft) 1845km/h (1146mph); service ceiling 15,240m (50,000ft); range 1740km (1081 miles)
Weights:	empty 6348kg (13,995lb); maximum take-off 13,170kg (29,035lb)
Dimensions:	wingspan (excluding missiles) 6.36m (21ft 9in); length 16.66m (54ft 8in); height 4.09m (13ft 5in); wing area 18.22sq m (196.10sq ft)
Armament:	one 20mm General Electric M61A1 cannon, provision for AIM-9 Sidewinder on fuselage, under wings or on tips, and/or stores up to a maximum of 1814kg (4000lb)

Lockheed F-117 Night Hawk

The F-117 is probably the most important aircraft to enter service in the past two decades, and has redefined our concept of what the flying machine of the 21st century will look like. The development program is shrouded in secrecy, but it is likely that research into stealth technology began in earnest in the wake of a number of successful radar guided missile attacks on US built F-4s during the 1973 Yom Kippur war. Both Lockheed and Northrop submitted proposals for the Experimental Stealth Technology requirement issued by the DOD; Lockheed's proposal was subsequently selected in 1977 and the plane was delivered five years later. In the 1991 Gulf War the Night Hawk really hit the headlines. Exploiting the low radar visibility, pilots were able to penetrate Iraqi airspace undetected and deliver useful quantities of ordnance with pinpoint accuracy.

Country of origin:	USA
Type:	single-seat stealth attack aircraft
Powerplant:	two 4899kg (10,800lb) General Electric F404-GE-F1D2 turbofans
Performance:	maximum speed about Mach 1at high altitude: combat radius about 1112km (691 miles) with maximum payload
Weights:	empty about 13,608kg (30,000lb); maximum take-off 23,814kg (52,500lb)
Dimensions:	wingspan 13.20m (43ft 4in); length 20.08m (65ft 11in); height 3.78m (12ft 5in); wing area about 105.9sq m (1,140sq ft)
Armament:	provision for 2268kg (5000lb) of stores on rotary dispenser in weapon bay; including the AGM-88 HARM anti-radiation missile; AGM-65 Maverick ASM, GBU-19 and GBU-27 optronically guided bombs, BLU-109 laser-guided bomb, and B61 free-fall nuclear bomb

Lockheed/Boeing F-22 Rapier

In April 1991, after a tightly fought competition to find a replacement for the F-15 Eagle, the Pratt & Whitney powered F-22 proposed by the Lockheed/Boeing partnership was declared the winner. The aircraft will incorporate all of the most advanced avionics and airframe technology at the disposal of the two companies, such as stealth, a long-range supersonic combat radius, high agility and STOL capability, and an advanced nav/attack system using artificial intelligence to filter data and so reduce the pilot's workload. The definitive airframe design was achieved in March 1992. The USAF plan to buy 648 aircraft, at a cost of $59.4 million each. Early in the next century the Raptor will begin replacing the F-15 Eagle as the USAF's premier air combat fighter. Flight testing is proceeding well, despite the loss of the second prototype (N22YX) in April 1992.

Country of origin:	USA
Type:	single-seat supersonic air superiority fighter
Powerplant:	two 15,876kg (35,000lb) Pratt & Whitney F119-P-100 turbofans
Performance:	maximum speed 2335km/h (1451mph); service ceiling 19,812m (65,000ft); combat radius 1285km (800miles)
Weights:	empty 14,061kg (31,000lb); maximum take-off 27,216 kg (60,000lb)
Dimensions:	wingspan 13.1m (43ft); length 19.55m (64ft 2in); height 5.39m (17ft 8in); wing area 77.1sq m (830sq ft)
Armament:	production aircraft will have cannon armament plus next generation air-to-air missiles in the internal weapons bay

Lockheed S-3A Viking

The development of deep-diving Soviet nuclear submarines highlighted the need within the US Navy for a new generation of hunter-killer ASW aircraft to replace the Grumman S-2. Lockheed was the winner of a contract awarded in 1969, for development of such an aircraft. The first flight was made in January 1972, and service deliveries began in October 1973. The aircraft is a remarkable exercise in packaging, and the cost of the airframe is far outweighed by the equipment it carries. On the original model this included the highly advanced APS-116 radar in the nose, CAINS (carrier aircraft inertial navigation system), comprehensive sonobuoy dispensing and control systems, doppler radar, very extensive radio navaid and altitude systems, radar warning and ECM systems. This aircraft was one delivered to Anti-submarine Squadron 21, aboard USS *John F. Kennedy*.

Country of origin:	USA
Type:	carrier-based patrol/attack aircraft
Powerplant:	two 4207kg (9275lb) General Electric TF34-GE-2 turbofans
Performance:	maximum cruising speed 814km/h (506mph); service celing 10,670m (35,000ft); combat range more than 3705km (2303 miles)
Weights:	empty 12,088kg (26,650lb); maximum take-off 19,278kg (42,500lb)
Dimensions:	wingspan 20.93m (68ft 8in); length 16.26m (53ft 4in); height 6.93m (2ft 9in); wing area 55.55 q m (598sq ft)
Armament:	internal weapons bay with provision for up to 907kg (2000lb) of stores, such as four Mk 46 torp does, four Mk 82 bombs, four depth bombs or four mines; two wing pylons can carry single or triple ejectors for bombs, rocket pods, missiles, tanks or other stores

Lockheed S-3B Viking

There is no more important part of the US Navy carrier air arm than the S-3A Viking, and as such the aircraft have been substantially upgraded during their service lives to maintain frontine combat capability. All aircraft now wear the low-visibility Tactical Paint Scheme. In 1980 Lockheed was awarded a contract to give the S-3As expanded ASW capability. Known as the Weapon System Improvement Program, this introduced a host of new avionics suites, including the AYS-1 Proteus acoustic signal processor, improved ESM, upgraded Texas Instruments AN/APS 137 (V) 1 radar, a new sonabouy telemetry receiver system, and provision to carry the AGM-64 Harpoon. Two aircraft were initially converted to S-3B standard by Lockheed and fully evaluated by the US Navy. In April 1988 Lockheed were contracted to supply S-3B conversion kits, all of which were delivered by August 1992.

Country of origin:	USA
Type:	carrier-based patrol/attack aircraft
Powerplant:	two 4207kg (9275lb) General Electric TF34-GE-2 turbofans
Performance:	maximum cruising speed 814km/h (506mph); service celing 10,670m (35,000ft); combat range more than 3705km (2303 miles)
Weights:	empty 12,088kg (26,650lb); maximum take-off 19,278kg (42,500lb)
Dimensions:	wingspan 20.93m (68ft 8in); length 16.26m (53ft 4in); height 6.93m (2ft 9in); wing area 55.55 sq m (598 sq ft)
Armament:	internal weapons bay with provision for up to 1814kg (4000lb) of stores, such as four Mk 46 torpedoes, four Mk 82 bombs, four depth bombs or four mines; two wing pylons can carry single or triple ejectors for bombs, rocket pods, missiles, tanks or other stores up to a weight of 1361kg (3000lb)

Lockheed SR-71 Blackbird

Even now, after 30 years in service, the SR-71 has looks and performance seemingly borne in the 21st century. Developed by a team led by Kelly Johnson at Lockheed's Skunk Works, the SR-71 was designed as a strategic reconnaissance aircraft to succeed the U-2. Although detailed design work began in 1959, the US Government did not formally acknowledge the existence of the SR-71 until 1964. By this time the aircraft had been evaluated as a possible experimental all-weather interceptor in the Improved Manned Interceptor programme. The three aircraft that had been provisionally ordered for the USAF were designated YF-12A for the duration of the programme, and were later allocated to the joint NASA/USAF AST (Advanced Supersonic Technology) programme. Production of the the the SR-71 began in 1963 and deliveries began to the 4200th Strategic Reconnaissance Wing in 1966.

Country of origin:	USA
Type:	strategic reconnaissance aircraft
Powerplant:	two 14,742kg (32,500lb) Pratt & Whitney JT11D-20B bleed-turbojets
Performance:	maximum speed at 24,385m (80,000ft) more than 3219km/h (2000mph); ceiling in excess of 24,385m (80,000ft); standard range 4800km (2983 miles)
Weights:	empty 27,216kg (60,000lb); maximum take-off 77,111kg (170,000lb)
Dimensions:	wingspan 16.94m (55ft 7in); length 32.74m 107ft 5in); height 5.64m (18ft 6in); wing area 167.22sq m (1800sq ft)

Lockheed TR-1A

The first U-2s were deployed to Lakenheath, England and Weisbaden, Germany in 1956. For a long period their true role was shrouded in secrecy. Official reports announced that the glider-like aircraft, the design of which intrigued aviation analysts at the time, were used by the National Advisory Committee for Aeronautics for atmospheric research. In truth they had a far more sinister role-overflying communist territory for clandestine reconnaissance missions. In 1978 the production line was reopened, and the first of 25 TR- 1A aircraft followed. The TR-1A is a development of the U-2R; its primary role is that of tactical surveillance. To this end it is equipped with high resolution radar such as the Hughes ASARS-2, which allows the TR-1A to loiter for many hours behind enemy lines searching for enemy tank concentrations and other installations at long oblique ranges.

Country of origin:	USA
Type:	single-seat high-altitude reconnaissance aircraft
Powerplant:	one 7711kg (17,000lb) Pratt & Whitney J75-P-13B turbojet
Performance:	maximum cruising speed at more than 21,335m (70,000ft); operational ceiling 27,430m (90,000ft); maximum range 10,050km (6250 miles)
Weights:	empty 7031kg (15,500lb); maximum take-off 18,733kg (41,300lb)
Dimensions:	wingspan 31.39m (103ft); length 19.13m (62ft 9in); height 4.88m (16ft); wing area 92.9sq m (1000sq ft)

McDonnell FH-1 Phantom

In 1942 the Bureau of Aeronautics entrusted McDonnell, at that time a relatively new and inexperienced aircraft manufacturer, with the task of designing and building the two prototypes of what would become the US Navy's first carrier-based turbojet-powered single-seat fighter. The resulting prototypes were low-wing monoplanes, with retractable landing gear, with power provided by two turbojets buried in the wing roots. The first flight on January 26, 1945, was made under the power of only one of these engines, as Westinghouse had been unable to deliver the second in sufficient time. Evaluation with the US Navy followed, during which the aircraft became the first US jet to be launched and recovered from an aircraft carrier. An initial contract for 100 FD-1s was placed, although the designation was changed to FH-1 before deliveries began in January 1947.

Country of origin:	USA
Type:	carrier-based fighter
Powerplant:	two 726kg (1600lb) Westinghouse J30-WE-20 turbojets
Performance:	maximum cruising speed 771km/h (479mph); service ceiling 12,525m (41,100ft); combat range 1118km (695 miles)
Weights:	empty 3031kg (6683lb); maximum take-off 5459kg (12,035lb)
Dimensions:	wingspan 12.42m (40ft 9in); length 11.35m (37ft 3in); height 4.32m (14ft 2in); wing area 24.64sq m (276sq ft)
Armament:	four 0.5in machine guns

McDonnell F2H-2 Banshee

The success of the FH-1 Phantom in US Navy and Marine Corps service meant that it was almost inevitable that McDonnell would be asked to submit a design to succeed the Phantom in service. The Banshee design team under G.V Covington kept to a broadly similar configuration to the aircraft's predecessor, with a low mid-set unswept wing, tricycle landing gear. The new aircraft was larger, incorporating folding wings and a lengthened fuselage to accommodate more fuel, and more powerful engines in fattened wing roots. The aircraft was initially designated F-2D, later F2H, and finally F-2. The first F2H-1 aircraft was delivered to the Navy in August 1948, and was followed into service by seven sub-variants. Almost all of the aircraft saw service in Korea, in a wide variety of roles. The F2H-2 was the second production version, with wingtip fuel tanks. Production total was 56.

Country of origin:	USA
Type:	carrier-based all-weather fighter
Powerplant:	one 1474kg (3,250lb) Westinghouse J34-WE-34 turbojet
Performance:	maximum cruising speed 933km/h (580mph); service ceiling 14,205m (46,600ft); combat range 1883km (1170 miles)
Weights:	empty 5980kg (13,183lb); maximum take-off 11,437kg (25,214lb)
Dimensions:	wingspan 12.73m (41ft 9in); length 14.68m (48ft 2in); height 4.42m (14ft 6in); wing area 27.31sq m (294sq ft)
Armament:	four 20-mm cannon; underwing racks with provision for two 227kg (500lb) or four 113kg (250lb) bombs

157

McDonnell F2H-2P Banshee

The success of the F2H-1 and -H2 fighter versions of the Banshee in operations over Korea led to a contract for a photo reconnaissance version. This aircraft was designated the F2H-2P and featured a lengthened nose housing up to six cameras. Eighty-nine were built, and they continued in service long after the fighter version of the Banshee had been superseded by more advanced types. This aircraft is displaying a mission tally of 122 operational sorties in the service of Marine Reconnaissance Squadron VMJ-1, which carried out surveillance work over Korea during 1950-53. The F2H-2P continued in service with the US Navy Reserve until the mid-1960s. McDonnell at one time also proposed a reconnaissance version of the all-weather fighter version, the F2H-3, but this never reached production.

Country of origin:	USA
Type:	single-seat carrier based reconnaissance aircraft
Powerplant:	two 1474kg (3250lb) Westinghouse J34-34 turbojets
Performance:	maximum speed 982km/h (610mph); service ceiling 17,000m (56,000ft); range 3220km (2000 miles)
Weights:	empty 5800kg (12,790lb); maximum take-off 8618kg (19,000lb)
Dimensions:	wingspan 13.67m (44ft 10in); length 15.48m (50ft 0.75in); height 4.4m (14ft 6in); wing area 27.31sq m (294sq ft)

McDonnell F3H-2 Demon

The F3H program was expected to give the US Navy a fighter at least as good as any USAF aircraft, but ultimately proved hugely costly and difficult. Despite the advanced airframe design, serious obstacles were encountered at an early stage. Chief amongst these problems was the failure of the Westinghouse XJ40 engine specifically designed for the aircraft which proved unreliable and unable to deliver sufficient thrust. The problems were compounded by the US Navy, who requested that the aircraft be redesigned as an all-weather night-fighter. The first production F3H-1N aircraft had a substitute J40-WE-22 turbojet, but after 11 accidents, two of them fatal, production was halted. The situation was resolved by installing the Allison J71 turbojet, and the F3H-1 aircraft were either used as ground trainers or retrofitted with the J71. Initial deliveries of the F3H-2 were made to VF-14 in 1956.

Country of origin:	USA
Type:	carrier-based strike fighter
Powerplant:	one 6350kg (14,000lb) Allison J71-A-2E turbojet
Performance:	maximum cruising speed 1041km/h (647mph); service ceiling 13,000m (42,650ft); combat range 2200km (1370 miles)
Weights:	empty 10,039kg (22,133lb); maximum take-off 15,377kg (33,900lb)
Dimensions:	wingspan 10.77m (35ft 4in); length 17.96m (58ft 11in); height 4.44m (14ft 7in); wing area 48.22sq m (519sq ft)
Armament:	four 20mm cannon; four underwing pylons with provision for up to 2722kg (6000lb) of stores, including bombs and rockets

McDonnell F-101A Voodoo

Originally intended a a long-range escort for Strategic Air Command, the early F-101A prototypes proved to have inadequate range for this role and the aircraft was subsequently adopted by Tactical Air Command as an attack aircraft. The first F-101A was flown in September 1954, and service delivery began in early 1957 with the 27th Tactical Fighter Wing at Bergstrom, Texas. At this time they were the heaviest and most powerful single-seat fighter in Air Force service. Fifty F101As were produced, followed by 47 improved 'C' models. The F-101A had only a limited front-line service life and all 'A' and 'C' models were converted to unarmed RF-101G and H reconnaissance aircraft for the Air National Guard. This aircraft wears a typically flamboyant colour scheme, and equipped the 81st Tactical Fighter Wing at Bentwaters and Woodbridge in England.

Country of origin:	USA
Type:	single-seat day ground attack aircraft
Powerplant:	two 6750kg (14,880lb) Pratt & Whitney J57-P-13 turbojets
Performance:	maximum speed at 10,675m (35,000ft) 1623km/h (1009mph); service ceiling 16,775m (55,800ft); range 3057km (1900 miles)
Weights:	empty 11,336kg (24,970lb); maximum take-off 23,768kg (52,400lb)
Dimensions:	wingspan 12.09m (39ft 8in); length 20.54m (67ft 4.75in); height 5.49m (18ft); wing area 34.19sq m (368sq ft)
Armament:	four 20mm cannon; one centreline pylon with provision for one MT tactical nuclear bomb and two wing pylons for two 907kg (2000lb) conventional bombs, or four 310kg (680lb) mines, or other ordnance

McDonnell F-101B Voodoo

The F-101B was a two-seat all-weather long range interceptor version of the Voodoo, accommodating a pilot and radar operator to work the MG-13 fire control system and more powerful engines. By fitting a tandem cockpit the company were forced to sacrifice internal fuel capacity, with the subsequent detrimental effect on combat range. An attempt to counter this problem was made by adding an inflight refuelling system. A total of 407 were built, with final delivery taking place in March 1961. In September 1962, McDonnell was awarded a contract to bring 153 F-101Bs up to F-101F standard by updating the fire control system and removing the inflight refuelling probe, amongst other modifications. This aircraft served with the 179th Fighter Interceptor Squadron of the Minnesota ANG at Deluth in 1973.

Country of origin:	USA
Type:	two-seat all-weather long-range interceptor
Powerplant:	two 7672kg (16,900lb) Pratt & Whitney J57-P-55 turbojets
Performance:	maximum speed at 12190m (40,000ft) 1965km/h (1221mph); service ceiling 16,705m (54,800ft); range 2494km (1550 miles)
Weights:	empty 13,141kg (28,970lb); maximum take-off 23,768kg (52,400lb)
Dimensions:	wingspan 12.09m (39ft 8in); length 20.54m (67ft 4.75in); height 5.49m (18ft); wing area 34.19sq m (368sq ft)
Armament:	two Mb-1 Genie missiles with nuclear warheads and four AIM-4C,-4D, or 4G Falcon missiles, or six Falcon missiles

McDonnell RF-101H Voodoo

Reconnaissance versions of the F-101 Voodoo enjoyed a far longer service life than any other, and are perhaps the most important variants. Two main types were produced, the RF-101A and -C. Both had a lengthened and modified nose housing either four KA-2 and three KA-46 cameras for night photography. Totals of 35 RF-101As and 166 RF-101Cs were built, and were used extensively during the Cuban Missile Crisis and in the Vietnam War. The first RF-101A unit was the 363rd Tactical Reconnaissance Wing at Shaw AFB in South Carolina. The majority of the 47 F-101C interceptor aircraft from which the reconnaissance models were derived were converted to RF-101H standard for use by the Air National Guard. The work was undertaken by Lockheed Aircraft Service Company, who also converted many F-101As to RF-101G standard for the ANG.

Country of origin:	USA
Type:	single-seat tactical reconnaissance aircraft
Powerplant:	two 6750kg (14,880lb) Pratt & Whitney J57-P-13 turbojets
Performance:	maximum speed at 10,675m (35,000ft) 1623km/h (1009mph); service ceiling 16,775m (55,800ft); range 3057km (1900 miles)
Weights:	empty 11,503kg (25,335lb); maximum take-off 23,768kg (52,400lb)
Dimensions:	wingspan 12.09m (39ft 8in); length 21.13m (69ft 4in); height 5.49m (18ft); wing area 34.19sq m (368sq ft)

McDonnell Douglas A-4F Skyhawk

During its long service career the Skyhawk has proved to be one of the most versatile combat aircraft ever built, disproving those who argued that the small, lightweight machine would be outclassed by bigger, heavier aircraft. The aircraft pictured is an A-4F, the final attack version for the US Navy, which is distinguished by the dorsal hump carrying additional avionics and the J52-P-8A engine. It bears the markings of Attack Squadron 212, Carrier Air Wing 21, and has the registration of the Air Wing Commander. While equipped with this model VAF-212 deployed four times to the Gulf of Tonkin aboard USS *Hancock*. The aircraft is loaded with a typical mixture external stores, including 500lb Mk 82 bombs, two 300 US gallon drop tanks and two AGM-12 Bullpup-A ASMs. One hundred aircraft were refitted with the 4990kg (11,000lb) J52-P-401.

Country of origin:	USA
Type:	single-seat attack bomber
Powerplant:	one 4218kg (9300lb) J52-8A turbojet
Performance:	maximum speed 1078km/h (670mph); service ceiling 14,935m (49,000ft); range with 4000lb load 1480km (920 miles)
Weights:	empty 4809kg (10,602lb); maximum take-off 12,437kg (27,420lb)
Dimensions:	wingspan 8.38m (27ft 6in); length excluding probe 12.22m (40ft 1.5in); height 4.66m (15ft 3in); wing area 24.15 q m (260sq ft)
Armament:	two 20mm Mk 12 cannon with 200 rpg; five external hardpoints with provision for 3720kg (8200lb) of stores including AGM-12 Bullpup air-to-surface missiles, AGM-45 Shrike anti-radar missiles, bombs, cluster bombs, dispenser weapons, rocket-launcher pods, cannon pods, drop tanks and ECM pods

McDonnell Douglas A-4K Skyhawk

The A-4 was exported to many different countries. The effectiveness of the aircraft during operations in Vietnam encouraged Argentina, Indonesia, Israel, Kuwait, Malaysia, New Zealand and Singapore to buy the aircraft for its armed forces. The Argentine air force used the Skyhawk in combat during the Falklands campaign. Two versions, designated A-4G and A-K, have been operated by the Royal New Zealand Air Force. The former aircraft were purchased from Australia in 1984, while 10 of the A-4K models were purchased direct from the manufacturer. The A-4K aircraft were fitted with the distinctive dorsal hump housing the considerably uprated avionics suite first introduced on the A-4F. In all other aspects the A-4K is broadly similar to the US A-4F, but is fitted with a braking parachute.

Country of origin:	USA
Type:	single-seat attack bomber
Powerplant:	one 4218kg (9300lb) J52-8A turbojet
Performance:	maximum speed 1078km/h (670mph); service ceiling 14,935m (49,000ft); range with 4000lb load 1480km (920 miles)
Weights:	empty 4809kg (10,602lb); maximum take-off 12,437kg (27,420lb)
Dimensions:	wingspan 8.38m (27ft 6in); length excluding probe 12.22m (40ft 1.5in); height 4.66m (15ft 3in); wing area 24.15sq m (260sq ft)
Armament:	two 20mm Mk 12 cannon with 200 rpg; five external hardpoints with provision for 2268kg (5000lb) of stores including air-to-surface missiles, bombs, cluster bombs, dispenser weapons, rocket-launcher pods, cannon pods, drop tanks and ECM pods

McDonnell Douglas TA-4J Skyhawk

Few people believed Ed Heinemann, then chief designer at what was Douglas El Segundo when he said he could build a jet attack bomber for the Navy at half of the 30,000lb weight they specified. The first Skyhawk, nicknamed Heinemann's Hot Rod, gained a world record by flying a 500km circuit at over 695mph. The aircraft stayed in production for over 20 years, in a multiplicity of different versions. The TA-4J was a variant built for the US Navy, one of the main operators of the type. The fuselage is lengthened by approximately 2.5ft to accommodate the instructor in a tandem cockpit, reducing the internal fuel capacity. The tactical avionics suite is also reduced, and only one cannon is fitted. A version was also produced for the New Zealand air force, designated the TA-4K and also for the Kuwaiti air force (TA-4KU).

Country of origin:	USA
Type:	two-seat carrier trainer
Powerplant:	one 3856kg (8500lb) J52-P-6 turbojet
Performance:	maximum speed 1084km/h (675mph); service ceiling 14,935m (49,000ft); range 1287km (800 miles)
Weights:	empty 4809kg (10,602lb); maximum take-off 11,113kg (24,500lb)
Dimensions:	wingspan 8.38m (27ft 6in); length excluding probe 12.98m (42ft 7.25in); height 4.66m (15ft 3in); wing area 24.15sq m (260sq ft)
Armament:	one 20mm cannon

McDonnell Douglas A-4P Skyhawk

In April 1967 the McDonnell company and Douglas Aircraft merged. The A-4 model produced by the latter remained in production under the new company name until February 1979, by which time a total of 2960 aircraft had been completed. The A4D-2 (later A-4B) version had strengthened rear fuselage, inflight refuelling equipment, provision for the Martin Bullpup air-to-surface missile, navigation and bombing computer and the J65-W-16A turbojet. Some 542 aircraft were built for the US Navy and US Marine Corps, 66 of which were rebuilt in the late 1960s for the Argentine air force and navy as the A-4P and A-4Q. The A-4Q is detailed on p.167. The A-4P serves with the Argentine Air Force, and was extensively used during the 1982 Falklands War. This aircraft served with Grupo 4 in the early 1970s.

Country of origin:	USA
Type:	single-seat attack bomber
Powerplant:	one 3538kg (7800lb) J65-W-16A turbojet
Performance:	maximum speed 1078km/h (670mph); service ceiling 14,935m (49,000ft); range with 4000lb load 1480km (920 miles)
Weights:	empty 4809kg (10,602lb); maximum take-off 12,437kg (27,420lb)
Dimensions:	wingspan 8.38m (27ft 6in); length excluding probe 12.22m (40ft 1.5in); height 4.66m (15ft 3in); wing area 24.15sq m (260 q ft)
Armament:	two 20mm Mk 12 cannon with 200 rpg; five external hardpoints with provision for 2268kg (5000lb) of stores including air-to-surface missiles, bombs, cluster bombs, dispenser weapons, rocket-launcher pods, cannon pods, drop tanks and ECM pods

McDonnell Douglas A-4Q Skyhawk

Argentina has been one of the largest users of the Skyhawk, acquiring many ex-US Navy aircraft for its own air forces. During the late 1960s they acquired 66 A-4B aircraft, which were refurbished and redesignated A-4P and A-4Q. The A-4B was an improved version with the ability to carry the Martin Bullpup ASM, a navigation and bombing computer, powered rudder, and the capacity for inflight refuelling, both as receiver and tanker aircraft. In total 542 were built for the US Navy and US Marine Corps. In Argentine use, the 'P' designation indicates an air force aircraft; 'Q' a naval air arm machine. During the Falklands conflict they were used extensively in attacks on British shipping, and despite suffering heavy losses at the hands of the Royal Navy Sea Harrier pilots Argentine pilots inflicted some damage on the British fleet at San Carlos.

Country of origin:	USA
Type:	single-seat attack bomber
Powerplant:	one 3538kg (7800lb) J65-W-16A turbojet
Performance:	maximum speed 1078km/h (670mph); service ceiling 14,935m (49,000ft); range with 4000lb load 1480km (920 miles)
Weights:	empty 4809kg (10,602lb); maximum take-off 12,437kg (27,420lb)
Dimensions:	wingspan 8.38m (27ft 6in); length excluding probe 12.22m (40ft 1.5in); height 4.66m (15ft 3in); wing area 24.15sq m (260sq ft)
Armament:	two 20mm Mk 12 cannon with 200 rpg; five external hardpoints with provision for 2268kg (5000lb) of stores including air-to-surface missiles, bombs, cluster bombs, dispenser weapons, rocket-launcher pods, cannon pods, drop tanks and ECM pods

McDonnell Douglas CF-17A Globemaster III

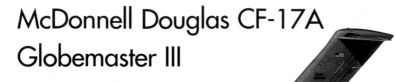

After a difficult development programme, the Globemaster III now occupies a position as the finest heavy-lift transport aircraft in current service. The early teething problems encountered during development have been ironed out and the aircraft can look forward to a long service life with MAC. The aircraft was designed and developed during the early 1980s to replace the C-141 Starlifter fleet. Cabin volume is similar to the much larger C-5 Galaxy, coupled with the short-field capability of the C-130 Hercules. Service deliveries began in 1994 and confidence in the aircraft's abilities have grown steadily. Although technically a highly complex aircraft, maintenance hours per flying hour are impressively low. All aircraft serve with Air Mobility Command. MDC are likely to win a contract to lease the Globemaster to the Royal Air Force.

Country of origin:	USA
Type:	heavy strategic transport
Powerplant:	four 18,195kg (41,700lb) Pratt & Whitney F117-P-100 turbofans
Performance:	maximum cruising speed at 10,670m (35,000ft) 829km/h (515mph); service ceiling 13,715m (45,000ft); range with 56,245kg (124,000lb) payload 5190km (3225 miles)
Weights:	empty 122,016kg (269,000lb); maximum take-off 263,083kg (580,000lb)
Dimensions:	wingspan 50.29m (165ft); length 53.04m (174ft); height 16.79m (55ft 1in); wing area 353sq m (3800sq ft)

McDonnell Douglas F-4C Phantom II

The greatest fighter of the post-war era was designed by McDonnell during the 1950s as part of a private venture study to meet anticipated future needs for an aircraft to replace the McDonnell F3H Demon in US Navy service. Although planned as an attack aircraft with four 20mm guns, it was changed into a very advanced gunless all-weather interceptor with missile armament. In this form it entered service as the F-4A (February 1960). In 1961 the F-4B was compared with Air Force fighters then in service and found to outperform all of them, particularly in terms of weapon load and radar performance. As a result it was ordered in modified form as the F-110, later designated the F-4C. This is generally similar to the F-4B but has dual controls, J79-GE-15 engines and a number of systems changes. A total of 635 were built to equip 16 of the 23 Tactical Air Command Wings.

Country of origin:	USA
Type:	two seat all-weather fighter/attack aircraft
Powerplant:	two 7718kg (17,000lb) General Electric J79-GE-15 turbojets
Performance:	maximum speed at high altitude 2414km/h (1500mph); service ceiling 18,300m (60,000ft); range on internal fuel with no weapon load 2817km (1750 miles)
Weights:	empty 12,700kg (28,000lb); maximum take-off 26,308kg (58,000lb)
Dimensions:	span 11.7m (38ft 5in); length 17.76m (58ft 3in); height 4.96m (16ft 3in); wing area 49.24sq m (530sq ft)
Armament:	four AIM-7 Sparrow recessed under fuselage; two wing pylons for two AIM-7, or four AIM-9 Sidewinder, provision for 20mm M-61 cannon in external centreline pod; four wing pylons for tanks, bombs, or other stores to a maximum weight of 6219kg (13,500lb)

McDonnell Douglas F-4D Phantom II

Both the F-4C and F-4D enjoyed remarkable service records. In the late 1980s, twenty-odd years after production of the latter aircraft ended, some were still being operated with the Air National Guard and the air forces of Iran and South Korea. The F-4D was a much improved version for the US Air Force, and much better suited to their needs. The F-4C's APQ-100 radar and optical sight were replaced by the APQ-109, which improved bombing accuracy immensely. Pilots complained of the lack of inbuilt gun armament (although a cannon pod could be carried on the centreline pylon), a problem not rectified until the introduction of the F-4E. The Air Force received a total of 793, with deliveries beginning in March 1966. Thirty-two were sold to Iran in 1969, and 18 to the Republic of South Korea in 1972.

Country of origin:	USA
Type:	two seat all-weather fighter/attack aircraft
Powerplant:	two 7718kg (17,000lb) General Electric J79-GE-15 turbojets
Performance:	maximum speed at high altitude 2414km/h (1500mph); service ceiling 18,300m (60,000ft); range on internal fuel with no weapon load 2817km (1750 miles)
Weights:	empty 12,700kg (28,000lb); maximum take-off 26,308kg (58,000lb)
Dimensions:	span 11.7m (38ft 5in); length 17.76m (58ft 3in); height 4.96m (16ft 3in); wing area 49.24sq m (530sq ft)
Armament:	four AIM-7 Sparrow recessed under fuselage; two wing pylons for two AIM-7, or four AIM-9 Sidewinder, provision for 20mm M-61 cannon in external centreline pod; four wing pylons for tanks, bombs, or other stores to a maximum weight of 6219kg (13,500lb)

McDonnell Douglas F-4D Phantom II

In the late 1960s the US supplied Iran with 32 ex-USAF F-4Ds as part of a modernisation plan of it's armed forces. These were later supplemented by approximately 200 F-4Es. After the discontinuation of American support in the wake of the Islamic revolution, the Iranian armed forces found it increasingly difficult to maintain serviceability. A number were lost during the first Gulf war with Iraq and by the mid 1980s Iran had barely a fifth of its F-4 fleet available. To compound the problem further, the aircraft were spread thinly across 13 squadrons. It is highly unlikely that any aircraft remain serviceable, although a large number remain on the Iranian armed forces inventory. The aircraft pictured is typically bereft of squadron markings, and carries a centreline M61A1 six-barrel cannon.

Country of origin:	USA
Type:	two-seat all-weather fighter/attack aircraft
Powerplant:	two 7718kg (17,000lb) General Electric J79-GE-15 turbojets
Performance:	maximum speed at high altitude 2414km/h (1500mph); service ceiling 18,300m (60,000ft); range on internal fuel with no weapon load 2817km (1750 miles)
Weights:	empty 12,700kg (28,000lb); maximum take-off 26,308kg (58,000lb)
Dimensions:	span 11.7m (38ft 5in); length 17.76m (58ft 3in); height 4.96m (16ft 3in); wing area 49.24sq m (530sq ft)
Armament:	four AIM-7 Sparrow recessed under fuselage; two wing pylons for two AIM-7, or four AIM-9 Sidewinder, provision for 20mm M61A1 cannon in external centreline pod; four wing pylons for tanks, bombs, or other stores to a maximum weight of 6219kg (13,500lb)

McDonnell Douglas F-4E Phantom II

The F-4E represented a significant improvement over the F-4D, and was the most prolific model built, with some 1329 produced for the USAF alone. It had been hoped to fit the APQ-109/CORDS (Coherent On Receive Doppler System) to this model, but in the event CORDS was cancelled and McDonnell Douglas adopted the Westinghouse APQ-120 radar. Another welcome improvement was the inclusion of an integral 20mm multi-barrel Vulcan cannon in a fairing on the centreline. To compensate for the change in the centre of gravity this caused, an additional fuel cell was added to the rear fuselage. Slats on the wing leading edges improved take-off/landing performance. Most significant of the upgrades to the avionics suite was the installation of ASX-1 TISEO (Target Identification System, Electro-Optical, and improved ASG-26 bomb-sight.

Country of origin:	USA
Type:	two-seat all-weather fighter/attack aircraft
Powerplant:	two 8119kg (17,900lb) General Electric J79-GE-17 turbojets
Performance:	maximum speed at high altitude 2390km/h (1485mph); service ceiling 19,685m (60,000ft); range on internal fuel with no weapon load 2817km (1750 miles)
Weights:	empty 12,700kg (28,000lb); maximum take-off 26,308kg (58,000lb)
Dimensions:	span 11.7m (38ft 5in); length 17.76m (58ft 3in); height 4.96m (16ft 3in); wing area 49.24sq m (530sq ft)
Armament:	one 20mm M61A1 Vulcan cannon and four AIM-7 Sparrow recessed under fuselage or other weapons up to 1370kg (3020lb) on centreline pylon; four wing pylons for two AIM-7, or four AIM-9 Sidewinder, for tanks, bombs, or other stores to a maximum weight of 5888kg (12,980lb)

McDonnell Douglas F-4E Phantom II

The successes of the Israeli Defence Force/Air Force during the 1973 Yom Kippur war helped to seal the Phantom's reputation as the finest combat aircraft of its generation. Israel purchased 204 F-4Es during the early 1970s, and they remained in front-line operation for many years. Modifications include adoption of the indigenously produced Elta EL/M-2021 multi-mode radar, and it is widely believed that the aircraft were modified to carry the Luz stand-off nuclear weapon. The aircraft pictured is painted in standard 'bleached' two-tone sand and peppermint green with squadron markings carried on the fin. A Shrike anti-radiation missile is carried. This weapon helped redress the balance with the SA-2 'guideline' air-to-surface missile, which had caused such devastating losses during the 1967 Six-Day War.

Country of origin:	USA
Type:	two-seat all-weather fighter/attack aircraft
Powerplant:	two 8119kg (17,900lb) General Electric J79-GE-17 turbojets
Performance:	maximum speed at high altitude 2390km/h (1485mph); service ceiling 19,685m (60,000ft); range on internal fuel with no weapon load 2817km (1750 miles)
Weights:	empty 12,700kg (28,000lb); maximum take-off 26,308kg (58,000lb)
Dimensions:	span 11.7m (38ft 5in); length 17.76m (58ft 3in); height 4.96m (16ft 3in); wing area 49.24sq m (530sq ft)
Armament:	one 20mm M61A1 Vulcan cannon and four AIM-7 Sparrow recessed under fuselage or other weapons up to 1370kg (3020lb) on centreline pylon; four wing pylons for two AIM-7, or four AIM-9 Sidewinder, anti-radiation missiles, bombs, tanks, or other stores up to a maximum weight of 5888kg (12,980lb)

McDonnell Douglas F-4EJ Phantom II

One of the largest operators of the Phantom has been the Japanese Air Self Defence Force. The EJ is a licence-built air-defence version of the F-4E. The original F-4E(J) model was built by McDonnell Douglas (13) and the remainder under licence by Mitsubishi with Kawasaki as a subcontractor (126), with the last delivered in May 1981. The original batch of 45 was then updated to F-4EJ Kai standard with improved weapon and avionics systems such as digital displays, revised Head-Up-Display, fire control system, and nose mounted Texas Instruments AN/APQ-172 radar. The aircraft have a limited lookdown/shootdown capability with Sparrow and Sidewinder AAMs. The aircraft equipped five squadrons of the JASDF, where they share the air-defence task with McDonnell Douglas F-15 Eagles. Japan also operates an unarmed reconnaissance version of the F-4EJ, designated RF-4EJ.

Country of origin:	USA
Type:	two-seat all-weather fighter/attack aircraft
Powerplant:	two 8119kg (17,900lb) General Electric J79-GE-17 turbojets
Performance:	maximum speed at high altitude 2390km/h (1485mph); service ceiling 19,685m (60,000ft); range on internal fuel with no weapon load 2817km (1750 miles)
Weights:	empty 12,700kg (28,000lb); maximum take-off 26,308kg (58,000lb)
Dimensions:	span 11.7m (38ft 5in); length 17.76m (58ft 3in); height 4.96m (16ft 3in); wing area 49.24sq m (530sq ft)
Armament:	one 20mm M61A1 Vulcan cannon and four AIM-7 Sparrow recessed under fuselage or other weapons up to 1370kg (3020lb) on centreline pylon; four wing pylons for two AIM-7, or four AIM-9 Sidewinder, for tanks, bombs, or other stores to a maximum weight of 5888kg (12,980lb)

McDonnell Douglas F-4F Phantom II

West Germany also enthusiastically adopted the Phantom, initially as a dedicated QRF strike/fighter aircraft, and later solely in the air-defence role. Designation of German built and operated F-4s is F-4F. Although most airframe parts for the aircraft were manufactured in Germany, final assembly took place in the US. Delivery of the 175 aircraft began during 1975 with completion the following year. One of the major features of the F-4F was the inclusion of leading edge slats to improve low-speed manoeuvring. A simplified APQ-100 radar system replaced the air-to-ground weapons system on the F-4E, which the F-4F otherwise resembles. The aircraft equipped four *Jagdgeschwader* and *Jagdbombergeschwader* in the interception and quick reaction strike roles respectively.

Country of origin:	USA/Germany
Type:	two-seat all-weather fighter/attack aircraft
Powerplant:	two 8119kg (17,900lb) General Electric J79-GE-17 turbojets
Performance:	maximum speed at high altitude 2390km/h (1485mph); service ceiling 19,685m (60,000ft); range on internal fuel with no weapon load 2817km (1750 miles)
Weights:	empty 12,700kg (28,000lb); maximum take-off 26,308kg (58,000lb)
Dimensions:	span 11.7m (38ft 5in); length 17.76m (58ft 3in); height 4.96m (16ft 3in); wing area 49.24sq m (530sq ft)
Armament:	one 20mm M61A1 Vulcan cannon and four AIM-7 Sparrow recessed under fuselage or other weapons up to 1370kg (3020lb) on centreline pylon; four wing pylons for two AIM-7, or four AIM-9 Sidewinder, or four AIM-120 AMRAAM, and/or tanks, bombs, or other stores to a maximum weight of 5888kg (12,980lb)

McDonnell Douglas F-4G Phantom II

The F-4G was designed and built specifically for the radar suppression role in the wake of significant USAF losses to Soviet supplied SA-2 'Guideline' SAMs over Vietnam. With the combat-proven performance of the Phantom II it was perhaps inevitable that it should be chosen for this role at some stage. By 1972 about 12 F-4C 'Wild Weasels' had been introduced to service. These were equipped with Westinghouse ECM pods and had provision to carry the AGM-45 Shrike anti-radiation missile. The F-4G was the result of a much more extensive modification programme, and were produced by modifying F-4Es when they were returned to MDC for life-extension programmes. The avionics and ECM systems are too extensive to list here but include the APR-38 radar warning, homing and missiles management system and a Texas Instruments computer management system.

Country of origin:	USA
Type:	two-seat EW/radar-surpression aircraft
Powerplant:	two 8119kg (17,900lb) General Electric J79-GE-17 turbojets
Performance:	maximum speed at high altitude 2390km/h (1485mph); service ceiling over 18,975m (62,250ft); range on internal fuel with weapon load 958km (595 miles)
Weights:	empty 13,300kg (29,321lb); maximum take-off 28,300kg (62,390lb)
Dimensions:	span 11.7m (38ft 5in); length 19.20m (63ft); height 5.02m (16ft 5.5in); wing area 49.24sq m (530sq ft)
Armament:	two AIM-7 Sparrow recessed under rear fuselage; wing pylons for radar suppression weapons such as AGM-45 Shrike, AGM-65

McDonnell Douglas F-4S Phantom II

One of the lesser known of the F-4 variants, the F-4S was a development of the F-4J models constructed in small numbers for the US Navy. The F-4J had the AWG-10 pulse-doppler radar, drooping ailerons, slatted tail, and J79-GE-10 engines. Also incorporated was an automatic carrier landing system. The F-4S was the redesignation of the remaining aircraft from the original delivery of 12 F-4Js, which were updated with a strengthened structure and leading edge slats. Production of the carrier based Phantoms lasted for a remarkable 17 years. The Phantom was eventually replaced in service by the McDonnell Douglas F/A 18 Hornet. Marine Phantoms were primarily used to support ground units. Pictured here is one of the aircraft operated by UMFA-33 USMC, based at MCAS Beaufort, South Carolina.

Country of origin:	USA
Type:	two-seat all-weather fighter/attack carrier-borne aircraft
Powerplant:	two 8119kg (17,900lb) General Electric J79-GE-10 turbojets
Performance:	maximum speed at high altitude 2414km/h (1500mph); service ceiling over 18,300m (60,000ft); range on internal fuel with no weapon load 2817km (1750 miles)
Weights:	empty 12,700kg (28,000lb); maximum take-off 26,308kg (58,000lb)
Dimensions:	span 11.7m (38ft 5in); length 17.76m (58ft 3in); height 4.96m (16ft 3in); wing area 49.24 q m (530sq ft)
Armament:	four AIM-7 Sparrow recessed under fuselage; two wing pylons for two AIM-7, or four AIM-9 Sidewinder, provision for 20mm M61A1 cannon in external centreline pod; four wing pylons for tanks, bombs, or other stores to a maximum weight of 6219kg (13,500lb)

McDonnell Douglas RF-4C Phantom II

The importance of tactical reconnaissance was brought home to the USAF during the Korean War, and much emphasis was placed on this aspect of air operations in the following years. The exceptional performance of the Phantom II made it an ideal tool for reconnaissance work, leading to the development of the RF-4B. The aircraft were generally similar to the F-4B, but with lengthened nose to accommodate cameras, sideways-looking radar and infra-red sensors, which replaced the standard avionics equipment. Some 46 were built for the US Marine Corps with deliveries commencing in 1965. Confusingly, the USAF took delivery of 499 RF-4C aircraft (basically an F-4C airframe with the RF-4B equipment fit) from 1964. A reconnaissance version was also offered for export (RF-4E) in 1967 and was subsequently operated by Federal Germany, Greece, Turkey, Iran, Israel and Japan.

Country of origin:	USA
Type:	two-seat tactical reconnaissance aircraft
Powerplant:	two 7711kg (17,000lb) General Electric J79-GE-8 turbojets
Performance:	maximum speed at 14,630m (48,000ft) 2390km/h (1485mph); service ceiling 18,900m (62,000ft); range 800km (500 miles)
Weights:	empty 13,768kg (30,328lb); maximum loaded 24,766kg (54,600lb)
Dimensions:	wingspan 11.7m (38ft 5in); length 18m (59ft); height 4.96m (16ft 3in); wing area 49.24sq m (530sq ft)

McDonnell Douglas Phantom FG.Mk 1

The Royal Navy's decision to buy the Phantom was governed by a requirement that the aircraft be equipped with British built engines. To this end, an Anglicised version of the F-4J was produced, designated the F-4K, that was powered by two Rolls-Royce Spey turbofans. Fitting these engines necessitated widening the fuselage. Twenty-eight aircraft were delivered to the Navy from 1964, with a further 20 for the Royal Air Force. These aircraft are designated FG.Mk 1 in British use. The RAF also received a further 120 F-4M models, which incorporated the British features with those of the F-4C mentioned previously; these aircraft were designated FGR.Mk 2 and also had the option to carry a centreline recce pod for tactical reconnaissance. The last aircraft in Royal Navy service was withdrawn in September 1978.

Country of origin:	USA
Type:	two-seat all-weather fighter/attack carrier-borne aircraft
Powerplant:	two 9305kg (20,515lb) Rolls-Royce Spey 202 turbofans
Performance:	maximum speed at high altitude 2230km/h (1386mph); service ceiling over 18,300m (60,000ft); range on internal fuel with no weapon load 2817km (1750 miles)
Weights:	empty 12,700kg (28,000lb); maximum take-off 26,308kg (58,000lb)
Dimensions:	span 11.7m (38ft 5in); length 17.55m (57ft 7in); height 4.96m (16ft 3in); wing area 49.24sq m (530sq ft)
Armament:	four AIM-7 Sparrow recessed under fuselage; two wing pylons for two AIM-7, or four AIM-9 Sidewinder, provision for 20mm M61A1 cannon in external centreline pod; four wing pylons for tanks, bombs, or other stores to a maximum weight of 7257kg (16,000lb)

McDonnell Douglas F-15A Eagle

To succeed the F-4 Phantom in US service McDonnell Douglas produced the F-15 Eagle. Since its inception, this aircraft has assumed the crown as the world's greatest air superiority fighter, although it has now been superseded by later F-15C and -B variants in US service. The first prototype of the F-15A, a single-seat twin turbofan swept wing aircraft flew in July 1972. The powerful Pratt & Whitney engines and extensive use of titanium in construction (more than twenty percent of the airframe weight of production aircraft) enabled high sustained speeds (Mach 2.5 plus) at high altitude. Impressive flying characteristics became immediately apparent during flight testing, with exceptional time-to- height performance. Deliveries began to the 555th Tactical Fighter Training Wing at Langley AFB, Virginia, in November 1974. Production continued until 1979 with 385 built.

Country of origin:	USA
Type:	single-seat air superiority fighter with secondary strike/attack role
Powerplant:	two 10,885kg (23,810lb) Pratt & Whitney F100-PW-100 turbofans
Performance:	maximum speed at high altitude 2655km/h (1650mph); initial climb rate over 15,240m (50,000ft)/min; ceiling 30,500m (100,000ft); range on internal fuel 1930km (1200 miles)
Weights:	empty 12,700kg (28,000lb); with maximum load 25,424kg (56,000lb)
Dimensions:	wingspan 13.05m (42ft 9.75in); length 19.43in (63ft 9in); height 5.63m (18ft 5in); wing area 56.48sq m (608sq ft)
Armament:	one 20mm M61A1 cannon with 960 rounds, external pylons with provision for up to 7620kg (16,800lb) of stores, for example four AIM-7 Sparrow air-to-air missiles and four AIM-9 Sidewinder AAMs; when configured for attack role conventional and guided bombs, rockets, air-to-surface missiles; tanks and/or ECM pods

McDonnell Douglas F-15DJ Eagle

The tandem seat F-15B Eagle was developed alongside the single-seat F-15A, to provide the USAF with a fully conformal trainer version. First flown in July 1973, a little over a year after the F-15A, the F-15B features an extended cockpit to accommodate the student. This was effected with little structural modification, and without changes to the overall airframe dimensions. The complete avionics suite from the F-15A was retained to enable full operational conversion training to be carried out and combat capability to be retained. The F-15DJ is the two-seat version of the F-15C (the upgraded version of the F-15A and the principal production version) for the Japanese Air Self-Defence Force. This aircraft is configured to carry conformal fuel tanks which fit flush with the fuselage, leaving all store hardpoints available for the carriage of weapons. Twelve were delivered.

Country of origin:	USA
Type:	twin-seat air superiority fighter trainer with secondary strike/attack role
Powerplant:	two 10,782kg (23,700lb) Pratt & Whitney F100-PW-220 turbofans
Performance:	maximum speed at high altitude 2655km/h (1650mph); initial climb rate over 15,240m (50,000ft)/min; ceiling 30,500m (100,000ft); range on internal fuel 4631km (2878 miles)
Weights:	empty 13,336kg (29,400lb); maximum take-off 30,844kg (68,000lb)
Dimensions:	wingspan 13.05m (42ft 9.75in); length 19.43m (63ft 9in); height 5.63m (18ft 5in); wing area 56.48sq m (608sq ft)
Armament:	one 20mm M61A1 cannon with 960 rounds, external pylons with provision for up to 10,705kg (23,600lb) of stores, for example four AIM-7 Sparrow air-to-air missiles and four AIM-9 Sidewinder AAMs; when configured for attack role conventional and guided bombs, rockets, air-to-surface missiles; tanks and/or ECM pods

McDonnell Douglas F-15J Eagle

By the late 1970s, the USAF had accepted the increasing tactical necessity for an interceptor that could provide top cover during long range strike missions, but defence budget cuts precluded the immediate development of a new aircraft. Instead, the USAF asked McDonnell to adapt the existing F-15A design to include a host of upgrades. The F- 15C progressively replaced the F-15A in service with front line USAF units between 1980-89. The most obvious change to the aircraft is the provision for two low-drag conformal fuel tanks (CFTs) that attach to the engine air inlet trunks without affecting the existing external stores stations. The tanks are fitted with stub pylons to allow an extra 5448kg (12,000lb) of stores. Avionics include APG-70 radar, which trebled the processing speed of the APG 63 it replaced. The aircraft was also built under licence in Japan as the F-15J.

Country of origin:	USA/Japan
Type:	single-seat strike/attack aircraft and air superiority fighter
Powerplant:	two 10,782kg (23,770lb) Pratt & Whitney F100-PW-220 turbofans
Performance:	maximum speed at high altitude 2655km/h (1,650mph); initial climb rate over 15,240m (50,000ft)/min; ceiling 30,500m (100,000ft); range with conformal fuel tanks 5745km (3570 miles)
Weights:	empty 12,793kg (23,770lb); maximum take-off 30,844kg (68,000lb)
Dimensions:	wingspan 13.05m (42ft 9.75in); length 19.43in (63ft 9in); height 5.63m (18ft 5in); wing area 56.48sq m (608sq ft)
Armament:	one 20mm M61A1 cannon with 960 rounds, external pylons with provision for up to 10,705kg (23,600lb) of stores, typically four AIM-7 Sparrow air-to-air missiles and four AIM-9 Sidewinder AAMs, or eight AIM-120A AMRAAMs; many combinations of conventional and guided bombs, rockets, air-to-surface missiles; tanks and/or ECM pods

McDonnell Douglas F-15E Strike Eagle

The Strike Eagle was initially developed as a private venture by MDC, who recognised the potential of the F-15 for performing a far wider range of combat tasks than originally conceived. The F-15E prototype, based on a significantly upgraded F-15B, was first flown in 1982. After evaluation against the General Dynamics F-16XL the USAF decided to proceed with procurement of the McDonnell Douglas aircraft. The Strike Eagle is operated by a crew of two, the pilot and the rear-seat weapons and defensive systems operator. The avionics suite is substantial, and to accommodate it one of the fuselage fuel tanks has been reduced. More powerful engines have been fitted without need for extensive airframe modifications. Strengthened airframe and landing gear allow a higher weapon load. F-15E units were at the forefront of precision bombing during the 1991 Gulf war.

Country of origin:	USA
Type:	twin-seat strike/attack aircraft and air superiority fighter
Powerplant:	two 10,885kg (23,810lb) Pratt & Whitney F100-PW-229 turbofans
Performance:	maximum speed at high altitude 2655km/h (1650mph); initial climb rate over 15,240m (50,000ft)/min; ceiling 30,500m (100,000ft); range with conformal fuel tanks 5745km (3570 miles)
Weights:	empty 14,379kg (31,700lb); maximum take-off 36,741kg (81,000lb)
Dimensions:	wingspan 13.05m (42ft 9.75in); length 19.43in (63ft 9in); height 5.63m (18ft 5in); wing area 56.48sq m (608sq ft)
Armament:	one 20mm M61A1 cannon with 960 rounds, external pylons with provision for up to 11,100kg (24,500lb) of stores, AIM-7 Sparrow air-to-air missiles, AIM-9 Sidewinder AAMs and AIM-120 AMRAAMs; many combinations of conventional and guided bombs, rockets, air-to-surface missiles; tanks and/or ECM pods

McDonnell Douglas F/A-18A Hornet

In the early 1970s the US Navy had a requirement for a lightweight, inexpensive carrier-based aircraft that could be adapted for a variety of roles and used in conjunction with the more sophisticated and heavier Grumman F-14 Tomcat and as a replacement for the F-4 Phantom II and Vought A-7 Corsair II aircraft then in service. The USAF had a similar requirement to complement the F-15 Eagle, but opted for the rival F-16 Fighting Falcon. The Hornet was originally derived from the private venture Northrop YF-17. Northrop undertook development work in conjunction with McDonnell Douglas and are also involved in production. Although the aircraft was originally to have been produced in both fighter and attack versions, service aircraft are easily adapted to either role. Deliveries began in May 1980 to the US Navy and were completed in 1987.

Country of origin:	USA
Type:	single-seat fighter and strike aircraft
Powerplant:	two 7264kg (16,000lb) General Electric F404-GE-400 turbofans
Performance:	maximum speed at 12,190m (40,000ft) 1912km/h (1183mph); combat ceiling 15,240m (50,000ft); combat radius 1065km (662 miles)
Weights:	empty 10,455kg (23,050lb); maximum take-off 25,401kg (56,000lb)
Dimensions:	wingspan 11.43m (37ft 6in); length 17.07m (56ft); height 4.66m (15ft 3.5in); wing area 37.16sq m (400sq ft)
Armament:	one 20mm M61A1 Vulcan rotary cannon with 570 rounds; nine external hardpoints with provision for up to 7711kg (17,000kg) of stores, including air-to-air missiles, air-to-surface missiles, anti-ship missiles, free-fall or guided bombs, cluster bombs, dispenser weapons, napalm tanks, rocket launchers, drop tanks and ECM pods

McDonnell Douglas F/A-18D Hornet

The decision to proceed with the F/A-18A Hornet lightweight carrier fighter prompted the US Navy to request development of a two-seat conversion trainer. Among the first batch of 11 Hornets completed by MDC at Missouri were two combat-capable tandem-seat trainer aircraft, designated F/A-18B. The aircraft is produced with the same navigation/attack systems as the single-seat variant, although internal fuel capacity has been reduced due to the inclusion of a second seat under a longer canopy. Performance is similar to the single-seat variant, with the exception of range. The first pilots began training on the type in the summer of 1982 with VFA-125 at Naval Air Station Leemore. The US Navy plans a procurement of 165 F/A-18Bs. The aircraft pictured is one of the F/A-18D attack versions in service with the UMFA (AW)-225 of the US Marine Corps.

Country of origin:	USA
Type:	tandem-seat conversion trainer with combat capability
Powerplant:	two 7257kg (16,000lb) General Electric F404-GE-400 turbofans
Performance:	maximum speed at 12,190m (40,000ft) 1912km/h (1183mph); combat ceiling about 15,240m (50,000ft); combat radius 1020km (634 miles) on attack mission
Weights:	empty 10,455kg (23,050lb); maximum take-off 25,401kg (56,000lb)
Dimensions:	wingspan 11.43m (37ft 6in); length 17.07m (56ft); height 4.66m (15ft 3.5in); wing area 37.16sq m (400sq ft)
Armament:	one 20mm M61A1 Vulcan six-barrell rotary cannon with 570 rounds, nine external hardpoints with provision for up to 7711kg (17,000lb) of stores, including AIM-7M and AIM-9L air-to-air missiles, air-to-surface missiles, anti-ship missiles, Mk 82 conventional and guided bombs, Hunting BL755 CBU cluster bombs, LAU-5003 rocket pods containing 19 CRV-7 70mm rockets, tanks and ECM pods

McDonnell Douglas CF-18A Hornet

On April 10, 1980, the Canadian Armed Forces minister announced his country's decision to buy 138 single-seat F-18A and 40 tandem seat F-18B aircraft, to replace its ageing CF-104 Starfighters. The order for the single-seat F-18A was progressively cut back to 98, but deliveries of trainer aircraft, designated CF-18B, began in October 1982. Each squadron operates a mixture of the two types, to enhance its multi-role capability. By comparison with the aircraft operated by the US Navy, the CF-18 has different Inertial Landing System, an added spotlight on the port side of the fuselage for ready identification during night formation flying, and provision to carry rocket pods. A comprehensive cold weather survival pack is provided for the pilot/crew. The aircraft pictured carries Sidewinder AAMs on the wingtip rails.

Country of origin:	USA
Type:	single-seat multi-mission fighter
Powerplant:	two 7257kg (16,000lb) General Electric F404-GE-400 turbofans
Perfromance:	maximum speed at 12,190m (40,000ft) 1912km/h (1183mph); combat ceiling about 15,240m (50,000ft); combat radius 740km (460 miles) on escort mission or 1065km (662 miles) in attack role
Weights:	empty 10,455kg (23,050lb); maximum take-off 25,401kg (56,000lb)
Dimensions:	wingspan 11.43m (37ft 6in); length 17.07m (56ft); height 4.66m (15ft 3.5in); wing area 37.16sq m (400sq ft)
Armament:	one 20mm M61A1 Vulcan six-barrell rotary cannon with 570 rounds, nine external hardpoints with provision for up to 7711kg (17,000lb) of stores, including AIM-7M and AIM-9L air-to-air missiles, air-to-surface missiles, anti-ship missiles, Mk 82 conventional and guided bombs, Hunting BL755 CBU cluster bombs, LAU-5003 rocket pods containing 19 CRV-7 70mm rockets, tanks and ECM pods

Martin B57-B

The decision by the US Air Force to adopt the English Electric (BAC) Canberra was swiftly followed by the choice of Martin and development of the B-57A as a version built to US standards. The main batch comprised B-57B tandem seaters. First flown in June 1954, this model ran to 202 examples and equipped Tactical Air Command from January 1955. This variant was followed into service by 67 improved B-57Es. The TAC aircraft saw little serious employment until the outbreak of the war in Vietnam, when B-57Bs then serving with the Air National Guard units were recalled fir first-line use as strike bombers. Many were later transferred to the Pakistan Air Force, were they saw service during cross-border conflicts with India. This aircraft wears the colours of No. 7 Squadron, Pakistan Air Force, who operated it in the light bomber and maritime surveillance role.

Country of origin:	USA
Type:	two-seat night intruder bomber
Powerplant:	two 3226kg (7,200lb) Wright J65-W5 turbojets
Performance:	maximum speed at 12,190m (40,000ft) 937km/h (582 mph); service ceiling 14,630m (48,000ft); range 3701km (2300 miles)
Weights:	empty 12,200kg (26,000lb); maximum take-off 24,950kg (55,000lb)
Dimensions:	wingspan 19.51m (64ft); length 19.96m (66ft 6in); height 4.75m (15ft 7in); wing area 89.18sq m (960sq ft)
Armament:	eight 0.5in machine guns, or four 20mm cannon; 16 underwing rockets and up to 2722kg (6000lb) of bombs in internal bomb bay

Martin EB-57

The operational flexibility of the British Canberra, its versatility, outstanding manoeuvrability, long range and endurance, was a primary motive for the USAF's decision to adopt the aircraft. The B-57E was an improved version of the B-57B, which was developed to encompass a wider range of offensive and non-offensive roles for the USAF. The aircraft was in fact very similar in configuration, powered by the same Wright-built version of the Armstrong Siddeley Sapphire. Many B, C, and E models were updated by the fitment of modern night and all-weather sensing, target designation and weapons aiming systems. These rebuilt aircraft were designated B-57G. A number were equipped with ECM systems during the Vietnam War. This aircraft is an EB-57, fitted with ECM and EW equipment to test defence systems in the USA and abroad in the 1960s and 1970s.

Country of origin:	USA
Type:	two-seat night intruder bomber
Powerplant:	two 3226kg (7,200lb) Wright J65-W5 turbojets
Performance:	maximum speed at 12,190m (40,000ft) 937km/h (582 mph); service ceiling 14,630m (48,000ft); range 3701km (2300 miles)
Weights:	empty 12,200kg (26,000lb); maximum take-off 24,950kg (55,000lb)
Dimensions:	wingspan 19.51m (64ft); length 19.96m (65ft 6in); height 4.75m (15ft 7in); wing area 89.18sq m (960sq ft)
Armament:	eight 0.5in machine guns, or four 20mm cannon; 16 underwing rockets and up to 2722kg (6000lb) of bombs in internal bomb bay

Martin B-57F

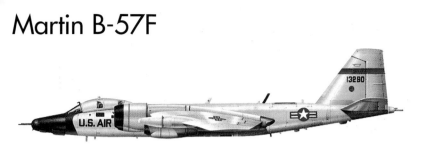

In 1960 Martin entrusted General Dynamics with the task of designing and building a high-altitude version of the B-57, the B-57F, to replace the interim B-57D (all of which were grounded by 1963 due to structural fatigue). Twenty-one of the B-57F models were converted from B and D aircraft, but little of the old is evident. The wing is entirely new, with more than double the area of the original Canberra wing and new fatigue resistant multi-spar structure. Most of the fuselage is new, as is the vertical tail. Four underwing hardpoints for pylons were incorporated, two of which were often occupied by J60 boost engine pods to supplement the turbofans. The nose is packed with electronics, and multi-sensor equipment can be seen all over the fuselage. As well as the US, the aircraft have operated from Japan, Panama, Argentina, Alaska and various Middle Eastern countries.

Country of origin:	USA
Type:	two-seat strategic reconnaissance aircraft
Powerplant:	two 8165kg (18,200lb) Pratt & Whitney TF33-11A turbofans and two 1500kg (3300lb) Pratt & Whitney J60-9 single-shaft turbojets
Performance:	maximum speed over 800km/h (500mph); service ceiling 22,860m (75,000ft); range 5955km (3700 miles)
Weights:	empty 16,330kg (36,000lb); maximum take-off 28,576kg (63,000lb)
Dimensions:	wingspan 37.32m (122ft 5in); length 21.03m (69ft); height 5.79m (19ft); wing area 186sq m (2000sq ft)

Messerschmitt Me 163B Komet 1

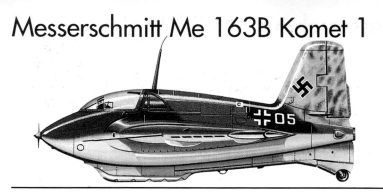

O f all the aircraft engaged in World War II the Me 163 was perhaps the most radical and futuristic. The concept of the short endurance high speed interceptor powered by a rocket engine was certainly valid and could have been more of a adversary than it was. The first flight of Dr Alex Lippisch's radical fighter, bereft of a horizontal tail and with an incredibly short fuselage, was made in glider form in the spring of 1941. To propel the aircraft, two extremely volatile liquids were employed, which ignited when they came into contact. To save weight the Komet took off from a wheeled trolley and landed on a sprung skid. The landing impact often caused residual propellants to 'slosh' together causing a violent explosion. Many aircraft were lost this way, but nevertheless by May 1944 these tiny aircraft were devastating US bomber formations.

Country of origin:	Germany
Type:	single-seat interceptor
Powerplant:	one 1700kg (3750lb) Walter HWK 509A-2 bi-propellant rocket burning concentrated hydrogen peroxide and hydrazine/methanol
Performance:	maximum speed at 10,000m (32,800ft) 960km/h (596mph); service ceiling 16,500m (54,000ft); range under 100km (62 miles); endurance about eight minutes in total
Weights:	empty 1905kg (4191lb); maximum loaded 4110kg (9042lb)
Dimensions:	wingspan 9.3m (30ft 7in); length 5.69m (18ft 8in); height 2.74m (9ft)
Armament:	two 300mm MK 108 cannon with 60 rounds each

Messerschmitt Me 262A-1a

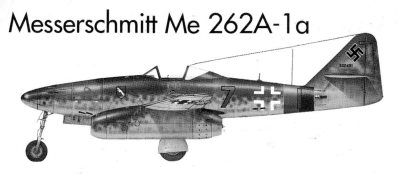

The Me 262 was undoubtedly the most advanced jet aircraft to see combat service during the World War II, and certainly the most successful in combat. Messerschmitt were somewhat late in getting off the mark in designing a jet combat aircraft. Heinkel were well advanced with the development of the He 280 prototype when in January 1939 Messerschmitt were ordered by the RLM to begin development of a similar type of aircraft. The turbojet engines then available lacked sufficient power to be used single, and so the design mounted twin-turbojets in underwing nacelles. The Me 262 V7 was the immediate precursor to a production model, the Me 262A-1a. This aircraft was the standard interceptor version, and first flew in combat on October 3, 1944. The aircraft pictured is in the colours of the 9. Staffel Jagdgeschwader Nr. 7 based at Parchim in early 1945.

Country of origin:	Germany
Type:	single-seat air-superiority fighter
Powerplant:	two 900kg (1984lb) Junkers Jumo 004B-1, 2, or -3 turbojets
Performance:	maximum speed at 6000m (19,685ft) 869km/h (540mph); service ceiling above 12,190m (40,000ft); range 1050km (652 miles)
Weights:	empty 3795kg (8,378lb); maximum take-off 6387kg (14,080lb)
Dimensions:	wingspan 12.5m (40ft 11½in); length 10.58m (34ft 9.5in); height 3.83m (12ft 7in); wing area 21.73sq m (234sq ft)
Armament:	four 30mm Rheinmetall-Borsig Mk 108A-3 cannon with 100 rounds for upper pair and 80 rounds for lower; provision for 12 R4M air-to-air rockets under each wing

Messerschmitt Me 262 A-2a

Allied air power during the North African and Italian landings effectively kept the Luftwaffe and German naval forces at bay, forcing a reappraisal of the role of the Me 262. Senior German commanders, Hitler included, were adamant that the new jet should be adapted to the role of fighter-bomber. By the autumn of 1943 of course, the outcome of the war was already decided, but nonetheless the decision was taken to convert many Me 262-A1a's in service to the later A-2a standard, by fitting Schloss 503A-1 bomb racks under the wings. The first unit to use the Me-262A-2a in battle was *Erprobugskommando Schenk*, led by Major Wolfgang Schenk, who formed at Lechfeld in July 1944. Four more fighter/bomber units were formed on January 30, 1945, although only I/KG(J)54, II/KG(J)54 and III/KG(J)6 saw any combat.

Country of origin:	Germany
Type:	single-seat fighter-bomber
Powerplant:	two 900kg (1984lb) Junkers Jumo 004B-1, -2, or -3 turbojets
Performance:	maximum speed at 6000m (19,685ft) 869km/h (540mph); service ceiling above 12,190m (40,000ft); range 1050km (652 miles)
Weights:	empty 3795kg (8,378lb); maximum take-off 6387kg (14,080lb)
Dimensions:	wingspan 12.5m (40ft 11.5in); length 10.58m (34ft 9.5in); height 3.83m (12ft 7in); wing area 21.73sq m (234sq ft)
Armament:	two 30mm Rheinmetall-Borsig Mk 108A-3 cannon with 100rounds for upper pair and 80 rounds for lower; provision for two 250kg (551lb) bombs under the wings

Messerschmitt Me 262B-1a/U1

Consideration of the Me 262 in the night-fighting role stemmed from a series of trials performed in October 1944 at Rechlin. These trials were conducted with single-seat A-1a fitted with FuG 220 intercept radar and a four-pole *Hirschgeweih* antenna array. Successful testing led to the decision to adopt a modified two-seat B-1a conversion trainer, designated Me 262B-1a/U1, as an interim night fighter, prior to the availability of a specialised model (Me 262B-2a). The B-1a/U1 aircraft were fitted with FuG 218 *Neptun V* radar with a *Hirschgeweih* array, and FuG 350 ZC *Naxos* for homing onto the emissions from British H2S radar equipment. The first unit to receive the aircraft were *Kommando Welter* (later 10./NJG 11), a specialised unit staffed by experienced *Wild Sau* (night-fighting) personnel, who took delivery of fewer than a dozen Me 262B-1a/U1s during February-March 1945.

Country of origin:	Germany
Type:	two-seat night fighter
Powerplant:	two 900kg (1984lb) Junkers Jumo 004B-1, -2, or -3 turbojets
Performance:	maximum speed at 6000m (19,685ft) 869km/h (540mph); service ceiling above 12,190m (40,000ft); range 1050km (652 miles)
Weights:	empty 3795kg (8,378lb); maximum take-off 6387kg (14,080lb)
Dimensions:	wingspan 12.5m (40ft 11.5in); length 10.58m (34ft 9.5in); height 3.83m (12ft 7in); wing area 21.73sq m (234sq ft)
Armament:	two 30mm Rheinmetall-Borsig Mk 108A-3 cannon with 100 rounds for upper pair and 80 rounds for lower

Mikoyan-Gurevich MiG-15 'Fagot'

No aircraft in history has had a bigger impact on the world scene than the MiG-15. Its existence was unsuspected in the West until American fighter pilots found themselves confronted by all-swept silver fighters that could fly faster, climb and dive faster, and turn more tightly. The development of the aircraft could be traced back to the decision of the post-war British government to send to the Soviet Union the latest British turbojet, the Rolls-Royce Nene, long before it was in service with any British service aircraft. This removed Mikoyan's problem of finding a suitable engine and by the end of December 1947 the prototype was flying, powered by an unlicensed version of the Nene. Losses in Korea were high, mainly because of pilot inexperience, but as late as 1960 the MiG-15 was still used as a fighter by 15 countries.

Country of origin:	USSR
Type:	single-seat fighter
Powerplant:	one 2700kg (5952lb) Klimov VK-1 turbojet
Performance:	maximum speed 1100km/h (684 mph); service ceiling 15,545m (51,000ft); range at height with slipper tanks 1424km (885 miles)
Weights:	empty 4000kg (8820lb); maximum loaded 5700kg (12,566lb)
Dimensions:	wingspan 10.08m (33ft 0.75in); length 11.05m (36ft 3.75in); height 3.4m (11ft 1.75in); wing area 20.60msq m (221.74sq ft)
Armament:	one 37mm N-37 cannon and two 23mm NS-23 cannon, plus up to 500kg (1102lb) of mixed stores on underwing pylons

Mikoyan-Gurevich MiG-17F 'Fresco-C'

Although outwardly similar to the MiG-15, the -17 was in fact a completely different aircraft. Western observers believed the aircraft had been hastily designed to rectify deficiencies shown in the MiG-15s performance during the Korean War, particularly the instability at speed which made it a difficult gun platform. In fact design of the -17 began in 1949, and was probably the last aircraft design in which Mikhail I. Gurevich had a direct personal role. The most important aspect of the new design was the wing, with the thickness reduced, a different section and platform and with three fences high speed behaviour was much improved. With a new tail on a longer rear fuselage, the transformation was completed by complete revision of the avionics fit. Service deliveries commenced in 1952 to the Soviet Air Force, with total production in excess of 5000.

Country of origin:	USSR
Type:	single-seat fighter
Powerplant:	one 3383kg (7,452lb) Klimov VK-1F turbojet
Performance:	maximum speed at 3000m (9,840ft) 1145km/h (711mph); service ceiling 16,600m (54,560ft); range at height with slipper tanks 1470km (913 miles)
Weights:	empty 4100kg (9040lb); maximum loaded 6,00kg (14,770lb)
Dimensions:	wingspan 9.45m (31ft); length 11.05m (36ft 3.75in); height 3.35m (11ft); wing area 20.60msq m (221.74sq ft)
Armament:	one 37mm N-37 cannon and two 23mm NS-23 cannon, plus up to 500kg (1102lb) of mixed stores on underwing pylons

Mikoyan-Gurevich MiG-19PM 'Farmer-D'

With the unveiling of the Mig-19 the Mikoyan-Gurevich bureau established itself at the forefront of the world's fighter design teams. The new fighter was in the preliminary design stage before the Mig-15 had been encountered over Korea, with five prototypes ordered in July 1951. The first flew in September 1953, powered by twin AM-5 engines. With afterburning engines the MiG-19 became the first supersonic engines in Soviet service. Steadily improved versions culminated in the MiG-19PM, with guns removed and pylons for four early beam-rider air-to-air missiles. In 1960 this simple, extremely potent aircraft was judged obsolete by Western observers. By 1970 the performance of Chinese-built F-6 (MiG-19SF) in North Vietnamese and Pakistani service led to it being reappraised by NATO. In the late 1990s some aircraft remained in service with training units.

Country of origin:	USSR
Type:	single-seat all-weather interceptor
Powerplant:	two 3250kg (7165lb) Klimov RD-9B turbojets
Performance:	maximum speed at 9080m (20,000ft) 1480km/h (920mph); service ceiling 17,900m (58,725ft); maximum range at high altitude with two drop tanks 2200km (1367 miles)
Weights:	empty 5760kg (12,698lb); maximum take-off 9500kg (20,944lb)
Dimensions:	wingspan 9m (29ft 6.5in); length 13.58m (44ft 7in); height 4.02m (13ft 2.25in); wing area 25sq m (269.11sq ft)
Armament:	underwing pylons for four AA-1 Alkali air-to-air-missiles, or AA-2 Atoll

Mikoyan-Gurevich MiG-21bis 'Fishbed-N'

The MiG-21 established a reputation as one of the most versatile combat aircraft of the post-war era. With production totalling a figure estimated at more than 11,000 the 'Fishbed' has served with 39 air arms. The aircraft was developed in 18 months following the Korean War. At least 30 pre-production aircraft were manufactured, before service deliveries of the MiG-21F 'Fishbed-C' began in 1958. The MiG-21bis 'Fishbed-N' pictured here was an improved version of the MiG-21bis 'Fishbed-L', which first appeared in 1971 and introduced new advanced construction techniques, greater fuel capacity and updated avionics for multi role air combat and ground attack. In 1975 the 'Fishbed-N' was introduced and in addition to these improvements the 'N' had more powerful turbojets and further uprated avionics.

Country of origin:	USSR
Type:	single-seat all-weather multi role fighter
Powerplant:	one 7507kg (16,535lb) Tumanskii R-25 turbojets
Performance:	maximum speed above 11,000m (36,090ft) 2229km/h (1385mph); service ceiling 17,500m (57,400ft); range on internal fuel 1160km (721 miles)
Weights:	empty 5200kg (11,464lb); maximum take-off 10,400kg (22,925lb)
Dimensions:	wingspan 7.15m (23ft 5.5in); length (including probe) 15.76m (51ft 8.5in); height 4.10m (13ft 5.5in); wing area 23sq m (247.58sq ft)
Armament:	one 23mm GSh-23 twin-barrell cannon in underbelly pack, four underwing pylons with provision for about 1500kg (3307kg) of stores, including AA-2 Atoll or AA-8 Aphid air-to-air missiles, UV-16-57 rocket pods, napalm tanks, or drop tanks

Mikoyan-Gurevich MiG-21U 'Mongol'

The two seat trainer version of the MiG-21F was known in the West by the NATO designated name 'Mongol'. Aside from the airframe modifications necessary to accommodate the instructor, the -21U is similar in configuration to the initial major production version, the -21F. The first prototype is reported to have flown in 1960. Variations from the single-seater include a one-piece forward airbrake, deletion of the cannon armament, repositioning of the pilot boom, adoption of larger mainwheels first introduced on the MiG-21PF. Further revisions were adopted on the -21US and -21UM models. These included vertical tail surfaces of revised design and a deeper dorsal spine. The aircraft is still used widely throughout in former Eastern Bloc countries and in India, were it was built under licence by HAL. This is one of the aircraft operated by the Finnish Air Force.

Country of origin:	USSR
Type:	two-seat trainer
Powerplant:	one 5950kg (13,118lb) Tumanskii R-11F2S-300 turbojet
Performance:	maximum speed above 12,200m (40,025ft) 2145km/h (1333mph); service ceiling 17,500m (57,400ft); range on internal fuel 1160km (721 miles)
Weights:	not released
Dimensions:	wingspan 7.15m (23ft 5.5in); length (including probe) 15.76m (51ft 8.5in); height 4.10m (13ft 5.5in); wing area 23sq m (247.58sq ft)

Mikoyan-Gurevich MiG-23M 'Flogger-B'

Although undoubtedly a fine aircraft, the MiG-21 was hampered by limited payload/range performance. In 1965 a requirement was issued for a replacement to help try and rectify these problems. Mikoyan-Gurevich submitted two proposals, one for an enlarged version of the MiG-21, and an alternative which was later realised as the Ye-23-11/1 prototype. The aircraft formed the basis for the MiG-23 and was first publicly displayed at the 1967 Aviation Day flypast. Apart from the variable geometry wing, the other major variation on early MiG jet aircraft were side inlets to allow incorporation of search radar and allow for greater internal fuel capacity. The MiG-23M 'Flogger-B' was the first series production version, and entered service in 1972 with the USSR and later Warsaw pact air forces.

Country of origin:	USSR
Type:	single-seat air combat fighter
Powerplant:	one 10,208kg (22,485lb) Khachaturov R-29-300 turbojet
Performance:	maximum speed at altitude about 2445km/h (1520mph); service ceiling over 18,290m (60,000ft); combat radius on hi-lo-hi mission 966km (600 miles)
Weights:	empty 10,400kg (22,932lb); maximum loaded 18,145kg (40,000lb)
Dimensions:	wingspan 13.97m (45ft 10in) spread and 7.78m (25ft 6.25in) swept; length (including probe) 16.71m (54ft 10in); height 4.82m (15ft 9.75in); wing area 37.25sq m (402sq ft)spread
Armament:	one 23mm GSh-23L cannon, underwing pylons for AA-3 Anab, AA-7 Apex, and/or AA-8 Aphid air-to-air missiles

Mikoyan-Gurevich MiG-23MF 'Flogger-B'

The MiG-23 and related MiG-27 ground attack aircraft superseded the MiG-21 as primary equipment for the Soviet tactical air forces and Voyska PVO home defence interceptor force. The aircraft is still flown by all of the former Warsaw Pact air forces, though it is now a little long in the tooth when compared to European and American aircraft. This aircraft served with the East German Air Force and has the designation MiG-23MF. This was the major production version from 1978, with improved radar and an infra-red sensor pod. The ventral fin folds prior to landing. Most MiG-23MFs serve in the fighter role, and are configured for high performance with modest weapons loads. With the disbandment of the East German Air Force, most were placed in long-term storage. Their long-term future, if they have any, is at present unknown.

Country of origin:	USSR
Type:	single-seat air combat fighter
Powerplant:	one 10,000kg (22,046lb) Rumanskii R-27F2M-300
Performance:	maximum speed at altitude about 2445km/h (1520mph); service ceiling over 18,290m (60,000ft); combat radius on hi-lo-hi mission 966km 600 miles)
Weights:	empty 10,400kg (22,932lb); maximum loaded 18,145kg (40,000lb)
Dimensions:	wingspan 13.97m (45ft 10in) spread and 7.78m (25ft 6.25in) swept; length (including probe) 16.71m (54ft 10in); height 4.82m (15ft 9.75in); wing area 37.25sq m (402sq ft) spread
Armament:	one 23mm GSh-23L cannon, underwing pylons for AA-3 Anab, AA-7 Apex, and/or AA-8 Aphid air-to-air missiles

Mikoyan-Gurevich MiG-23M 'Flogger-B'

By 1975 several hundred MiG-23s, including the attack and trainer versions, had been delivered to Warsaw Pact air forces. Production continued until the mid-1980s; by far the largest operator was the Soviet Union. It was reported during the late-1980s that the US had acquired former Egyptian operated MiG-23s for realistic air-to-air combat training of USAF and NATO pilots. Soviet operated aircraft differ from export models by having the Sapfir-23D-Sh 'High Lark' fire-control radar, and infra-red search/track system and pulse Doppler navigation. These aircraft are numerically still the most important Russian interceptors, though the fleet as a whole is in a poor state due to shortages of funding. The engine – one of the most powerful to be fitted to a combat aircraft – gives good short field performance and high top speed.

Country of origin:	USSR
Type:	single-seat air combat fighter
Powerplant:	one 10,208kg (22,485lb) Khachaturov R-29-300 turbojet
Performance:	maximum speed at altitude about 2445km/h (1520mph); service ceiling over 18,290m (60,000ft); combat radius on hi-lo-hi mission 966km (600 miles)
Weights:	empty 10,400kg (22,932lb); maximum loaded 18,145kg (40,000lb)
Dimensions:	wingspan 13.97m (45ft 10in) spread and 7.78m (25ft 6.25in) swept; length (including probe) 16.71m (54ft 10in); height 4.82m (15ft 9.75in); wing area 37.25sq m (402sq ft) spread
Armament:	one 23mm GSh-23L cannon, underwing pylons for AA-3 Anab, AA-7 Apex, and/or AA-8 Aphid air-to-air missiles

Mikoyan-Gurevich MiG-27 'Flogger-D'

The MiG-27 was a highly developed version of the MiG-23. The aircraft was designed from the outset as a dedicated ground attack aircraft and is optimised for operations over the battlefield. The most obvious difference is the nose, which was designed to give the pilot an enhanced view of the ground during approaches. Because it was only necessary to house a laser rangefinder and marked-target seeker in the nose, it was possible for the MiG designers to taper the nose steeply, as can be seen above. The pilot is protected from small-arms fire by armour plating on the side of the cockpit, and to enhance low-level performance, the variable geometry inlets and variable nozzle are replaced by lighter fixed units. The aircraft began to enter service in the late 1970s; improved versions are the MiG-27K and -27D 'Flogger-J'.

Country of origin:	USSR
Type:	single-seat ground attack aircraft
Powerplant:	one 11,500kg (23,353lb) Tumanskii R-29B-300 turbojet
Performance:	maximum speed at 8000m (26,250ft) 1885km/h (1170mph); service ceiling over 14,000m (45,900ft); combat radius on lo-lo-lo mission with full weapon load and three tanks 540km (335 miles)
Weights:	empty 11,908kg (26,252lb); maximum loaded 20,300kg (44,750lb)
Dimensions:	wingspan 13.97m (45ft 10in) spread and 7.78m (25ft 6.25in) swept; length 17.07m (56ft 0.75in); height 5.0m (16ft 5in); wing area 37.35sq m (402sq ft) spread
Armament:	one 23mm GSh-23L cannon with 200 rounds, seven external hardpoints with provision for up to 4000kg (8818lb) of stores, Kh-29 air-to-surface missiles, AS-7 Kerry air-to-surface missiles, cannon pods, rocket launcher pods, large calibre rockets, napalm tanks, drop tanks, ECM pods, conventional and guided bombs

Mikoyan-Gurevich MiG-23 'Flogger-E'

Libya and a number of other Arab countries have purchased a much simplified export version of the MiG-23M 'Flogger-B', designated MiG-23 'Flogger-E'. The aircraft retains the same basic airframe as its predecessor, but is powered by the 10,000kg (22,046lb) Tumanskii R-27F2M-300 turbojet. It is also equipped with a far less capable version of the 'Jay Bird' radar in a shorter nose radome. This has search and tracking ranges of about 29km and 18km respectively and no look-down capability. The avionics suite is also simplified, with no Doppler navigation or IR sensor pod. Another version with slightly different equipment fit is also in service with numerous Arab countries. Both export models are considerably less capable than the aircraft in CIS service. This aircraft wears the Islamic green insignia adopted in 1978 in place of the red-white-black roundels shared with Egypt.

Country of origin:	USSR
Type:	single-seat air combat fighter
Powerplant:	one 10,000kg (22,046lb) Tumanskii R-27F2M-300 turbojet
Performance:	maximum speed at altitude about 2445km/h (1520mph); service ceiling over 18,290m (60,000ft); combat radius on hi-lo-hi mission 966km (600 miles)
Weights:	empty 10,400kg (22,932lb); maximum loaded 18,145kg (40,000lb)
Dimensions:	wingspan 13.97m (45ft 10in) spread and 7.78m (25ft 6.25in) swept; length (including probe) 16.71m (54ft 10in); height 4.82m (15ft 9.75in); wing area 37.25sq m (402sq ft) spread
Armament:	one 23mm GSh-23L cannon with 200 rounds, six external hardpoints with provision for up to 3000kg (6614lb) of stores, including AA-2 Atoll air-to-air missiles, cannon pods, rocket launcher pods, large calibre rockets, and bombs

Mikoyan-Gurevich MiG-23UB 'Flogger-C'

A two-seat version of the MiG-23 was produced for conversion training, powered by the Tumanskii R-27 turbojet and equipped with the 'Jay Bird' radar of export. The second cockpit, for the instructor, is to the rear of the standard cockpit. The seat is slightly raised and is provided with a retractable periscopic sight to give a more comprehensive forward view. Like most Soviet military aircraft produced during the Cold War, it retains full combat capability and has the NATO reporting name MiG-23UB 'Flogger-C'. Libya was one of the first countries to take delivery of the aircraft, which is also in service with several other Arab nations. Though these nations have taken delivery of what are advanced combat aircraft, pilot training and servicing provision on the ground remains poor, thus affecting overall effectiveness.

Country of origin:	USSR
Type:	two-seat conversion trainer
Powerplant:	one Tumanskii 10,000kg (22,046lb) R-27F2M-300 turbojet
Performance:	maximum speed at altitude about 2445km/h (1,520mph); service ceiling over 18,290m (60,000ft); operational radius about 966km (600 miles)
Weights:	empty 11,000kg (24,200lb); maximum loaded 18,145kg (40,000lb)
Dimensions:	wingspan 13.97m (45ft 10in) spread and 7.78m (25ft 6.25in) swept; length (including probe) 16.71m (54ft 10in); height 4.82m (15ft 9.75in); wing area 37.25sq m (402sq ft) (spread)
Armament:	one 23mm GSh-23L cannon with 200 rounds; six external hardpoints with provision for up to 3000kg (6614lb) of stores, including air-to-air missiles, cannon pods, rocket-launcher pods, and bombs

Mikoyan-Gurevich MiG-23BN 'Flogger-F'

The Mikoyan-Gurevich MiG-23BN/BM 'Flogger-F' are basically fighter-bomber versions of the MiG-23 for the export market. The aircraft have similar nose shape, the same laser rangefinder, raised seat, cockpit external armour plate, and low pressure tyres of the Soviet air forces' MiG-27 'Flogger-D', but retains the powerplant, variable geometry intakes and cannon armament of the MiG-23MF 'Flogger-B' interceptor (an improved version of the MiG-23M 'Flogger-B' detailed previously). The aircraft can be configured to carry the AS-7 Kerry air-to-surface missile, and was supplied to Algeria, Cuba, Egypt, Ethiopia, Iraq, Libya, Syria and Vietnam, as well as the Warsaw Pact versions. This aircraft was operated by a unit of the Czech Air Force based at Pardubice, 100km (62 miles) east of Prague, during the late 1970s.

Country of origin:	USSR
Type:	single-seat fighter bomber
Powerplant:	one 10,000kg (22,046lb) Tumanskii R-27F2M-300 turbojet
Performance:	maximum speed at altitude about 2445km/h (1520mph); service ceiling over 18,290m (60,000ft); combat radius on hi-lo-hi mission 966km (600 miles)
Weights:	empty 10,400kg (22,932lb); maximum loaded 18,145kg (40,000lb)
Dimensions:	wingspan 13.97m (45ft 10in) spread and 7.78m (25ft 6.25in) swept; length (including probe) 16.71m (54ft 10in); height 4.82m (15ft 9.75in); wing area 37.25sq m (402sq ft) spread
Armament:	one 23mm GSh-23L cannon with 200 rounds, six external hardpoints with provision for up to 3000kg (6614lb) of stores, including AA-2 Atoll air-to-air missiles, AS-7 Kerry air-to-surface missiles, cannon pods, rocket launcher pods, large calibre rockets, and bombs

Mikoyan-Gurevich MiG-25P 'Foxbat-A'

Reports of the development of a long-range, high-speed strategic bomber in the US in the late 1950s – the B-70 Valkyrie – prompted the Soviet authorities to give highest priority to the design and development of an interceptor that could be operational to meet the B-70s planned 1964 in-service date. Even when the B-70 programme was cancelled in 1961, work continued on the development of the interceptor known as the MiG-25 and was given the NATO reporting name 'Foxbat'. The aircraft was unveiled publicly at the 1967 Moscow Aviation Day. The prototypes blazed a trail of world records in 1965-67, and when the MiG-25P production aircraft entered service in 1970 it far outclassed any Western aircraft in terms of speed and height. This aircraft is also operated by Libya, Algeria, India, Iraq and Syria.

Country of origin:	USSR
Type:	single-seat interceptor
Powerplant:	two 10,200kg (22,487lb) Tumanskii R-15B-300 turbojets
Performance:	maximum speed at altitude about 2974km/h (1848mph); service ceiling over 24,385m (80,000ft); combat radius 1130km (702 miles)
Weights:	empty 20,000kg (44,092lb); maximum take-off 37,425kg (82,508lb)
Dimensions:	wingspan 14.02m (45ft 11.75in); length 23.82m (78ft 1.75in); height 6.10m (20ft 0.5in); wing area 61.40sq m (660.9sq ft)
Armament:	external pylons for four air-to-air missiles in the form of either two each of the IR- and radar-homing AA-6 'Acrid', or two AA-7 'Apex' and two AA-8 'Aphid' weapons

Mikoyan-Gurevich MiG-25RB 'Foxbat-B'

Shortly after they entered service in the Soviet Union four MiG-25P 'Foxbat-A's were deployed to Egypt, were they provided reconnaissance support to the Egyptian Air Force. Over a four-year period the aircraft proved invulnerable to interception by Israeli F-4. This hastened development of a dedicated reconnaissance version, which entered service with the Soviet Air Force in 1971. The aircraft differs from the interceptor version by having a new nose structure to house five optical cameras, a slightly reduced span wing with a constant planform (the leading edge of the MiG-25P has a compound sweep), and with a full Elint suite and inertial navigation system. A number of sub-variants were produced, with a production total of Foxbat-B and -D models estimated at 170. Algeria have been supplied with four MiG-25R 'Foxbat-B' aircraft, one of which is pictured.

Country of origin:	USSR
Type:	single-seat reconnaissance aircraft
Powerplant:	two 11,200kg (24,691lb) Tumanskii R-15BD-300 turbojets
Performance:	maximum speed at altitude about 3339km/h (2112mph); service ceiling 27,000m (88,585ft); operational radius 900km (559 miles)
Weights:	empty 19,600kg (43,211lb); maximum take-off 33,400kg (73,634lb)
Dimensions:	wingspan 13.42m (44ft 0.75in); length 23.82m (78ft 1.75in); height 6.10m (20ft 0.5in); wing area not disclosed
Armament:	six external pylons for six 500kg (1102lb) bombs

Mikoyan-Gurevich MiG-25R 'Foxbat-D'

The MiG-25RB was later joined in service by two sub-variants, the MiG-25RBT with slightly different equipment fit and the MiG-25RBV with the SRS-9 Elint suite. Three further developments were deemed sufficiently different by NATO intelligence officers for them to be designated 'Foxbat D'. This series includes the MiG-25RBK, the MiG-25RBS, and the MiG-25RBSh (an upgraded version of the -25RBS). The Foxbat D series is used for non-optical reconnaissance and retains the limited bombing capability of the RB. The side of the nose has flush dielectric panels, and on the starboard side there is a large Side-Looking Airborne Radar that can record surface detail up to a range of 200km (124 miles). A development of the MiG-25 known as the E.266M still holds the world absolute height record for aeroplanes at 37,650m (123,524ft), which was set in 1977.

Country of origin:	USSR
Type:	single-seat reconnaissance aircraft
Powerplant:	two 11,200kg (24,691lb) Tumanskii R-15BD-300 turbojets
Performance:	maximum speed at altitude about 3339km/h (2112mph); service ceiling 27,000m (88,585ft); operational radius 900km (559 miles)
Weights:	empty 19,600kg (43,211lb); maximum take-off 33,400kg (73,634lb)
Dimensions:	wingspan 13.42m (44ft 0.25in); length 23.82m (78ft 1.75in); height 6.10m (20ft 0.5in); wing area not disclosed
Armament:	six external pylons for six 500kg (1102lb) bombs

Mikoyan-Gurevich MiG-29 'Fulcrum-A'

In 1972 the Soviet Air Force began seeking a replacement for the MiG-21, -23, Sukhoi Su-15, and -17 fleets then in service. The MiG bureau submitted the winning entry and flight testing of the new fighter, designated 'Ram L' (later 'Fulcrum') by Western intelligence, began in October 1977. First deliveries of the aircraft were made to Soviet Frontal Aviation units in 1983 and the type became operational in 1985. A more detailed analysis of the aircraft was not possible until 1986, when a detachment of the aircraft visited Finland. The visit confirmed many estimates at to the size and configuration of the aircraft. More than 600 of the first production model, the 'Fulcrum-A', were delivered, with two important export orders to Syria and India. Deliveries to No. 28 Squadron and No. 47 Squadron of the Indian Air Force began in 1986.

Country of origin:	USSR
Type:	single-seat air-superiority fighter with secondary ground attack capability
Powerplant:	two 8300kg (18,298lb) Sarkisov RD-33 turbofans
Performance:	maximum speed above 11000m (36,090ft) 2443km/h (1518mph); service ceiling 17,000m (55,775ft); range with internal fuel 1500km (932 miles)
Weights:	empty 10,900kg (24,030lb); maximum take-off 18,500kg (40,785lb)
Dimensions:	wingspan 11.36m (37ft 3.75in); length (including probe) 17.32m (56ft 10in); height 7.78m (25ft 6.25in); wing area 35.2sq m (378.9sq ft)
Armament:	one 30mm GSh-30 cannon with 150 rounds, eight external hardpoints with provision for up to 4500kg (9921lb) of stores, including six AA-11 'Archer' and AA-10 'Alamo' infra-red or radar guided air-to-air missiles, rocket launcher pods, large calibre rockets, napalm tanks, drop tanks, ECM pods, conventional and guided bombs

Mikoyan-Gurevich MiG-29M 'Fulcrum-D'

Work commenced on advanced versions of the MiG-29 at the end of the 1970s, with work concentrated on improving the range and versatility of the aircraft. One of the most significant changes was the incorporation of an advanced analog fly-by-wire control system, coupled with improved Head-Up and Head-Down displays. Physical appearance is similar, although the MiG-29M has an extended chord tailplane, and a recontoured dorsal fairing. Other changes are a more reliable and fuel efficient version of the Sarkisov turbofans, updated avionics with an advanced radar data processor four times the power of its predecessor, rearward shift in the C of G to complement the fly-by-wire system, and two extra underwing hardpoints. These improvements all make for a better aircraft, but despite its potential it has not been ordered by the Russian Air Force.

Country of origin:	USSR
Type:	single-seat air-superiority fighter with secondary ground attack capability
Powerplant:	two 9,409kg (20,725lb) Sarkisov RD-33K turbofans
Performance:	maximum speed above 11000m (36,090ft) 2300km/h (1,430mph); service ceiling 17,000m (55,775ft); range with internal fuel 1500km (932 miles)
Weights:	empty 10,900kg (24,030lb); maximum take-off 18,500kg (40,785lb)
Dimensions:	wingspan 11.36m (37ft 3.75in); length (including probe) 17.32m (56ft 10in); height 7.78m (25ft 6.25in); wing area 35.2sq m (378.9sq ft)
Armament:	one 30mm GSh-30 cannon with 150 rounds, six external hardpoints with provision for up to 3000kg (6614lb) of stores, including six AA-11 'Archer' and AA-10 'Alamo' infra-red or radar guided air-to-air missiles, rocket launcher pods, large calibre rockets, napalm tanks, drop tanks, ECM pods, conventional and guided bombs

Mikoyan-Gurevich MiG-31 'Foxhound-A'

The MiG-31 was developed during the 1970s from the impressive MiG-25 'Foxbat' to counter the threat from low-flying cruise missiles and bombers. A prototype first flew in September 1975, but it gradually became clear that the new aircraft was far more than a new-generation 'Foxbat'. In fact the MiG-31 was a vast improvement over its older stablemate, with tandem seat cockpit, IR search and tracking sensor, and the Zaslon 'Flash Dance' pulse-Doppler radar providing genuine fire-and-forget engagement capability against multiple targets flying at lower altitudes. The 'Foxhound-A' entered service in 1983 with the Voyska PVO. The aircraft pictured wears the colours of the former Soviet air force, based in the Arkhangel'sk district. Further development of the aircraft has been hampered by cut-backs in defence expenditure.

Country of origin:	USSR
Type:	two-seat all weather interceptor and ECM aircraft
Powerplant:	two 15,500kg (34,171lb) Soloviev D-30F6 turbofans
Performance:	maximum speed at 17,500m (57,400ft) 3000km/h (1865mph); service ceiling 20,600m (67,600ft); combat radius with four AAMs and two drop tanks 1400km (840 miles)
Weights:	empty 21,825kg (48,415lb); maximum take-off 46,200kg (101,850lb)
Dimensions:	wingspan 13.46m (44ft 2in); length 22.68m (74ft 5.25in); height 6.15m (20ft 2.25in); wing area 61.6sq m (663sq ft)
Armament:	one 23mm GSh-23-6 cannon with 260 rounds, eight external hardpoints with provision for four AA-9 'Amos' and two AA-6 'Acrid' or four AA-8 'Aphid' air-to-air missiles, ECM pods, or drop tanks

Mitsubishi F-1

Japan followed a somewhat unusual, but ultimately far-sighted route by developing the T-2 jet trainer before the F-1. Following the successful development of the T-2 Mitsubishi converted the second and third prototypes to single seat configuration, with the aim of producing a close-support fighter version. The first flight took place in 1975, and after evaluation by the JASDF Air Proving Wing at Gifu the aircraft was ordered into full time production. A total of 77 F-1S were ordered with deliveries commencing in September 1977. The final aircraft was received in March 1987, replacing the ageing North American F-86 Sabres then in service. This particular aircraft served with the 3rd Air Squadron of the 3rd Air Wing of the Japanese Air Self Defence Force (JASDF) at Misawa in the early 1980s.

Country of origin:	Japan
Type:	close-support and anti-ship attack fighter
Powerplant:	two 3315kg (7,308lb) Ishikawajima-Harima TF40-IHI-801A turbofans
Performance:	maximum speed at 10,675m (35,000ft) 1708km/h (1,061mph); service ceiling 15,240m (50,000ft); combat radius on hi-lo-hi mission with 1816kg (4,000lb) load 350km (218 miles)
Weights:	empty 6358kg (14,017lb); maximum take-off 13,700kg (30,203lb)
Dimensions:	wingspan 7.88m (25ft 10.2in); length 17.86m (58ft 7in); height 4.39m (14ft 4.75in); wing area 21.17sq m (227.88sq ft)
Armament:	one 20mm JM61Vulcan six-barrell cannon with 750 rounds, five external hardpoints with provision for 2722kg (6000lb) of stores, including air-to-surface missiles, conventional and guided bombs, rocket-launcher pods, drop tanks, ECM pods; two wingtip pylons for air-to-air missiles

Mitsubishi T-2

To replace the T-1 tandem-seat trainer (Japan's first post-war military aircraft) a team led by Dr Kenji Ikeda designed the T-2, using the Anglo-French SEPECAT Jaguar as a basis. After flight trials had proved the validity of the design a single-seat version, the FST-2 - Kai was ordered (see F-1). The two aircraft are almost identical apart from the rear cockpit and addition of tubular passive warning radar aerial along the top of the fin. By mid-1975, orders had been placed for the T-2, powered by Ishikawajima-Harima built versions of the Rolls-Royce Turbomeca Adour turbofans. The aircraft entered service in 1976 with the 4th Air Wing at Mitsushima; its success in operational service has underlined the benefits of commonality with the F-1 fighter. This aircraft wears the colours of the 'Blue Impulse' aerobatic team of the JASDF, a component of the 4th Kokudan.

Country of origin:	Japan
Type:	two-seat advanced flying, weapon and combat trainer
Powerplant:	two 3315kg (7308lb) Ishikawajima-Harima TF40-IHI-801A turbofans
Performance:	maximum speed at 10,675m (35,000ft) 1708km/h (1,061mph); service ceiling 15,240m (50,000ft); combat radius on hi-lo-hi mission with 1816kg (4000lb) load 350km (218 miles)
Weights:	empty 6307kg (13,904lb); maximum take-off 12,800kg (28,219lb)
Dimensions:	wingspan 7.88m (25ft 10.2in); length 17.86m (58ft 7in); height 4.39m (14ft 4.75in); wing area 21.17sq m (227.88sq ft)
Armament:	one 20mm JM61Vulcan six-barrell cannon with 750 rounds, five external hardpoints with provision for 2722kg (6000lb) of stores, including air-to-surface missiles, conventional and guided bombs, rocket-launcher pods, drop tanks, ECM pods; two wingtip pylons for air-to-air missiles

Morame-Saulnier MS.760 Paris

The MS.760 is the more successful four-seater version of the MS.755 Fleuret, which made an unsuccessful bid to win the early 1950s Armée de l'Air competition for a jet trainer. The Morane-Saulnier company, which later became part of Potez in 1963, proceeded with development of the low-wing cabin monoplane and the first prototype flew in July 1954. Orders were received from both the Armée de l'Air and the Aeronavale as well as a number of overseas clients, including Brazil and Argentina. In 1961 production switched to the MS.760B Paris II, with more powerful engines, leading edge fuel tanks and improved baggage space. A total of 165 Paris Is and IIs were completed before production ended in 1964. A handful still serve as liaison aircraft with the Aeronavale and Argentina.

Country of origin:	France
Type:	four/five-seat liason and light transport aircraft
Powerplant:	two 400kg (882lb) Turbomeca Marbore turbojets
Performance:	maximum speed at 7620m (25,000ft) 695km/h (432mph); service ceiling 12,000m (39,370ft); range 1740km (1,081 miles)
Weights:	empty 2067kg (4557lb); maximum take-off 3920kg (8642lb)
Dimensions:	wingspan 10.15m (33ft 6.75in); length 10.24m (33ft 7in); height 2.6m (8ft 6.5in); wing area 18sq m (193.76sq ft)
Armament:	none in liason/transport role; Argentina have used theirs in COIN role with two 7.62mm machine guns in nose, and two 50kg (110lb) bombs or four 90mm rockets under wings

Myasischev M-4 'Bison-C'

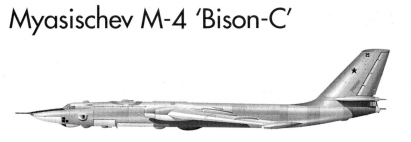

Asingle example of this large aircraft took part in the 1954 May Day parade over Moscow. It was expected to appear in large numbers in the inventories of the various Soviet air arms, but nothing was heard of it in the West for years. In fact the aircraft was produced in some numbers as the 'Bison-A' strategic bomber, and in 1959 a modified example set up new payload to height records. The Mya-4 bombers were subsequently adapted to the role of long-range strategic reconnaissance and ECM duties. In the 'Bison-C' sub-type a large search radar was fitted inside a lengthened and modified nose. The 'C' model was most frequently encountered on high- and low-level missions over the Arctic, and the Atlantic and Pacific oceans. Soviet bomber aircraft in operation during the 1960s wore a natural finish.

Country of origin:	USSR
Type:	multi-role reconnaissance bomber
Powerplant:	four 13,000kg (28,660lb) Soloviev D-15 turbojets
Performance:	maximum speed 900km/h (560mph); service ceiling 15,000m (49,200ft); range with 4,500kg (9920lb) of electronic gear or bombs 11,000km (6835 miles)
Weights:	empty 80,000kg (176,400lb); maximum loaded 170,000kg (375,000lb)
Dimensions:	wing span 50.48m (165ft 7.5in); length 47.2m (154ft 10in); height 14.1m (46ft); wing area 309sq m (3,326.16sq ft)
Armament:	six 23mm cannon in two forward turrets and tail turret; internal bay with provision over 4500kg (10,000lb) of stores

Myasishchev M-50 'Bounder'

Vladimir M. Myasishchev was involved in the design of a number of Soviet aircraft designs from 1924 before forming the design bureau that bears his name in 1951. His design for the M-50 was extremely advanced and was considered a considerable potential threat when details of its capabilities first became known. The aircraft was only ever built in prototype form, but it demonstrated extremely advanced design and construction techniques. A shoulder-mounted cropped delta wing was coupled with a conventional tail unit with all-swept surfaces. The fuselage was pressurised and incorporated a large weapons bay. The flight of the first prototype probably took place in 1957, and the last of several prototypes took part in the 1961 Aviation Day fly-past. This last prototype, designated M-52, differed from the others by having the two outer re-heated engines moved to the wing-tips.

Country of origin:	USSR
Type:	prototype supersonic strategic bomber
Powerplant:	four wing-mounted 13,000kg (28,860lb) Soloviev D-15 turbojets
Performance:	(estimated) maximum speed at altitude 1950km/h (1,212mph)
Weights:	(not released)
Dimensions:	(not released)
Armament:	probably at least one cannon; internal bomb bay carrying stand-off nuclear weapons

Nanchang Q-5 'Fantan'

The basic design of the Fantan close-support fighter was derived from the Mikoyan-Gurevich MiG-19. Design of the aircraft began in 1958, which retains a similar wing and rear fuselage configuration. Power is provided by two turbojets mounted side-by-side in the fuselage, with an attack radar mounted in the nose. Service deliveries began in 1970, and by 1980 approximately 100 were in service. Export customers have included Pakistan (52 A-5C), Bangladesh (20 A-5C), and North Korea (Q-5 IA). More than 900 of the aircraft now serve with the People's Liberation Army air force and navy. The Nanchang factory, based in Kiangsi province, has also developed a modernised version of the basic model pictured equipped with an Alenia FIAR Pointer 2500 ranging radar for export. This is designated A-5M.

Country of origin:	China
Type:	single-seat close support fighter with secondary air combat capability
Powerplant:	two 3250kg (7165lb) Shenyang WP-6 turbojets
Performance:	maximum speed at 11,000m (36,090ft) 1190km/h (739mph); service ceiling 16,000m (52,500ft); combat radius on low level mission with maximum load 400km (249 miles)
Weights:	empty 6375kg (14,054lb); maximum take-off 11,830kg (26,080lb)
Dimensions:	wingspan 9.68m (31ft 9in); length (including probe) 15.65m (51ft 4.25in); height 4.33m (14ft 2.75in); wing area 27.95sq m (300.85sq ft)
Armament:	two 23mm Type 23-2K cannon with 100rpg; ten external hardpoints with provision for up to 2000kg (4409lb) of stores, including air-to-air missiles, fee-fall bombs, rocket launcher pods, napalm tanks, drop tanks and ECM pods

North American FJ-1 Fury

The FJ-1 Fury was one of three jet-powered aircraft ordered for evaluation purposes by the US Navy. The three prototypes were heavily influenced by German wartime research; the North American NA-134, which was to become the FJ-1 Fury, flew in November 1946. One hundred production aircraft had been ordered in May 1945, but this was subsequently cut to 30. Production deliveries began in March 1948 to Naval Squadron VF-5A, who made the first carrier landings with the aircraft on the tenth day of that month on USS *Boxer*. Although it had a relatively undistinguished career the Fury was the first aircraft to complete an operational tour at sea, and paved the way for the more aesthetically pleasing F-86 Sabre. For a brief period it could also claim to be the fastest aircraft in US Navy service.

Country of origin:	USA
Type:	single-seat carrier-borne fighter
Powerplant:	one 1816kg (4000lb) Allison J35-A-2 turbojet
Performance:	maximum speed at 2743m (9000ft) 880km/h (547mph); service ceiling 9754m (32,000ft); range 2414km (1500 miles)
Weights:	empty 4011kg (8843lb); maximum loaded 7076kg (15,600lb)
Dimensions:	wingspan 9.8m (38ft 2in); length 10.5m (34ft 5in); height 4.5m (14ft 10in); wing area 20.5sq m (221sq ft)
Armament:	six 0.5in machine guns

North American F-86D Sabre

One of the most famous combat aircraft of the post war era, the Sabre was developed to meet a US Army Air Force requirement for a day fighter that could also be used as an escort fighter or dive-bomber. The F-86D was designed as an all-weather interceptor, and although development did not commence until 1949 the first prototype flew from Muroc Dry Lake on December 22 of that year. The F-86D was highly complex for its time, and introduced the new concept of gunless collision-course interception directed by a AN/APG-36 search radar above the nose intake and an autopilot. This was the most extensively built of all the Sabre series, with 2,054 completed. At the peak of its deployment in the 1950s some 20 Air Defence Command wings were equipped with the type. This aircraft was supplied to many NATO countries under the Military Aid Program.

Country of origin:	USA
Type:	single-seat all-weather/night interceptor
Powerplant:	one 3402kg (7500lb) General Electric J47-GE-17B or -33 turbojet
Performance:	maximum speed at sea level 1138km/h (707mph); service ceiling 16,640m (54,600ft); range 1344km (835 miles)
Weights:	empty 5656kg (12,470lb); maximum take-off 7756kg (17,100lb)
Dimensions:	wingspan 11.30m (37ft 1in); length 12.29m (40ft 4in); height 4.57m (15ft); wing area 27.76sq m (288sq ft)
Armament:	24 2.75in 'Mighty Mouse' air-to-air rocket projectiles in retractable tray under cockpit floor

North American F-86F Sabre

The F-86F Sabre was basically an uprated version of the F-84E, which had introduced the powered all-flying tailplane and slatted wing. The F-86F had further refinements, such as an extended leading edge, increased chord and a small wing fence. Both aircraft saw extensive service in the Vietnam conflict. The first Sabre units in Korea were equipped with the earlier 'A' model; the 'F' began to arrive in theatre with the 8th and 18th Fighter Bomber Wings in early 1953. The aircraft was flown brilliantly against the MiG-15. Despite having marginally inferior performance to the Russian aircraft, the disparity was more than matched by the superior training and experience of American pilots. Total production of the F-86F totalled 1,079; from 1954 many were delivered to America's allies under the Military Aid Program.

Country of origin:	USA
Type:	single-seat fighter-bomber
Powerplant:	one 2710kg (5970lb) General Electric J47-GE-27turbojet
Performance:	maximum speed at sea level 1091km/h (678mph); service ceiling 15,240m (50,000ft); range 1344km (835 miles)
Weights:	empty 5045kg (11,125lb); maximum loaded 9350kg (20,611lb)
Dimensions:	wingspan 11.30m (37ft 1in); length 11.43m (37ft 6in); height 4.47m (14ft 8.75in); wing area 27.76sq m (288sq ft)
Armament:	six 0.5 Colt-Browning M-3 with 267 rpg, underwing hardpoints for two tanks or two stores of 454kg (1000lb), plus eight rockets

North American FJ-3M Fury

Both Army and Navy contracts were awarded to North American in 1944 for a jet fighter, but the land-based programme moved fastest. After the land-based program had discarded the straight-wing configuration of the early design for an all-swept format, the naval team persisted with it and produced the unremarkable FJ-1 Fury. Before this aircraft had even entered service, the US Navy was seeking its replacement. This aircraft, the FJ-2, was in essence a navalised version of the company's land-based F-86E Sabre, with folding wings, strengthened landing gear and catapult hitches, and arrestor gear. Some 200 were produced and served with the US Marines. They were superseded by the FJ-3, which had a larger, more powerful engine which necessitated increasing the depth of the fuselage, a new canopy, extended leading edge, and increased weapon load.

Country of origin:	USA
Type:	single-seat fighter-bomber
Powerplant:	one 3648kg (7800lb) Wright J65-W-2 turbojet
Performance:	maximum speed at sea level 1091km/h (678mph); service ceiling 16,640m (54,600ft); range 1344km (835 miles)
Weights:	empty 5051kg (11,125lb); maximum loaded 9350kg (20,611lb)
Dimensions:	wingspan 11.30m (37ft 1in); length 11.43m (37ft 6in); height 4.47m (14ft 8.75in); wing area 27.76sq m (288sq ft)
Armament:	six 0.5 Colt-Browning M-3 with 267 rpg, underwing hardpoints for two tanks or two stores of 454kg (1000lb), plus eight rockets

North American F-100D Super Sabre

The resounding success of the Sabre made it only natural that North American would attempt to build a successor. This was planned from 1949 as a larger and more powerful machine able to exceed the speed of sound in level flight. After a very rapid development programme and with the first (479th) wing operational, the F-100A was grounded in November 1954 due to stability problems. After modifications to the wings and fin, the F-100 enjoyed a trouble-free and successful career. The 203 A fighter versions produced were followed by structurally strengthened C fighter-bombers, a flap and autopilot equipped D variant and a tandem seat F model. Total production was 2,294, with many aircraft serving in Vietnam. The F-100D was an improved version with larger fin and rudder, increased external stores capacity, and for the first time, landing flaps.

Country of origin:	USA
Type:	single-seat fighter-bomber
Powerplant:	one 7711kg (17,000lb) Pratt & Whitney J57-P-21A turbojet
Performance:	maximum speed at 10,670m (35,000ft) 1390km/h (864mph); service ceiling 14,020m (46,000ft); range with inernal fuel 966km (600 miles)
Weights:	empty 9525kg (21,000lb); maximum take-off 15,800kg (34,832lb)
Dimensions:	wingspan 11.82m (38ft 9.5in); length excluding probe 14.36m (47ft 1.25in); height 4.95m (16ft 3in); wing area 35.77sq m (385sq ft)
Armament:	four 20mm cannon; eight external hardpoints with provision for two drop tanks and up to 3402kg (7500lb) of stores, bombs, cluster bombs, dispenser weapons, rocket-launcher pods, cannon pods, and ECM pods

North American A-5A Vigilante

When it was introduced the Vigilante boasted some of the newest technology of any aircraft, including automatically scheduled engine inlets and nozzles, single surface vertical tail, differential slab tailplanes, linear bomb bay between the engines and a comprehensive radar-inertial navigation system. The aircraft was designed for carrier-based all-weather nuclear strike operations, and it became operational in this role in June 1961 with Navy Squadron VAH-7. The primary weapon of the A-5A was a free-fall nuclear weapon ejected rearwards from the bomb bay. The A-5A had only a short career as a strike aircraft as the US carrier force was relieved of its nuclear strike role; most were converted to reconnaissance aircraft. Total production was 57 aircraft, before the type was superseded by the improved A-5B.

Country of origin:	USA
Type:	carrier-based attack aircraft
Powerplant:	two 7332kg (16,150lb) General Electric J79-2 turbojets
Performance:	maximum speed at altitude 2230km/h (1385mph); service ceiling 20,400m (67,000ft); range with drop tanks 5150km (3200 miles)
Weights: empty	17,240kg (38,000lb); maximum loaded 36,285kg (80,000lb)
Dimensions:	wingspan 16.15m (53ft); length 23.11m (75ft 10in); height 5.92m (19ft 5in); wing area 70.05sq m (754sq ft)
Armament:	internal bomb bay with provision for nuclear weapons

North American RA-5C Vigilante

When the US Navy gave up its nuclear strike role, the 57 A-5A Vigilantes were followed into service by a reconnaissance version designated the RA-5C. These aircraft formed the airborne element of an integrated intelligence system serving the whole fleet and other forces. Originally designated A3J-3P, the RA-5C flew in prototype form in June 1962. Integrated into the aircraft were all the improvements in range and aerodynamic design that had been developed for the abandoned A-5B project. Fifty-five new production aircraft were built, and all but four of the original A-5A bomber aircraft were converted to RA-5C standard. RVAH-5, operating from USS *Ranger*, were the first unit to operate the aircraft. The aircraft pictured was operated by Heavy Recon Attack Squadron 6, known as the 'Fleurs'. The 'NL' tail code denotes the USS *Constellation*.

Country of origin:	USA
Type:	carrier-based long-range reconnaissance aircraft
Powerplant:	two 8101kg (17,860lb) General Electric J79-GE-10 turbojets
Performance:	maximum speed at altitude 2230km/h (1385mph); service ceiling 20,400m (67,000ft); range with drop tanks 5150km (3200 miles)
Weights:	empty 17,009kg (37,498lb); maximum loaded 36,285kg (80,000lb)
Dimensions:	wingspan 16.15m (53ft); length 23.11m (75ft 10in); height 5.92m (19ft 5in); wing area 70.05sq m (754sq ft)

North American XB-70 Valkyrie

Unquestionably one of the most impressive aircraft ever built, the XB-70 was a large delta-wing Mach 3 strategic bomber designed to replace Strategic Air Command B-52s in service in the mid-1960s. The initial US Air Force requirement was issued in 1954, and the North American design was selected for development in 1957. Budgetary cut-backs meant that by 1959 the programme had been reduced to a single prototype, although this was partially restored in 1960 with a further $265 million made available for development. The first prototype flew in September 1964, with Mach 3 achieved just over 12 months later. Tragically, the second prototype was lost in a mid-air collision with an F-104 chase plane in June 1966. The surviving aircraft passed to NASA and the programme was terminated in 1969.

Country of origin:	USA
Type:	long-range strategic bomber
Powerplant:	six 14,074kg (31,000lb) General Electric YJ93-GE-3 turbojets
Performance:	maximum speed at 24,400m (80,000ft) 3185km/h (1,980mph); service ceiling 24,400m (80,000ft); range 12,067km (7500 miles)
Weights:	maximum loaded 238,350kg (525,000lb)
Dimensions:	wingspan 32.03m (105ft); length 57.64m (189ft); height 9.15m (30ft); wing area 585.62sq m (6,297sq ft)

Northrop T-38A Talon

The T-38A trainer aircraft was derived from a requirement issued by the US government in the mid-1950s for a lightweight fighter to supply to friendly nations under the Military Assistance Program. The initial privately funded Northrop design formed the basis for a family of aircraft which also included the F-5A Freedom Fighter, to which the T-38 bears a strong physical similarity. Three YT-38 prototypes were ordered as part of a provisional contract awarded to Northrop in 1956. After three years of development, flight trials were undertaken to assess the performance of different powerplants, before service began with the USAF in March 1961. The aircraft has proved highly successful in service, with 1,139 completed. Approximately 700 are still in service. Portugal and Turkey also use the aircraft and are likely to continue doing so for some years.

Country of origin:	USA
Type:	two-seat supersonic basic trainer
Powerplant:	two 1746kg (3850lb) General Electric J85-GE-5 turbojets
Performance:	maximum speed at 10,975m (36,000ft) 1381km/h (858mph); service ceiling 16,340m (53,600ft); range with internal fuel 1759km (1093 miles)
Weights:	empty 3254kg (7174lb); maximum take-off 5361kg (11,820lb)
Dimensions:	wingspan 7.7m (25ft 3in); length 14.14m (46ft 4.5in); height 3.92m (12ft 10.5in); wing area 15.79sq m (170sq ft)

Northrop F-5A Freedom Fighter

In 1955, Northrop began the design of a lightweight fighter powered by two underslung J85 missile engines. This was yet another of the countless projects born during the Korean era when pilots were calling for lighter, simpler fighters with higher performance. The design team led by Welko Gasich refined the design, putting the engines in the fuselage and increasing their size. From this aircraft, the T-38 Talon, was developed the F-5A, which was largely a privately funded project by Northrop. In October 1962 the US Department of Defense decided to buy the aircraft in large numbers to supply to friendly countries on advantageous terms. More than 1,000 were supplied to Iran, Taiwan, Greece, South Korea, Phillipines, Turkey, Ethiopia, Morocco, Norway, Thailand, Libya, and South Vietnam. The aircraft pictured is an F-5A of the 341 Mira, Hellenic (Greek) Air Force.

Country of origin:	USA
Type:	light tactical fighter
Powerplant:	two 1850kg (4080lb) General Electric J85-GE-13 turbojets
Performance:	maximum speed at 10,975m (36,000ft) 1487km/h (924mph); service ceiling 15,390m (50,500ft); combat radius with maximum warload 314km (195 miles)
Weights:	empty 3667kg (8085lb); maximum take-off 9374kg (20,667lb)
Dimensions:	wingspan 7.7m (25ft 3in); length 14.38m (47ft 2in); height 4.01m (13ft 2in); wing area 15.79sq m (170sq ft)
Armament:	two 20mm M39 cannon with 280 rpg; provision for 1996kg (4400lb) of stores on external pylons, (including two air-to-air missiles on wingtip pylons), bombs, cluster bombs, rocket launcher pods

Northrop CF-5A

In partnership with the Netherlands, the Canadair company licence built versions of the single-seat F-5A and two-seat F-5B for the Canadian Armed Forces, and Netherlands air force. The Canadian aircraft are designated CF-5A/CF-5D. In 1987, Bristol Aerospace Ltd of Winnipeg received a contract to upgrade and extend the service life of 56 CF-5A and -D aircraft and optimise them for lead-in training for CF-18 Hornets. This program involved reskinning the wings and vertical stabiliser, reinforcement of various fuselage parts and replacement of the landing gear. With airframe life extended by another 4000 hours, installation of advance avionics, and incorporation of aerodynamic improvements, the Bristol re-furbished F-5A/B becomes the F5-2000, indicating continuation of service beyond the year 2000. Cost of the first modified aircraft, returned to service in 1991, was quoted as $4 million.

Country of origin:	USA
Type:	light tactical fighter
Powerplant:	two 1950kg (4300lb) Orenda (General Electric) J85-CAN-13 turbojets
Performance:	maximum speed at 10,975m (36,000ft) 1487km/h (924mph); service ceiling 15,390m (50,500ft); combat radius with maximum warload 314km (195 miles)
Weights:	empty 3667kg (8085lb); maximum take-off 9374kg (20,667lb)
Dimensions:	wingspan 7.7m (25ft 3in); length 14.38m (47ft 2in); height 4.01m (13ft 2in); wing area 15.79sq m (170sq ft)
Armament:	two 20mm M39 cannon with 280 rpg; provision for 1996kg (4400lb) of stores on external pylons, (including two air-to-air missiles on wingtip pylons), bombs, cluster bombs, rocket launcher pods

Northrop F-5E Tiger II

The F-5E Tiger II won a US industry competition in November 1970 for a follow-on International Fighter Aircraft to replace the F-5A. The improved aircraft is equipped with more powerful powerplants, extending nosegear to improve short field performance, extra fuel in a longer fuselage, new inlet ducts, widened fuselage and wing, root extensions ad manoeuvring flaps. Deliveries began in 1972. The US Air Force operates the aircraft for aggressor training in the USA, UK and the Philippines. The aircraft pictured is operated by the US Navy's Fighter Weapons School at Naval Air Station Miramar in California. The manoeuvrability of the F-5 makes it a formidable opponent in air combat training. A two-seat trainer version is also produced with designation F-JF. Both aircraft retain full combat capability. The F-5E has also been supplied to the Royal Saudi Air Force.

Country of origin:	USA
Type:	light tactical fighter
Powerplant:	two 2268kg (5000lb) General Electric J85-GE-21B turbojets
Performance:	maximum speed at 10,975m (36,000ft) 1741km/h (1082mph); service ceiling 15,790m (51,800ft); combat radius with maximum warload 306km (190 miles)
Weights:	empty 4410kg (9723lb); maximum take-off 11,214kg (24,722lb)
Dimensions:	wingspan 8.13m (26ft 8in); length 14.45m (47ft 4.75in); height 4.07m (13ft 4.25in); wing area 17.28sq m (186sq ft)
Armament:	two 20mm M39 cannon with 280 rpg; two air-to-air missiles on wingtip pylons, five external pylons with provision for 3175kg (7000lb) of stores, including air-to-surface missiles, bombs, cluster bombs, rocket launcher pods, ECM pods, and drop tanks

Northrop RF-5E TigerEye

The RF-5E is a reconnaissance version of the F-5E Tiger, the improved version of the Freedom Fighter detailed elsewhere. The export success of this aircraft led to the development of a specialised tactical reconnaissance version, which first appeared at the Paris Air Show in 1978. Externally, the RF-5E is similar to the fighter, except for an extended 'chisel' nose housing camera equipment and refuelling probe. Internally, the aircraft can carry a wide range of reconnaissance equipment, on easily interchangeable pallets. The pilot also has the benefit of advanced navigation and communications systems, to allow him to concentrate on operation of the reconnaissance equipment. The aircraft pictured is operated by the Royal Saudi Air Force, who along with Malaysia, were the only two countries to buy the aircraft.

Country of origin:	USA
Type:	light tactical reconnaissance fighter
Powerplant:	two 2268kg (5000lb) General Electric J85-GE-21B turbojets
Performance:	maximum speed at 10,975m (36,000ft) 1741km/h (1082mph); service ceiling 15,390m (50,500ft); combat radius on internal fuel 463km (288 miles)
Weights:	empty 4423kg (9750lb); maximum take-off 11,192kg (24,765lb)
Dimensions:	wingspan 8.13m (26ft 8in); length 14.65m (48ft 0.75in); height 4.07m (13ft 4.25in); wing area 17.28sq m (186sq ft)
Armament:	one 20mm M39 cannon with 140 rounds; two air-to-air missiles on wingtip pylons, five external pylons with provision for 3175kg (7000lb) of stores, including air-to-surface missiles, bombs, cluster bombs, rocket launcher pods, ECM pods, and drop tanks

Northrop-Grumman B-2 Spirit

The B-2 has been developed from 1978 to a US Air Force requirement for a strategic penetration bomber to complement and replace the Rockwell B-1 Lancer and the Boeing B-52 Stratofortress. The aircraft was designed to incorporate low-observables (stealth technology), with Northrop as the prime contractor. The characteristic flying-wing stems from the extensive research carried out by the company in the 1950s. The B-2s radar reflectivity is very low because of smooth blended surfaces and the use of radiation-absorbent materials. Careful mixing of hot exhaust gases with cold airstream air reduces thermal and acoustic signals to a very significant extent. The original production order was cut from 132 to approximately 20 aircraft, partly because of the enormous unit costs (over $1 billion), and also because of the reduced threat from the former USSR.

Country of origin:	USA
Type:	strategic bomber and missile-launch platform
Powerplant:	four 8618kg (19,000lb) General Electric F118-GE-110 turbofans
Performance:	maximum speed at high altitude 764km/h (475mph); service ceiling 15,240m (50,000ft); range on high level mission with standard fuel and 16,919kg (37,300lb) warload 11,675km (7255 miles)
Weights:	empty 45,360kg (100,000lb); maximum take-off 181,437kg (400,000lb)
Dimensions:	wingspan 52.43m (172ft); length 21.03m (69ft); height 5.18m (17ft); wing area more than 464.50sq m (5,000sq ft)
Armament:	two internal bomb bays with provision for up to 22,680kg (50,000lb) of stores; each bay can carry one eight-round Boeing Rotary launcher for a total of 16 1.1 megaton B83 thermonuclear free-fall bombs, 22 680kg (1500lb) bombs, or 80 227kg (500lb) free-fall bombs

Northrop/McDonnell Douglas YF-23A

In the 1981 the US Air Force issued a requirement for an Advanced Tactical Fighter to replace the McDonnell Douglas F-15 Eagle. Two rival consortia submitted designs, one led by Lockheed and including Boeing and General Dynamics, and the other led by Northrop in association with McDonnell Douglas. The Northrop design incorporated many stealth features seen on the B-2 Spirit bomber; the first of two prototype aircraft, dubbed the 'Grey Ghost', flew in August 1990. After a successful flight testing programme involving both YF-23A prototypes (designated PAV-1 and -2) the aircraft was rejected in favour of the Lockheed YF-22. The two Northrop aircraft were subsequently placed in secure storage at Edwards AFB. It is interesting to compare Northrop's approach to stealth with Lockheed's F-117 Night Hawk.

Country of origin:	USA
Type:	single-seat tactical fighter
Powerplant:	one aircraft with two 15,890kg (35,000lb) Pratt & Whitney YF119-PW-100 turbofans; one with General Electric YF120-GE-100 turbofans
Performance:	maximum speed approximately Mach 2; service ceiling 19,812m (65,000ft); range on internal fuel 1200km (750 miles)
Weights:	empty 16,783kg (37,000lb); combat take-off 29,030kg (64,000lb)
Dimensions:	wingspan 13.2m (43ft 7in); length 20.5m (67ft 4in); height 4.2m (13ft 10in); wing area 87.8sq m (945.07sq ft)
Armament:	(planned) one 20mm M61 cannon, internal bay for AIM-9 Sidewinder air-to-air missiles and AIM-120 AMRAAMS, 'Have Dash 2' AAMs and 'Have Slick' air-to-surface missiles

PZL Mielec TS-11 Iskra-bis B

The Polish-designed TS-11 Iskra (spark) two-seat trainer was selected by the Polish Air Force for production in 1961, despite having lost a Soviet air force competition for such an aircraft to the Aero L-29. The aircraft became operational in 1964; improvements were made to the basic powerplant and production of the two-seat version continued until mid-1979. A single-seat reconnaissance version was also produced before this time. Production resumed in 1982 of an improved combat/reconnaissance version, and ceased in the late 1980s, with more than 600 aircraft completed. The aircraft was also produced for the Indian air force who took delivery of 50. The aircraft has now been almost completely replaced in Polish service by the I-22 Iryda, and it is likely that the IAF will replace their aircraft in the near future.

Country of origin:	Poland
Type:	two-seat combat/reconnaissance trainer
Powerplant:	one 1100kg (2425lb) IL SO-3W turbojet
Performance:	maximum speed at 5000m (16,405ft) 770km/h (478mph); service ceiling 11,000m (36,090ft); range on internal fuel 1260km (783 miles)
Weights:	empty 2560kg (5644lb); maximum take-off 3840kg (8,66lb)
Dimensions:	wingspan 10.06m (33ft); length 11.15m (36ft 7in); height 3.5m (11ft 5.75in); wing area 17.50sq m (188.37sq ft)
Armament:	one 23mm cannon, four external hardpoints for a variety of weapons up to a total of 400kg (882lb)

PZL I-22 Iryda

The PZL I-22 Iryda was designed by a team at the Istytut Lotnictwa led by Alfred Baron to replace the TS-11 Iskra as the primary jet trainer of the Polish Air Force. The I-22 is a far more versatile aircraft, with the capability for advanced pilot training in roles such as ground attack, air combat and reconnaissance. The aircraft has a useful weapons load and can also undertake light attack missions. The aircraft is similar in both configuration and appearance to the Dassault/Dornier Alpha Jet, and has broadly similar performance. Pictured is one of the prototype aircraft; production deliveries to the Polish air force began in 1993, although with the dominance of the Aero L-29 in the inventories of former Eastern Bloc nations it is unlikely to enjoy major export success. The aircraft pictured is the first of the two prototypes, and first flew in March 1985.

Country of origin:	Poland
Type:	two-seat multi-role trainer and light close-support aircraft
Powerplant:	two 1100kg (2425lb) PZL-Rzeszow SO-3W22 turbojets
Performance:	maximum speed at 5000m (16,405ft) 840km/h (522mph); service ceiling 11,000m (36,090ft); range with maximum warload 420km (261 miles)
Weights:	empty 4700kg (10,361lb); maximum take-off 6900kg (15,211lb)
Dimensions:	wingspan 9.6m (31ft 6in); length 13.22m (43ft 4.5in); height 4.3m (14ft 1.25in); wing area 19.92sq m (214.42sq ft)
Armament:	one 23mm GSh-23L cannon with 200 rds, four external hardpoints with provision for 1200kg (2645lb) of stores, including bombs, rocket launcher pods and drop tanks

Panavia Tornado Gr.Mk 1

A huge amount of planning went into the Tornado Multi-Role Combat Aircraft. Feasibility studies began in 1967, with the tri-national Panavia company formed in 1969 by collaboration between BAC, MBB and Aeritalia. The RB.199 turbofan was selected as the powerplant, to be built by the Turbo-Union (Rolls-Royce, MTU and Fiat) conglomerate. Each of the participating nations wanted different things from the aircraft, and the resolution of a design to meet the majority of these requirements in a single airframe represents a triumph for collaboration. The first prototype flew in August 1974, with service deliveries to the Tri-National Tornado Training Establishment at RAF Cottesmore in 1981. The RAF received 229 Gr.Mk 1 strike aircraft; the Lufwaffe received 212 which are used in a similar role; the Marineflieger (German naval air arm) ordered 112, and the Italian Air Force 100.

Country of origin:	Germany, Italy and UK
Type:	multi-role combat aircraft
Powerplant:	two 7292kg (16,075lb) Turbo-Union RB.199-34R Mk 103 turbofans
Performance:	maximum speed above 11,000m (36,090ft) 2337km/h (1,452mph); service ceiling 15,240m (50,000ft); combat radius with weapon load on hi-lo-hi mission 1390km (864 miles)
Weights:	empty 14,091kg (31,065lb); maximum take-off 27,216kg (60,000lb)
Dimensions:	wingspan 13.91m (45ft 7in) spread and 8.6m (28ft 2.5in) swept; length 16.72m (54ft 10in); height 5.95m (19ft 6.25in); wing area 26.60sq m (286.3sq ft)
Armament:	two 27mm IWKA-Mauser cannon with 180 rpg, seven external hard-points with provision for up to 9000kg (19,840lb) of stores, including nuclear and JP233 runway denial weapon, ALARM anti-radiation missiles, air-to-air, air-to-surface and anti-ship missiles, conventional and guided bombs, cluster bombs, ECM pods and drop tanks

Panavia Tornado GR.Mk 1A

Germany and Italy provided the driving force for development of a centreline reconnaissance system that could be fitted to the Tornado Gr.Mk 1, and such a device was developed by Messerschmitt-Bolkow-Blohm in the early 1980s. The RAF began flight trials with a GR.Mk 1 equipped with a reconnaissance pack fitted in the cannon ammunition bay in 1985. The pack contains infrared cameras, line-scan, and thermal imaging modules, which conforms with a reconnaissance management system. These aircraft are designated GR.Mk 1A. They are readily identifiable by the small underbelly blister fairing and transparent side panels for the sideways-looking surveillance equipment. Thirty were delivered to the RAF; 15 were converted from GR.Mk 1s and 14 were built from new. Deliveries of new-built aircraft to UK based squadrons began in January 1990.

Country of origin:	Germany, Italy and UK
Type:	all-weather day/night reconnaissance aircraft
Powerplant:	two 7292kg (16,075lb) Turbo-Union RB.199-34R Mk 103 turbofans
Performance:	maximum speed above 11,000m (36,090ft) 2337km/h (1,452mph); service ceiling 15,240m (50,000ft); combat radius with weapon load on hi-lo-hi mission 1390km (864 miles)
Weights:	empty 14,091kg (31,065lb); maximum take-off 27,216kg (60,000lb)
Dimensions:	wingspan 13.91m (45ft 7.75in) spread and 8.6m (28ft 2.5in) swept; length 16.72m (54ft 10in); height 5.95m (19ft 6.25in); wing area 26.60sq m (286.3sq ft)
Armament:	seven external hardpoints with provision for up to 9000kg (19,840lb) of stores, including nuclear weapons, JP233 runway denial weapon, ALARM anti-radiation missiles, air-to-air missiles, air-to-surface missiles, anti-ship missiles, conventional and guided bombs, cluster bombs, ECM pods and drop tanks

Panavia Tornado ADV

In the late 1960s the RAF saw the need to replace its McDonnell Douglas Phantom II and BAe Lighting interceptors, and ordered the development of the Tornado ADV (Air Defence Variant), a dedicated air-defence aircraft with all-weather capability, in based on the same airframe as the GR.Mk 1 ground attack aircraft. It was realised early in the programme that to attain adequate fighter performance it would be necessary to recess the primary armament of the aircraft, the BAe Sky Flash air-to-air missile, under the fuselage centreline. Full development was authorised in March 1976, and the aircraft shares 80 percent commonality with its predecessor. Structural changes include a lengthened nose for the Foxhunter radar, and a slight increase in the fuselage length. Deliveries of 18 F.Mk 2s to the RAF were followed by 155 F.Mk 3 aircraft with Mk 104 engines.

Country of origin:	Germany, Italy and UK
Type:	all-weather air defence aircraft
Powerplant:	two 7493kg (16,520lb) Turbo-Union RB.199-34R Mk 104 turbofans
Performance:	maximum speed above 11,000m (36,090ft) 2337km/h (1452mph); operational ceiling about 21,335m (70,000ft); intercept radius more than 1853km (1150 miles)
Weights:	empty 14,501kg (31,970lb); maximum take-off 27,987kg (61,700lb)
Dimensions:	wingspan 13.91m (45ft 7.75in) spread and 8.6m (28ft 2.5in) swept; length 18.68m (61ft 3in); height 5.95m (19ft 6.25in); wing area 26.60sq m (286.3sq ft)
Armament:	two 27mm IWKA-Mauser cannon with 180 rpg, six external hardpoints with provision for up to 5806kg (12,800lb) of stores, including Sky Flash medium-range air-to-air missiles, AIM-9L Sidewinder short range air-to-air missiles and drop tanks

Republic F-84G Thunderjet

Last of the 'straight-wing' F-84 family, and the most numerous production version, was the F-84G, of which 3025 were built. This was the first single-seat US fighter aircraft capable of delivering nuclear weapons. The aircraft had provision for inflight refuelling and was equipped with an autopilot. In September 1954, using its refuelling capability, the F-84G became the first turbojet powered single-seat fighter to record a non-stop crossing of the Atlantic. Strategic Air Command retired its F-84Gs by 1956, although Tactical Air Command retained its aircraft for some time afterward. Of the total built, 1,936 were supplied to NATO air forces. Take-off with full weapons load was very long and often marginal, but the aircraft provided an effective foil to the Eastern Bloc in central Europe.

Country of origin:	USA
Type:	single-seat fighter-bomber
Powerplant:	one 2542kg (5600lb) Wright J65-A-29 turbojet
Performance:	maximum speed 973km/h (605mph) at 1220m (4,000ft); service ceiling 12,353m (40,500ft); combat radius with drop tanks 1609km (1000 miles)
Weights:	empty 5203kg (11,460lb); maximum take-off 12,701kg (28,000lb)
Dimensions:	wingspan 11.05m (36ft 4in); length 11.71m (38ft 5in); height 3.9m (12ft 10in); wing area 24.18sq m (260sq ft)
Armament:	six 0.5in Browning M3 machine-guns, external hardpoints with provision for up to 1814kg (4000lb) of stores including rockets and bombs

Republic F-84F Thunderstreak

In 1944 Republic began development of the Thunderjet, an aircraft which they conceived as a replacement for the piston-engined P-47 Thunderbolt. The first of three prototype aircraft was flown at the Muroc Dry Lake test centre on February 28, 1946. The first production aircraft were designated F-84B and entered full-scale production for the USAF in May 1947. Total production was 224. Introduction of a swept wing began with the F-84F variant, which first flew in June 1950, although problems with the Allison powerplant delayed development and service deliveries. Some 2713 F-84Fs were completed, of which 1,301 were supplied to NATO forces. The aircraft continued in service with Air National Guard units until 1971. The aircraft pictured served with the Belgian Air Force during the 1960s.

Country of origin:	USA
Type:	single-seat fighter-bomber
Powerplant:	one 3278kg (7220lb) Wright J65-W-3 turbojet
Performance:	maximum speed 1118km/h (695mph); service ceiling 14,020kg (46,000ft); combat radius with drop tanks 1304km (810 miles)
Weights:	empty 6273kg (13,830lb); maximum take-off 12,701kg (28,000lb)
Dimensions:	wingspan 10.24m (33ft 7.25in); length 13.23m (43ft 4.75in); height 4.39m (14ft 4.75in); wing area 30.19sq m (325sq ft)
Armament:	six 0.5in Browning M3 machine-guns, external hardpoints with provision for up to 2722kg (6000lb) of stores

Republic RF-84F Thunderflash

The final major production version of the swept-wing F-84 family was the RF-84F reconnaissance aircraft, with wing root air intakes and cameras in the nose. The prototype was designated YRF-84F and first flew in 1952. Deliveries to Strategic Air Command and Tactical Air Command reconnaissance units began in March 1954, and by the time the deliveries ended in 1958, production had reached 715, including 386 bought by the Air Force Mutual Defense programme and destined for users abroad. Some 25 aircraft were later modified for the FICON (Fighter Conveyor) project with a retractable hook in the nose, to provide long-range reconnaissance capability. The carrier aircraft was a modified Convair B-36 bomber. After hooking on to their long-range transport the aircraft (designated RF-84K) were carried to the reconnaissance area. Mission complete, they hooked up again for return to base.

Country of origin:	USA
Type:	single-seat photo-reconnaissance aircraft
Powerplant:	one 3541kg (7800lb) Wright J65-W-7 turbojet
Performance:	maximum speed 1118km/h (695mph); service ceiling 14,020kg (46,000ft); combat radius with drop tanks 1304km (810 miles)
Weights:	empty 6273kg (13,830lb); maximum take-off 12,701kg (28,000lb)
Dimensions:	wingspan 10.24m (33ft 7.25in); length 13.23m (43ft 4.75in); height 4.39m (14ft 4.75in); wing area 30.19sq m (325sq ft)
Armament:	six 0.5in Browning M3 machine-guns, external hardpoints with provision for up to 2722kg (6000lb) of stores

Republic XF-91 Thunderceptor

One of the rash of jet aircraft under development with Western design teams after World War II, the XF-91 was a bold attempt to produce a high altitude interceptor to a 1946 USAAF requirement. Republic introduced many unusual features, such as a variable-incidence inverse tapered wing with tandem-wheel main gears at the tips, and on one of the two prototypes a 'butterfly tail' was fitted for a time. Another unusual feature was the twin powerplant. The fairing for a Reaction Motors XLR-11-RM-9 rocket motor, visible under the tail, could be used to augment top speed for short periods. The aircraft was first flown on May 9, 1949, and achieved the then remarkable speed of 1812km/h (1126mph). However, the project was ultimately doomed. No production aircraft were built and the two prototypes ended their days as research aircraft.

Country of origin:	USA
Type:	experimental high-altitude interceptor
Powerplant:	one General Electric J47-GE-3 turbojet; Reaction Motors XLR-11-RM-9 rocket motor
Performance:	maximum speed attained 1812km/h (1126mph); ceiling (approximately) 15,250m (50,000ft)
Weights:	n/a
Dimensions:	n/a

Republic F-105B Thunderchief

Even before the F-84F Thunderstreak had entered service, Republic had begun studies on an aircraft which it was hoped would replace it in service. The primary mission of this new aircraft was perceived as the delivery of nuclear and conventional weapons in all weathers at high speeds and over long ranges. Contracts for two prototype aircraft were issued in 1954; the first flight was made in October 1955. No F105A production aircraft were built because of the availability of a more powerful powerplant, and the company subsequently built four YF-105B aircraft with these engines. The production F-105B entered service in August 1958 with the USAF's 335th Tactical Fighter Squadron, three years later than planned. Seventy-five were completed before the aircraft was superseded by the F-105D.

Country of origin:	USA
Type:	single-seat fighter-bomber
Powerplant:	one 10,660kg (23,500lb) Pratt & Whitney J75 turbojet
Performance:	maximum speed 2018km/h (1254mph); service ceiling 15,850m (52,000ft); combat radius with weapon load 370km (230 miles)
Weights:	empty 12,474kg (27,500lb); maximum take-off 18,144kg (40,000lb)
Dimensions:	wingspan 10.65m (34ft 11.25in); length 19.58m (64ft 3in); height 5.99m (19ft 8in); wing area 35.8sq m (385sq ft)
Armament:	one 20mm M61 cannon with 1029 rounds; internal bay with provision for up to 3629kg (8000lb) of bombs; five external pylons for additional load of 2722kg (6000lb)

Republic F-105D Thunderchief

The major production version of the Thunderchief, the aircraft known to a generation of pilots as the 'Thud', was the F-105D. The aircraft represented a significant improvement over the -B with a more powerful version of the J75 turbojet and advanced avionics, including NASARR monopulse radar and Doppler navigation system. This gave the aircraft true all-weather strike capability. Deliveries to the 4th Tactical Fighter Wing began in May 1960, but it was in Vietnam that the Thud cemented its reputation. The aircraft operating in that theatre bore a huge burden throughout the war, and built up a solid reputation with the men who flew them. Nevertheless about half of those built were destroyed. About 350 of the 600 production aircraft were modified during the conflict to carry the T-stick (Thunderstick) all-weather blind attack bombing system.

Country of origin:	USA
Type:	single-seat fighter-bomber
Powerplant:	one 11,113kg (24,500lb) Pratt & Whitney J75-19W turbojet
Performance:	maximum speed 2382km/h (1,480mph); service ceiling 15,850m (52,000ft); combat radius with 16 750lb bombs 370km (230 miles)
Weights:	empty 12,474kg (27,500lb); maximum take-off 23,834kg (52,546lb)
Dimensions:	wingspan 10.65m (34ft 11.25in); length 19.58m (64ft 3in); height 5.99m (19ft 8in); wing area 35.8sq m (385sq ft)
Armament:	one 20mm M61 cannon with 1029 rounds; internal bay with provision for up to 3629kg (8000lb) of bombs; five external pylons for additional load of 2722kg (6000lb)

Republic F-105F Thunderchief

In 1962, the USAF ordered 143 two-seat F-105F trainers. The aircraft were equipped with dual controls and full operational equipment. To incorporate the tandem cockpit, the fuselage was lengthened slightly. It was originally intended to use the aircraft for combat proficiency training and transition training, but the pressures of US involvement in the Vietnam conflict created an urgent requirement for these high-performance fighter-bombers and many were used operationally in theatre. Eighty-six of the F-104F aircraft were converted to Wild Weasel configuration for ECM operations over North Vietnam with Radar Homing and Warning equipment, jamming pods, a missile-launch warning receiver, and other specialised avionics to locate and identify the threat from North Vietnamese surface-to-air missiles.

Country of origin:	USA
Type:	two-seat operational trainer
Powerplant:	one 11,113kg (24,500lb) Pratt & Whitney J75-19W turbojet
Performance:	maximum speed 2382km/h (1480mph); service ceiling 15,850m (52,000ft); combat radius with 16 750lb bombs 370km (230 miles)
Weights:	empty 12,890kg (28,393lb); maximum take-off 24,516kg (54,000lb)
Dimensions:	wingspan 10.65m (34ft 11.25in); length 21.21m (69ft 7.5in); height 6.15m (20ft 2in); wing area 35.8sq m (385sq ft)
Armament:	one 20mm M61 cannon with 1029 rounds; internal bay with provision for up to 3629kg (8000lb) of bombs; five external pylons for additional load of 2722kg (6000lb)

Republic F-105G Thunderchief

The threat from Soviet-built SA-2 'Guideline' surface-to-air missiles operated by North Vietnamese forces led to the rapid development and introduction of the ECM equipped F-105G Wild Weasel. These aircraft were equipped with a large externally mounted pod containing electronics, RHAW (Radar Homing and Warning), a missile-launch warning receiver, and other specialised avionics. The 86 aircraft thus configured were designated EF-105F. A more comprehensive modification was undertaken on 60 of these aircraft, which have the designation F-105G. The aircraft carried out the bulk of anti-SAM missions until 1973, before passing on to the Air National Guard units that operated them until 1984. This is one of the aircraft operated by the 561st Tactical Fighter Squadron of the 23rd Tactical Fighter Wing, based at McConnell AFB in Kansas.

Country of origin:	USA
Type:	two-seat ECM aircraft
Powerplant:	one 11,113kg (24,500lb) Pratt & Whitney J75-19W turbojet
Performance:	maximum speed 2382km/h (1480mph); service ceiling 15,850m (52,000ft); ferry range 3486km (2390 miles)
Weights:	empty 12,890kg (28,393lb); maximum take-off 24,516kg (54,000lb)
Dimensions:	wingspan 10.65m (34ft 11¼in); length 21.21m (69ft 7.5in); height 6.15m (20ft 2in); wing area 35.8sq m (385sq ft)
Armament:	one 20mm M61 cannon with 1029 rounds; five external pylons for additional load of 2722kg (6000lb), including anti-radiation missiles, conventional and guided bombs, drop tanks and ECM pods

Rockwell B-1B Lancer

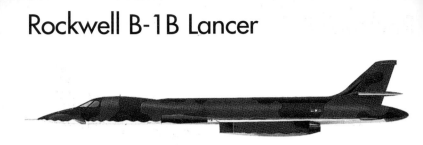

The B-1B long-range penetration bomber was originally conceived in the 1965 USAF Advanced Manned Strategic Aircraft requirement. North American Rockwell, as it then was, were selected as the prime contractor for the new bomber, which was designated B-1. General Electric were selected to build the F101 engines to power it. Prototype contracts were awarded in June 1970, with planned service delivery of all 244 aircraft scheduled before 1981. The first prototype made its maiden flight on December 23, 1974, but the programme was cancelled in 1977 because of escalating costs. A contract for 100 aircraft derived from the B-1, with a revised role as a cruise missile carrier, awarded in 1982. The aircraft incorporated a variable-geometry configuration with stealth technology and advanced avionics.

Country of origin:	USA
Type:	long-range multi-role strategic bomber
Powerplant:	four 13962kg (30,780lb) General Electric F101-GE-102 turbofans
Performance:	maximum speed at high altitude 1328km/h (825mph); service ceiling 15,240m (50,000ft); range on internal fuel 12,000km (7,455 miles)
Weights:	empty 87,090kg (192,000lb); maximum take-off 216,634kg (477,000lb)
Dimensions:	wingspan 41.67m (136ft 8.5in) unswept and 23.84m (78ft 2.5in) swept; length 44.81m (147ft); height 10.36m (34ft); wing area 181.16sq m (1,950sq ft)
Armament:	three internal bays with provision for up to 34,019kg (75,000lb) of weapons, plus eight underfuselage stations with a capacity of 26,762kg (59,000lb); weapons can include AGM-69 SRAMs, AGM-86B ALCMs, B-28, B-43, B-61 or B-83 nuclear bombs, and Mk 82 or Mk 84 conventional bombs

Rockwell B-1B Lancer

Since its service entry in June 1985 the B-1B has not been wholly free of problems. The first unit to equip the aircraft, the 96th BW at Dyess, suffered serviceability problems and fuel leaks with their aircraft. Several aircraft were lost after engine failures and groundings were frequent in early days. This is perhaps understandable on such a radically new aircraft, and these problems have largely been eradicated. Since then the B-1B has steadily been proving itself as a highly capable weapons system. Very low-level penetration missions are dependent on state-of-the-art avionics, including a satellite communications link, Doppler radar altimeter, forward-looking and terrain-following radars, and a defensive suite weighing over a ton. All aircraft have adopted the overall grey colour scheme seen on this aircraft of the 77th Bomb Squadron, 29th Bombardment Wing, South Dakota.

Country of origin:	USA
Type:	long-range multi-role strategic bomber
Powerplant:	four 13962kg (30,780lb) General Electric F101-GE-102 turbofans
Performance:	maximum speed at high altitude 1328km/h (825mph); service ceiling 15,240m (50,000ft); range on internal fuel 12,000km (7,455 miles)
Weights:	empty 87,090kg (192,000lb); maximum take-off 216,634kg (477,000lb)
Dimensions:	wingspan 41.67m (136ft 8.5in) unswept and 23.84m (78ft 2.5in) swept; length 44.81m (147ft); height 10.36m (34ft); wing area 181.16sq m (1950sq ft)
Armament:	three internal bays with provision for up to 34,019kg (75,000lb) of weapons, plus eight underfuselage stations with a capacity of 26,762kg (59,000lb); weapons can include AGM-69 SRAMs, AGM-86B ALCMs, B-28, B-43, B-61 or B-83 nuclear bombs, and Mk 82 or Mk 84 conventional bombs

Rockwell T-2 Buckeye

The T-2 began service as the primary jet trainer of the US Navy in 1960, and after nearly 40 years is now being replaced by the T-45A Goshawk. The wing of the aircraft was derived from the FJ-1 Fury and the control system is similar to that employed on the T-28 Trojan. The first aircraft flew on January 31, 1958 and service deliveries began the following July. A total of 217 T-2As were supplied to the US Navy under the name Buckeye. A more powerful version designated T-2B was also produced. The final version was the T-2C with yet more powerful General Electric engines. Two hundred and seventy three were built, some of which were supplied to Venezuela and Greece. Pictured is one of the T-2C aircraft operated by VT-23 of Training Wing 2, US Navy. Some of the aircraft in US service have been converted for use as drone directors.

Country of origin:	USA
Type:	two-seat multi-role jet trainer
Powerplant:	one 1338kg (2950lb) General Electric J85-GE-4 turbojets
Performance:	maximum speed at 7620m (25,000ft) 838km/h (521mph); service ceiling 13,535m (44,400ft); range 1465km (910 miles)
Weights:	empty 3681kg (8115lb); maximum take-off 5978kg (13,180lb)
Dimensions:	wingspan 11.63m (38ft 2in); length 11.79m (38ft 8in); height 4.51m (14ft 9.5in); wing area 23.70sq m (255sq ft)

Ryan XV-5A

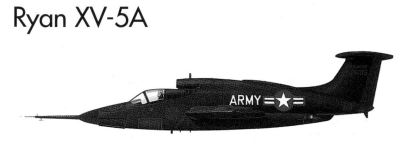

During the late 1950s, the race to develop a practical VTOL aircraft for military use intensified. Some of the more successful US efforts were developed by the Ryan company (who in the 1930s built the 'Spirit of St. Louis' which carried Lindbergh across the Atlantic). The XV-5A was the fourth in a series of experimental aircraft which had begun in 1955 with the successful X-13 Vertijet, which took off vertically with the nose pointed into the air and landed like a conventional aircraft. With the XV-5, Ryan approached the problem somewhat differently. The aircraft was in appearance a conventional mid-wing monoplane, with cabin accommodation for two in side-by-side ejection seats. Power was supplied by two turbojets, the efflux of which could be directed either to the wing fans for vertical flight, or for conventional jet propulsion in horizontal flight.

Country of origin:	USA
Type:	experimental VTOL aircraft
Powerplant:	two 1206kg (2658lb) General Electric J85-GE-5 turbojets
Performance:	n/a
Weights:	n/a
Dimensions:	n/a

SEPECAT Jaguar A

Developed jointly by BAC in Britain and Dassault-Breguet in France (Societé Européenne de Production de l'Avion Ecole de Combat at Appui Tactique), to meet a joint requirement of the Armée de l'Air and Royal Air Force, the Jaguar emerged from protracted development as a far more powerful and effective aircraft than originally envisaged. The original idea was for a light trainer and close-support machine with a 590kg (1300lb) load, but with British pressure, this was considerably upgraded. Power was provided by a turbofan developed jointly from the Rolls-Royce RB.172 by Rolls Royce and Turbomeca. The first French version to fly was the two-seat E, followed in March 1969 by the Jaguar A single-seat tactical support aircraft, which form the backbone of the French tactical nuclear strike force. Service deliveries began in 1973 with production of some 160 aircraft.

Country of origin:	France and UK
Type:	single-seat tactical support and strike aircraft
Powerplant:	two 3313kg (7305lb) Rolls-Royce/Turbomeca Adour Mk 102 turbofans
Performance:	maximum speed at 11,000m (36,090ft) 1593km/h (990mph); combat radius on lo-lo-lo mission with internal fuel 557km (357 miles)
Weights:	empty 7000kg (15,432lb); maximum take-off 15,500kg (34,172lb)
Dimensions:	wingspan 8.69m (28ft 6in); length 16.83m (55ft 2.5in); height 4.89m (16ft 0.5in); wing area 24sq m (258.34sq ft)
Armament:	two 30mm DEFA cannon with 150 rpg; five external hardpoints with provision for 4536kg (10,000lb) of stores, including one AN-52 tactical nuclear weapon or conventional loads such as one AS.37 Martel anti-radar missile and two drop tanks, or eight 454kg (1000lb) bombs, or combinations of ASMs, drop tanks and rocket-launcher pods, and a reconnaissance pod

SEPECAT Jaguar E

Forty of the two-seat Jaguar E advanced trainers were built for the Armée de l'Air; the first two prototypes flew in September 1968 and February 1969 respectively. During initial flight trials, Mach 1 plus was achieved, and confirmed the validity of the high-set monoplane wing design. The two crew are accommodated in a pressurised and air-conditioned cockpit, with the rear (instructor's) seat raised by 0.38m (15in). Deliveries began in May 1972. The RAF version of the French aircraft (pictured above) has the service designation Jaguar T.Mk 2, which retains full operational capability and is equipped to the same standard as the GR.Mk 1. The RAF received 38 T.Mk 2s, three more than originally planned. Updated aircraft are T.Mk 2A. Pictured is a T.Mk 2 of No. 54 Squadron, based at Cottishall in East Anglia.

Country of origin:	France and UK
Type:	single-seat tactical support and strike aircraft
Powerplant:	two 3647kg (8040lb) Rolls-Royce/Turbomeca Adour Mk 104 turbofans
Performance:	maximum speed at 11,000m (36,090ft) 1593km/h (990mph); combat radius on lo-lo-lo mission with internal fuel 557km (357 miles)
Weights:	empty 7000kg (15,432lb); maximum take-off 15,500kg (34,172lb)
Dimensions:	wingspan 8.69m (28ft 6in); length 16.83m (55ft 2.5in); height 4.89m (16ft 0.5in); wing area 24sq m (258.34 q ft)
Armament:	two 30mm DEFA cannon with 150 rpg; five external hardpoints with provision for 4536kg (10,000lb) of stores, including one AN-52 tactical nuclear weapons or conventional loads such as one AS.37 Martel anti-radar missile and two drop tanks, or eight 454kg (1000lb) bombs, or combinations of ASMs, drop tanks and rocket-launcher pods, and a reconnaissance pod

SEPECAT Jaguar International

The outstanding versatility of the Jaguar encouraged the Anglo-French SEPECAT company to develop a version for the export market. The first Jaguar International took to the air in August 1976. Many different combinations of avionics and weapons fitment were offered, with the aircraft optimised for anti-shipping, air defence, ground attack and reconnaissance roles. Although substantial export orders were envisaged, a total of only 169 had been ordered by four nations by the mid-1990s. Indian company HAL assembled 45 from British-supplied kits before switching to domestic production. These aircraft have a highly advanced avionics suite which includes a Smiths HUD and weapons aiming system. Ecuador, Nigeria and Oman also operate the aircraft. Pictured is one of the 9 Ecuadorian aircraft, operated by 2111º Escuadron 'Agulas' near Quito.

Country of origin:	France and UK
Type:	single-seat tactical support and strike aircraft
Powerplant:	two 3810kg (8400lb) Rolls-Royce/Turbomeca Adour Mk 811 turbofans
Performance:	maximum speed at 11,000m (36,090ft) 1699km/h (1,056mph); combat radius on lo-lo-lo mission with internal fuel 537km (334 miles)
Weights:	empty 7700kg (16,976lb); maximum take-off 15,700kg (34,613lb)
Dimensions:	wingspan 8.69m (28ft 6in); length 16.83m (55ft 2.5in); height 4.89m (16ft 0.5in); wing area 24.18sq m (260.28 q ft)
Armament:	two 30mm Aden Mk.4 cannon with 150 rpg; seven external hardpoints with provision for 4763kg (10,500lb) of stores, including Sidewinder or Magic air-to-air missiles, Exocet or Sea Eagle anti-ship missiles, laser-guided or conventional bombs, cluster bombs, anit-airfield weapons, rocket-launcher pods, napalm tanks, drop tanks and ECM pods

SOKO G-2A Galeb

The SOKO company rose from the ashes of the Yugoslav aircraft industry, which had been comprehensively destroyed during World War II. In 1948 SOKO began licensed production of foreign designs before embarking on the design and construction of the G-2A Galeb trainer in 1957. This is a conventional low-wing monoplane of all-metal construction, retractable tricycle undercarriage, and turbojet power. The crew are seated in tandem seats in a heated and air-conditioned cockpit. The avionics suite is limited to a radio compass and communications transceiver, although full blind-flying system is standard. The first aircraft was flown in May 1961, and production for the Yugoslav air force under the designation G-2A Galeb began in 1963. Production of the uprated G-2A-E export model continued until 1983.

Country of origin:	Yugolavia
Type:	basic trainer
Powerplant:	one 1134kg (2500lb) Rolls-Royce Viper 11 Mk 226 turbojet
Performance:	maximum speed at 6000m (19,685ft) 730km/h (454mph); service ceiling 12,000m (39,370ft); range with maximum standard fuel 1240km (771 miles)
Weights:	empty 2620kg (5776lb); maximum take-off 4300kg (9480lb)
Dimensions:	wingspan 9.73m (31ft 11in); length 10.34m (33ft 11in); height 3.28m (10ft 9in); wing area 19.43sq m (209.15sq ft)
Armament:	two 12.7mm machine guns with 80 rpg; underwing racks for 150kg (331lb) bomblet containers, 100kg (220lb) bombs, 127mm rockets, and 55mm rocket-launcher pods

SOKO J-1 Jastreb

It was a relatively simple process for SOKO designers to convert the G-2A Galeb into a single-seat light attack aircraft. No major structural modifications needed to be made, and as the canopy had originally been designed as a two-piece unit it was necessary only to fair over the rear cockpit with sheet metal. To improve weapons-carrying ability, an uprated version of the Viper engine was introduced, but apart from some local airframe strengthening, uprated wing hardpoints and the installation of a braking parachute, little was changed. The first two versions to enter production were the J-1 attack and the RJ-1 reconnaissance aircraft for the Yugoslav air force, although neither of these aircraft remain in service. The aircraft pictured is the second of two prototypes, in Yugoslav air force markings. Libya and Zambia also bought the aircraft, although their status is uncertain.

Country of origin:	Yugolavia
Type:	single-seat light attack aircraft
Powerplant:	one 1361kg (3000lb) Rolls-Royce Viper Mk 531 turbojet
Performance:	maximum speed at 6000m (19,685ft) 820km/h (510mph); service ceiling 12,000m (39,370ft); combat radius with standard fuel 1520km (944 miles)
Weights:	empty 2820kg (6217lb); maximum take-off 5100kg (11,244lb)
Dimensions:	wingspan 11.68m (38ft 3.75in); length 10.88m (38ft 8.25in); height 3.64m (11ft 11.25in); wing area 19.43sq m (209.15sq ft)
Armament:	three 12.7mm machine guns with 135 rpg; inboard hardpoints with provision for 500kg (1102lb) of stores, including bombs, bomblet containers, flares, gun pods, rocket-launcher pods, and for six 127mm rockets on wing attachments

SOKO G-4 Super Galeb

Studies began on an improved version of the G-2A Galeb to replace this aircraft and the Lockheed T-33 in basic and advanced training units of the Yugoslav Air Force. Despite having a name in common with its predecessor, the G-4 is in fact a wholly new design, with a swept wing and all-swept tail, and a far more modern cockpit, housing the student and instructor in tandem seats. The rear seat is slightly raised, in a style similar to the BAe Hawk. Avionics equipment on the G-4 is far more comprehensive, with Distance Measuring Equipment, radio altimeter, radio compass, VHF radio, very high frequency Omni-directional Range/Instrument Landing System. Although the aircraft is some 25 percent heavier than the G-2A, it can carry a greater weapons load. A small number of the large order for the Yugoslav Air Force had been delivered before the break-up of the country.

Country of origin:	Yugolavia
Type:	basic trainer/light attack aircraft
Powerplant:	one 1814kg (4000lb) Rolls-Royce Viper Mk 632 turbojet
Performance:	maximum speed at 4000m (13,125ft) 910km/h (665mph); service ceiling 12,850m (42,160ft); range with internal fuel 1900km (1,80 miles)
Weights:	empty 3172kg (6993lb); maximum take-off 6300kg (13,889lb)
Dimensions:	wingspan 9.88m (32ft 5in); length 12.25m (40ft 2.25in); height 4.3m (14ft 1.25in); wing area 19.5sq m (209.9sq ft)
Armament:	one 23mm GSh-23L cannon with 200 rpg; four external hardpoints with provision for 2053kg of stores, including air-to-air missiles, bombs, cluster bombs, dispenser weapons, napalm tanks, large-calibre rockets, rocket-launcher pods, drop tanks and ECM pods

SOKO/Avioane IAR-93A

The J-22 was the result of a collaboration between the Romanian IAv (Intreprinderea De Avioane Bucuresti) company and SOKO of Yugoslavia, stemming from a common requirement in both countries for a twin-jet close-support and ground-attack aircraft. The initial design was contracted out to the Institute of Aviation in Romania and its counterpart in Yugoslavia. Each country constructed prototypes powered by two licence-built Rolls-Royce Viper Mk 632 41Rs, and the first flights took place simultaneously in October 1974. Production of the initial batch of 20 Romanian aircraft, which are designated IAR-93A, began in 1979, with SOKO commencing production of the similar J- 22 in 1980. An improved version with afterburning engines began production in 1984 and is designated J-22(M) or Orao 2, with production totalling 165 in both countries.

Country of origin:	Yugolavia
Type:	single-seat close-support/ground attack aircraft
Powerplant:	two 2268kg (5000lb) Turbomecanica (Rolls-Royce Viper Mk 633-47) turbojets
Performance:	maximum speed at sea level 1160km/h (721mph); service ceiling 12,500m (41,010ft); combat radius with four 250kg bombs and drop tanks 530km (329 miles)
Weights:	empty 5900kg (13,007lb); maximum take-off 10,100kg (22,267lb)
Dimensions:	wingspan 9.62m (31ft 6.75in); length 14.90m (48ft 10.75in); height 4.45m (14ft 7.25in); wing area 26sq m (279.87 q ft)
Armament:	two 23mm GSh-23L cannon with 200 rpg; five external hardpoints with provision for 2800kg (6173lb) of stores, including air-to-air missiles, air-to-surface missiles, bombs, cluster bombs, dispenser weapons, napalm tanks, rocket-launcher pods and drop tanks

Saab 105

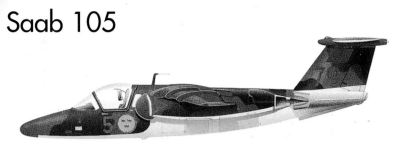

Saab established its reputation as a designer and manufacturer of first class jet aircraft wit the Draken. The success of this aircraft encouraged the Swedish manufacturer to extend their range of aircraft by developing the privately-funded 105. This aircraft is a swept shoulder- wing monoplane with side-by-side cabin accommodation for either two or four crew. Power is provided by twin turbojets. The first prototype flew in June 1963, and after successful evaluation by the Swedish Air Force, orders were placed for 150 production aircraft. The type began to enter service in 1966, initially with the primary flying training school at Ljungbyhed air base. In Swedish air force use, the aircraft are designated Sk 60A; the armed close-support variant is the Sk 60B, and the photo-recce version is the Sk 60C.

Country of origin:	Sweden
Type:	training/liason aircraft with secondary attack capability
Powerplant:	two 744kg (1640lb) Turbomeca Aubisque turbofans
Performance:	maximum speed at 6095m (20,000ft) 770km/h (480mph); service ceiling 13,500m (44,290ft); range 1400km (870 miles)
Weights:	empty 2510kg (5534lb); maximum take-off 4050kg (8929lb)
Dimensions:	wingspan 9.5m (31ft 2in); length 10.5m (34ft 5.375in); height 2.7m (8ft 10.25in); wing area 16.3sq m (175.46sq ft)
Armament:	six external hardpoints with provision for up to 700kg (1543lb) of stores, including two Saab Rb05 air-to-surface missiles, or two 30mm cannon pods, or 12 135mm rockets, or bombs, cluster bombs and rocket launcher pods

Saab A21R

Frid Wanstrom's design is the only aircraft in the world to have seen front-line service with both piston and jet power. The aircraft was initially conceived in March 1941, in response to a Swedish request for a replacement for the miscellaneous obsolescent fighters then in service. The piston-engined version went into production with German Daimler-Benz 605B power in 1945. The conversion to jet power proved remarkably straightforward. The tailplane was carried high on altered fins and the landing gear was shortened. Power was provided by a single de Havilland Goblin 2 turbojet (J21RA), and later with a licence-built version of the same engine (J21RB). Thirty of each type were built and after a short career as fighter aircraft, they were converted to attack aircraft and redesignated A21R and A21RB respectively.

Country of origin:	Sweden
Type:	single-seat fighter/attack aircraft
Powerplant:	one 1361kg (3000lb) de Havilland Goblin 2 turbojet
Performance:	maximum speed 800km/h (497mph); service ceiling 12,000m (39,400ft); range 720km (450 miles)
Weights:	empty 3200kg (7055lb); maximum take-off 5000kg (11,023lb)
Dimensions:	wingspan 11.37m (37ft 4in); length 10.45m (34ft 3in); height 2.90m (9ft 8in)
Armament:	one 20mm Bofors cannon and four 13.2mm M/39A, centreline pod housing eight 13.2mm guns, wing racks for 10 100mm or five 180mm Bofors rockets, or 10 80mm anti-tank rockets

Saab J32B Lansen

Designed to replace the Saab 18 light-bomber in service with the Swedish air force, the Type 32 was a large all-swept machine of outstanding quality, designed and developed ahead of similar aircraft elsewhere in Western Europe. Owing to its not inconsiderable size, it was capable of development for three dissimilar missions. The A 32A all-weather attack aircraft was the first into production in 1953, followed by the J 32B all-weather and night fighter, and the S 32C reconnaissance aircraft in mid-1958. The survivors of nearly 450 aircraft completed served well into the 1990s as aggressor aircraft, target tugs, and trials aircraft. The J 32B pictured here had a more powerful licence-built Rolls-Royce engine than its predecessor, and S6 radar fire control for lead/pursuit interception. Between 1958 and 1970 seven squadrons were equipped with the type.

Country of origin:	Sweden
Type:	all-weather and night fighter
Powerplant:	one 6890kg (15,190lb) Svenska Flygmotor (Rolls-Royce Avon) RM6A
Performance:	maximum speed 1114km/h (692mph); service ceiling 16,013m (52,500ft); range with external fuel 3220km (2000 miles)
Weights:	empty 7990kg (17,600lb); maximum loaded 13,529kg (29,800lb)
Dimensions:	wingspan 13m (42ft 7.75in); length 14.50m (47ft 6.75in); height 4.65m (15ft 3in); wing area 37.4sq m (402.58 q ft)
Armament:	four 30-mm Aden M/55 cannon; four Rb324 (Sidewinder) air-to-air missiles or FFAR (Folding Fin Air-launched Rocket) pods

Saab J35F Draken

The Draken was designed to a demanding Swedish Air Force specification for a single-seat interceptor which could operate from short air strips, have rapid time-to-height performance, and supersonic performance. The aircraft the Saab team, led by Erik Bratt, designed between 1949-51 is one of the most remarkable to arrive on the post-war aviation scene. The unique 'double-delta' is an ingenious method of arranging items one behind the other to give a long aircraft with small frontal area and correspondingly high aerodynamic efficiency. The aircraft was ten years in development, with the first J35A production models arriving in service in March 1960. Saab also offered the Draken for export under the designation Saab-35X, with increased fuel capacity and higher gross weight. Finland received 24 ex-Flyguapnet J34F single-seaters, one pictured here.

Country of origin:	Sweden
Type:	single-seat all-weather interceptor
Powerplant:	one 7761kg (17,110lb) Svenska Flygmotor RM6C turbojet
Performance:	maximum speed 2125km/h (1320mph); service ceiling 20,000m (65,000ft); range with maximum fuel 3250km (2020 miles)
Weights:	empty 7425kg (16,369lb); maximum take-off 16,000kg (35,274lb)
Dimensions:	wingspan 9.4m (30ft 10in); length 15.4m (50ft 4in); height 3.9m (12ft 9in); wing area 49.20sq m (526.6sq ft)
Armament:	one 30mm Aden M/55 cannon with 90 rds, two radar-homing Rb27 and two IR-homing Rb28 Falcon air-to-air missiles, or two of four Rb24 Sidewinder AAMs, or up to 4082kg of bombs on attack mission

Saab Sk 35C Draken

Ome of the two Draken variants developed for the Swedish Air Force was the Sk35C tandem two-seat operational conversion trainer. The other is the S 35E reconnaissance aircraft derived from the J 35D. The Sk 35C fleet mainly converted J35As, with armament removed and without any combat capability. In 1995, only 12 remained in service with Flygflottilj, 10 at Angelholm in southern Sweden. Eleven export versions of the same aircraft, designated Sk 35XD, were delivered to Denmark, and five J35CS (Swedish Sk 35C) went to Finland. Now virtually replaced by the Viggen, the Draken has the considerable distinction of being the first supersonic European combat aircraft. Pictured is a Swedish Sk 35C, carrying a centreline drop tank. Note the short tail configuration, adopted to accommodate the Type 55 afterburner.

Country of origin:	Sweden
Type:	two-seat operational trainer
Powerplant:	one 6804kg (15,000lb) Svenska Flygmotor RM6B turbojet
Performance:	maximum speed 2011km/h (1,250mph); service ceiling 20,000m (65,000ft); range with maximum fuel 3250km (2020 miles)
Weights:	empty 7425kg (16,369lb); maximum take-off 8262kg (18,200lb)
Dimensions:	wingspan 9.4m (30ft 10in); length 15.4m (50ft 4in); height 3.9m (12ft 9in); wing area 49.20sq m (526.6sq ft)

Saab J 35J Draken

The final new-build air defence version of the Draken was the J 35F, which was a development of the J 35D with more capable radar, collision course fire-control and a Hughes infra-red sensor to allow the carriage of licence-built Hughes Falcon AAMs. During the late 1980s, the decision was taken to update 64 J 35Fs to J 35J standard in order to allow three squadrons of F10 Wing, based near Angelholm in southern Sweden, to remain operational until the mid-1990s. Improvements were made to the weapons electronics, IR sensor, radar and IFF equipment. Two additional inboard pylons were added to the strengthened wing, together with an altitude warning system. Redeliveries were completed in 1990. Pictured is one of the aircraft operated by Flygflottilj 10, with Rb24 sidewinder missiles on both inboard and outer pylons.

Country of origin:	Sweden
Type:	single-seat all-weather interceptor
Powerplant:	one 7830kg (17,262lb) Svenska Flygmotor RM6C turbojet
Performance:	maximum speed at 11,000m (36,090ft) 2125km/h (1320mph); service ceiling 20,000m (65,000ft); range with internal fuel on hi-lo-hi mission 560km (348 miles)
Weights:	empty 7425kg (16,369lb); maximum take-off 16,000kg (35,274lb)
Dimensions:	wingspan 9.4m (30ft 10in); length 15.4m (50ft 4in); height 3.9m (12ft 9in); wing area 49.20sq m (526.6sq ft)
Armament:	one 30mm Aden M/55 cannon with 90 rds, two radar-homing Rb27 and two IR-homing Rb28 Falcon air-to-air missiles, or two of four Rb24 Sidewinder AAMs, or up to 4082kg (9000lb) of bombs on attack mission

Saab AJ 37 Viggen

Until the arrival of the Panavia Tornado it may be argued that the Viggen was the most advanced combat aircraft ever produced in Europe. When it entered service in 1971 the AJ37 had a far more advanced radar, a greater speed range, and a more comprehensive avionics fit than most of its contemporaries. The Royal Swedish Air Board planned System 37 in 1958-61 as a standardised weapon system to be integrated with the Stril 60 air-defence environment of radars, computers and displays. Included in this system is a standard platform (the Viggen family) produced in five versions, each tailored for a specific task. The AJ37 is a dedicated all-weather attack aircraft which provides the Swedish air force with its ground-attack capability, and has an avionics suite optimised for this role. This aircraft is operated by Flygflottilj 15, of the Swedish air force, based at Soderhamn.

Country of origin:	Sweden
Type:	single-seat all-weather attack aircraft
Powerplant:	one 11,800kg (26,015lb) Volvo Flygmotor RM8 turbofan
Performance:	maximum speed at high altitude 2124km/h (1320mph); service ceiling 18,290m (60,000ft); combat radius on hi-lo-hi mission with external armament 1000km (621 miles)
Weights:	empty 11,800kg (26,015lb); maximum take-off 20,500kg (45,194lb)
Dimensions:	wingspan 10.6m (34ft 9.25in); length 16.3m (53ft 5.75in); height 5.6m (18ft 4.5in); wing area 46sq m (495.16sq ft)
Armament:	seven external hardpoints with provision for 6000kg (13,228lb) of stores, including 30mm Aden cannon pods, 135mm rocket pods, Sidewinder or Falcon air-to-air missiles for self-defence, Maverick air-to-surface missiles, bombs, cluster bombs

Saab JA37 Viggen

The interceptor version of the Viggen, and an integral part of the System 37 series, was the single-seat JA37. Externally, the aircraft closely resembles the attack AJ37, although the fin is slightly taller and the interceptor has four elevon actuators under the wing instead of three as on other versions. A considerable amount of effort was made to optimise the Pratt & Whitney-designed Volvo turbofan for high altitude performance and high-stress combat manoeuvring, resulting in the RM8B unit fitted to the JA37. The other main area of development was the onboard avionics suite, most importantly the Ericsson UAP-1023 I/J-band long-range pulse-Doppler radar which provides target search and acquisition. Production of the JA37 totalled 149 aircraft with the last delivered in June 1990. The number 13 on the fuselage denotes Flygflottilj 13 of the Swedish air force.

Country of origin:	Sweden
Type:	single-seat all-weather interceptor aircraft with secondary attack capability
Powerplant:	one 12,750kg (28,109lb) Volvo Flygmotor RM8B turbofan
Performance:	maximum speed at high altitude 2124km/h (1320mph); service ceiling 18,290m (60,000ft); combat radius on lo-lo-lo mission with external armament 500km (311 miles)
Weights:	empty 15,000kg (33,060lb); maximum take-off 20,500kg (45,194lb)
Dimensions:	wingspan 10.6m (34ft 9.25in); length 16.3m (53ft 5.75in); height 5.9m (19ft 4.25in); wing area 46sq m (495.16sq ft)
Armament:	one 30mm Oerlikon KCA cannon with 150 rds; six external hardpoints with provision for 6000kg (13,228lb) of stores, including two Rb71 Sky Flash and four Rb24 Sidewinder air-to-air missiles, or bombs and/or 135mm rocket pods

Saab SF37 Viggen

The second variant in the System 37 series was the SF37, a dedicated single-seat reconnaissance version intended to replace the S 35E in service with the Swedish Air Force. The first prototype flew in May 1973,. Production aircraft are distinguished by a chisel nose (as can be seen from the artwork above) containing seven cameras, which are often supplemented by surveillance pods on the shoulder hardpoints. One forward-looking camera is used for infra-red photography, two are installed vertically for high altitude work and four are mounted in a downward facing arc for use at low-level. This provides horizon-to-horizon surveillance. The aircraft retain the full weapon capability of the JA37 interceptor, but the camera fit in the nose dispenses with radar of any kind. Deliveries of 26 SF37s began in April 1977.

Country of origin:	Sweden
Type:	single-seat all-weather photo-reconnaissance aircraft
Powerplant:	one 11,800kg (26,015lb) Volvo Flygmotor RM8 turbofan
Performance:	maximum speed at high altitude 2124km/h (1,320mph); service ceiling 18,290m (60,000ft); combat radius on hi-lo-hi mission with external armament 1000km (621 miles)
Weights:	empty 11,800kg (26,015lb); maximum take-off 17,000kg (37,479lb)
Dimensions:	wingspan 10.6m (34ft 9.25in); length 16.3m (53ft 5.75in); height 5.9m (19ft 4.25in); wing area 46sq m (495.16sq ft)
Armament:	(in secondary attack role) seven external hardpoints with provision for 6000kg (13,228lb) of stores, including 30mm Aden cannon pods, 135mm rocket pods, Sidewinder or Falcon air-to-air missiles for self-defence, Maverick air-to-surface missiles, bombs, cluster bombs

Saab JAS 39 Gripen

Saab has produced another excellent lightweight fighter in the form of the Gripen, and it is extremely surprising, given the outstanding performance demonstrated by the aircraft, that more export orders have not been forthcoming. The aircraft was conceived during the late 1970s as a replacement for the AJ, SH, SF and JA versions of the Saab 37 Viggen. Configuration follows Saab's tried and tested convention with an aft-mounted delta, and swept canard foreplanes. The flying surfaces are controlled via a fly-by-wire system. Advanced avionics, including pulse-Doppler search and acquisition radar, pod-mounted FLIR, head-up and -down displays (replacing normal flight instruments) and excellent ECM and navigation systems, give the aircraft multi-role all-weather capability. The JAS 39A became operational in 1995.

Country of origin:	Sweden
Type:	single-seat all-weather fighter, attack and reconnaissance aircraft
Powerplant:	one 8210kg (18,100lb) Volvo Flygmotor RM12 turbofan
Performance:	maximum speed more than Mach 2; range on hi-lo-hi mission with external armament 3250km (2020 miles)
Weights:	empty 6622kg (14,600lb); maximum take-off 12,473kg (27,500lb)
Dimensions:	wingspan 8m (26ft 3in); length 14.1m (46ft 3in); height 4.7m (15ft 5in)
Armament:	one 27mm Mauser BK27 cannon with 90 rounds, six external hardpoints with provision for Rb71 Sky Flash and Rb24 Sidewinder air-to-air missiles, Maverick air-to-surface missiles, Rb15F anti-ship missiles, bombs, cluster bombs, rocket-launcher pods, reconnaissance pods, drop tanks and ECM pods

Saunders-Roe SR.53

The SR.53 is worthy of comparison with the Republic XF-91, if only for the sake of posterity and to recall a golden age of aircraft design. After Britain's early lead in jet technology, there seemed little chance that British post-war austerity could match the financial and industrial might of the US. However, with ingenuity and technical skill, some impressive advances were made, most notably the BAC TSR.2. The Defence White Paper of 1957, the scourge of post-war British aircraft design, dashed forever any hope of parity with the Americans. The Saunders-Roe SR.53 was one of two mixed-power (rocket and turbojet-engined) short-range interceptors (along with the Avro 720) ordered in prototype form by the RAF. The SR.53 had a Viper turbojet and a Spectre rocket engine. The rocket engine was used for climb, and a turbojet for economical cruising and electrical power.

Country of origin:	United Kingdom
Type:	experimental high-speed interceptor
Powerplant:	one 794 kg (1750lb) Armstrong-Siddeley Viper turbojet; one 3632kg (8000lb) de Havilland Spectre rocket
Performance:	Mach 2 plus
Weights:	n/a
Dimensions:	n/a

State Aircraft Factory
Shenyang JJ-5

T he physical similarity of the Shenyang JJ-5 to the MiG-15 is no coincidence. China benefited from considerable Soviet assistance when the communist government refurbished the Shenyang factory after the Second World War, and this extended to licensing machines of Soviet design to the new republic. The first turbojet-powered aircraft to be built in China were single-seat and two-seat versions of the MiG-15 'Fagot' and the MiG-17F. Chinese designers at the Chengdu factory (where the aircraft were built) developed an indigenous aircraft which incorporated features of both aircraft, and powered it with a Chinese built copy of a Soviet engine. The aircraft flew in prototype form in May 1966 and currently serves in the air arm of the PLA as its standard advanced trainer. An export model for Pakistan, Bangladesh, Sudan and Tanzania is designated FT-5.

Country of origin:	China
Type:	two-seat advanced trainer
Powerplant:	one 2700kg (5952lb) Xian WP-5D turbojet
Perfomance:	normal operating speed 775km/h (482mph); service ceiling 14,300m (46,915ft); range with maximum fuel 1230km (764 miles)
Weights:	empty 4080kg (8995lb); maximum take-off 6215kg (13,702lb)
Dimensions:	wingspan 9.63m (31ft 7in); length 11.5m (37ft 8.75in); height 3.8m (12ft 5.5in)
Armament:	one 23mm Type 23-1 cannon in removable fuselage pack

State Aircraft Factory Shenyang J-6

The national aircraft company at Shenyang continued to assemble a version of the Mikoyan-Gurevich MiG-19S from knock-down kits supplied by the Soviet government until 1960. In that year, however, Sino-Soviet relations cooled and locally manufactured components were used instead. The Chinese-built MiG-19S was designated J-6 and entered service from mid-1962 with the Air Force of the People's Liberation Army and became its standard day fighter. The Nanchang Aircraft Manufacturing Company in Jiangxi province were also involved in the production of the aircraft, which numbered in their thousands. Pakistan was a major export customer for the F-6, many of which remain in service in the late 1990s. These aircraft have been fitted with Western avionics, though this does not compensate for their overall obsolescence.

Country of origin:	China
Type:	single-seat day fighter
Powerplant:	two 3250kg (7165lb) Shenyang WP-6 turbojets
Perfomance:	maximum speed 1540km/h (957mph); service ceiling 17,900m (58,725ft); range with internal fuel 1390km (864 miles)
Weights:	empty 5760kg (12,699lb); maximum take-off 10,000kg (22,046lb)
Dimensions:	wingspan 9.2m (30ft 2.25in); length 14.9m (48ft 10.5in); height 3.88m (12ft 8.75in); wing area 25sq m (269.11sq ft)
Armament:	three 30mm NR-30 cannon; four external hardpoints with provision for up to 500kg (1102lb) of stores, including air-to-air missiles, 250kg bombs, 55mm rocket-launcher pods, 212mm rockets or drop tanks

Sud-Ouest Aquilon 203

Although obviously derived from the de Havilland Venom, the Sud-Est Aquilon was significantly different and in many ways more capable than the carrier-based versions in service with the Royal Navy. The French company were suitably impressed with the proposed Sea Venom Mk 52, based on the Sea Venom FAW.Mk 20 to begin licensed production at Marignane, near Marseilles. This grew into an all-French family of aircraft using Westinghouse APQ-65 radar and Fiat-built de Havilland Ghost 48 engines. The single-seat Aquilon 203 had the pilot sitting slightly to starboard, a French APQ-65 radar and command-guidance Nord 5103 air-to-air missiles. Like the 202, it had full-air-conditioning (a source of much contention among British pilots), Martin-Baker ejector seat and Hispano 404 cannon. Forty were completed. This aircraft is painted in the colours of Aéronavale Flottila 16F.

Country of origin:	France/United Kingdom
Type:	single-seat carrier-based fighter
Powerplant:	one 2336kg (5150lb) de Havilland Ghost 48 turbojet
Performance:	maximum speed 1030km/h (640mph); service ceiling 14,630m (48,000ft); range with drop tanks 1730km (1075 miles)
Weights:	empty 4174kg (9202lb); maximum loaded 6945kg (15,310lb)
Dimensions:	wingspan (over tip tanks) 12.7m (41ft 8in); length 10.38m (32ft 4in); height 1.88m (6ft 2in); wing area 25.99sq m (279.75sq ft)
Armament:	four 20mm Hispano 404 cannon with 150 rpg, two wing pylons for Nord 5103 (AA.20) air-to-air missiles

Sud-Ouest Vautour IIB

A fter World War II, the French aircraft industry strived to make up for five lost years, particularly in the new science of jet propulsion. By mid-March 1951 Sud-Ouest had flown the prototype of an advanced high-performance twin-jet bomber, designated the S.O. 4000. From this was developed the S.O. 4050. The S.O. 4050 differed quite considerably from its predecessor, with swept-wing surfaces and the engines mounted in nacelles beneath the wing. One of the three S.O. 4050 prototypes was completed as a two-seat bomber, with Armstrong Siddeley Sapphire turbojets and a glazed bomb-aiming position in the nose. The aircraft was designated S.O. 4050-3, and first flew on December 5, 1954. Evaluation of the aircraft led to production orders for 40, powered by the SNECMA Atar turbojet that was common to all variants.

Country of origin:	France
Type:	two-seat medium bomber
Powerplant:	two 3503kg (7716lb) SNECMA Atar 101E-3 turbojets
Performance:	maximum speed 1105km/h (687mph); service ceiling more than 15000m (49,210ft)
Weights:	empty 10,000kg; maximum take-off 20,000kg (44,092lb)
Dimensions:	wingspan 15.09m (49ft 6in); length 15.57m (51ft 1in); height 4.5m (14ft 9in)
Armament:	internal bomb bay with provision for up to 10 bombs, and underwing pylons for two bombs up to 450kg (992lb), or two drop tanks

Sud-Ouest Vautour IIN

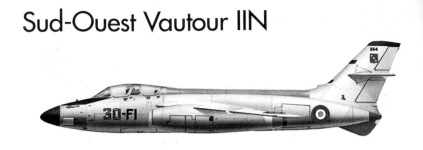

The S.O. 4050 seemed an unlikely candidate as a fighter aircraft, given the fact that it had been originally developed as a medium bomber. Nevertheless, one of the three prototypes ordered by the Armée de l'Air was completed as a two-seat all-weather interceptor, powered by SNECMA Atar 101B turbojets. This aircraft formed the basis for the Vautour II-N, which was powered by the Atar 101E, and first flew in October 1956. Armament consisted of cannon, missiles and rockets and also had radar equipment. Seventy were completed between 1957 and 1959, half of the original planned order. Most of these aircraft served with 30ième Eseadre Tout-Temps (all-weather wing) based at Tours. An upgraded version with all-moving slab tailplanes was designated Vautour II-1N. The aircraft was replaced by the Dassault Mirage F1 in the early 1970s.

Country of origin:	France
Type:	two-seat all-weather fighter
Powerplant:	two 3503kg (7716lb) SNECMA Atar 101E-3 turbojets
Performance:	maximum speed 1105km/h (687mph); service ceiling more than 15000m (49,210ft)
Weights:	empty 10,000kg; maximum take-off 20,000kg (44,092lb)
Dimensions:	wingspan 15.09m (49ft 6in); length 15.57m (51ft 1in); height 4.5m (14ft 9in)
Armament:	four 30mm DEFA cannon, internal bomb bay with provision for up to 240 rockets; underwing pylons for air-to-air missiles, MATRA M.116E rockets, or 24 120mm rockets, or two drop tanks

Sud-Ouest Vautour IIN

Israel established close links with the French aviation industry soon after the Second World War. In 1957, the Israeli government struck a deal with Sud-Oeust to supply 18 Vautour IIAs, which were followed into service with the Heyl Ha'Avir by seven IINs. These aircraft played a significant role in the 1967 Six-Day War, for both bombing and interceptor missions, and acquitted themselves with some distinction. An eighth IIN was purchased in 1966. This had a lengthened nose and was equipped for electronic warfare. Israel's air force had four Vautours shot down in the 1967 war, but the remaining aircraft saw almost constant service until August 1970. The camouflage scheme on the aircraft pictured is that applied to the current generation of Israeli tactical aircraft, which is indicative of the Vautour's long-service career.

Country of origin:	France
Type:	two-seat night/all-weather fighter
Powerplant:	two 3503kg (7716lb) SNECMA Atar 101E-3 turbojets
Performance:	maximum speed 1105km/h (687mph); service ceiling more than 15000m (49,210ft); range 4000km (2485 miles)
Weights:	empty 10,000kg; maximum take-off 20,700kg (45,635lb)
Dimensions:	wingspan 15.09m (49ft 6in); length 15.57m (51ft 1in); height 4.5m (14ft 9in)
Armament:	four 30mm DEFA cannon with 100rpg, internal bomb bay with provision for up to 240 SNEB rockets; four underwing pylons for four MATRA 5103 (R 511) air-to-air missiles, MATRA M.116E rockets, or 24 120mm rockets, or two drop tanks

Sukhoi Su-7B 'Fitter-A'

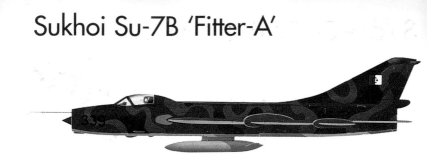

A large number of previously unknown Soviet aircraft were revealed at the 1956 Aviation Day at Tushino, among them a large swept-wing Sukhoi fighter (given the reporting name 'Fitter' by NATO). It has since become clear that the aircraft was planned as a fighter to intercept the North American F-100 and F-101 in service with the USAF, but subsequently became the standard tactical fighter-bomber of the Soviet air forces. The S-1 prototype aircraft was designed by Pavel Sukhoi after the re-establishment of Sukhoi OKB in 1953. Development work led to the S-2 and eventually to the S-22 pre-production aircraft. The Su-7B was ordered into production in 1958, and in a variety of sub-variants became the standard Soviet Bloc attack aircraft. Thousands were supplied to all Warsaw Pact nations and to Afghanistan, Algeria, Egypt, Cuba, India, Syria, Iraq and North Vietnam.

Country of origin:	USSR
Type:	ground attack fighter
Powerplant:	one 9008kg (19,842lb) Lyulka AL-7F turbojet
Performance:	maximum speed at 11,000m (36,090ft) approximately 1700km/h (1056mph); service ceiling 15,150m (49,700ft); typical combat radius 320km (199 miles)
Weights:	empty 8620kg (19,000lb); maximum take-off 13,500kg (29,750lb)
Dimensions:	wingspan 8.93m (29ft 3.5in); length 17.37m (57ft); height 4.7m (15ft 5in)
Armament:	two 30mm NR-30 cannon with 70 rpg; four external pylons for two 750kg (1653lb) and two 500kg (1102lb) bombs, but with two tanks on fuselage pylons, total external weapon load is reduced to 1000kg (2205lb)

Sukhoi Su-17M-4 'Fitter-K'

Early Soviet research into 'swing-wing' technology concentrated on the Su-7. The basic wing of the aircraft was found to be unsuitable for conversion, and so a completely redesigned variable-geometry wing was tested on a prototype, designated Su-7IG, which first flew in August 1966. Fitted with a more powerful engine, the new aircraft was found to have far superior performance than even the most developed Su-7, especially for short-field operations. The aircraft entered service in 1971 and was widely used by the Soviet air arms. The ultimate development of the aircraft was the Su-17M-4. These are distinguishable by an airscoop for the cooling system on the leading edge of the tailfin root, but also incorporate advanced avionics. About 165 of the aircraft in CIS service can carry a centreline reconnaissance pod, though many have been put into storage indefinitely.

Country of origin:	USSR
Type:	single-seat ground attack fighter
Powerplant:	one 11,250kg (24,802lb) Lyul'ka AL-21F-3 turbojet
Performance:	maximum speed above 11,000m (36,090ft) approximately 2220km/h (1380mph); service ceiling 15,200m (49,865ft); combat radius on hi-lo-hi mission with 2000kg (4409lb) load 675km (419 miles)
Weights:	empty 9,500kg (20,944lb); maximum take-off 19,500kg (42,990lb)
Dimensions:	wingspan 13.80m (45ft 3in) spread and 10m (32ft 10in) swept; length 18.75m (61ft 6in); height 5m (16ft 5in); wing area 40sq m (430sq ft)
Armament:	two 30mm NR-30 cannon with 80 rpg; nine external pylons with provision for up to 4250kg (9370lb) of stores, including tactical nuclear weapons, air-to-air missiles, air-to-surface missiles, guided bombs, cluster bombs, dispenser weapons, napalm tanks, large-calibre rockets, rocket-launcher pods, cannon pods, drop tanks and ECM pods

Sukhoi Su-20 'Fitter-C'

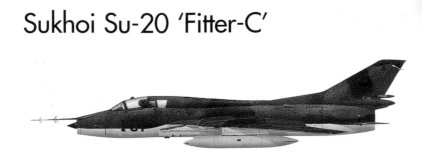

The first version of the variable-geometry wing Sukhoi Su-17 ground-attack aircraft made available for export was designated Su-20. This aircraft was basically similar to the Su-17M 'Fitter C', with inboard wing fences, broader-cord tailfin, a single brake parachute, and eight stores pylons. Poland was the only country to receive the full-standard 'Fitter-C', but a reduced equipment version was operated by Afghanistan, Algeria, Angola, Egypt, Iraq, North Korea and Vietnam. A later version, designated Su-22, was also produced, with an undernose pod housing terrain-avoidance radar and pulse-Doppler radar. Another feature which distinguishes the Su-22 from the Su-20, with its constant section rear fuselage, is the distinct bulge aft of the main wheels. This structural change was necessary to accommodate the Khachaturov turbojet, which replaces the Lyul'ka unit on the Su-20.

Country of origin:	USSR
Type:	single-seat ground attack fighter
Powerplant:	one 11,250kg (24,802lb) Lyul'ka AL-21F-3 turbojet
Performance:	maximum speed above 11,000m (36,090ft) approximately 2220km/h (1380mph); service ceiling 15,200m (49,865ft); combat radius on hi-lo-hi mission with 2000kg (4409lb) load 675km (419 miles)
Weights:	empty 9,500kg (20,944lb); maximum take-off 19,500kg (42,990lb)
Dimensions:	wingspan 13.80m (45ft 3in) spread and 10m (32ft 10in) swept; length 18.75m (61ft 6in); height 5m (16ft 5in); wing area 40 sq m (430 sq ft)
Armament:	two 30mm NR-30 cannon with 80 rpg; nine external pylons with provision for up to 4250kg (9370lb) of stores, icluding tactical nuclear weapons, air-to-air missiles, air-to-surface missiles, guided bombs, cluster bombs, dispenser weapons, napalm tanks, large calibre rockets, rocket-launcher pods, cannon pods, drop tanks and ECM pods

Sukhoi Su-15 'Flagon-A'

The Su-15 single-seat all-weather interceptor was developed to a requirement for a successor to the Sukhoi Su-11 (developed from the Su-7), and strongly resembles that aircraft in various aspects of its design. The most obvious similarities are the wings and tail. The initial T-5 prototype from which the Su-15 was developed was basically an enlarged version of the Su-11 with two engines, and the same pitot nose intake. The T-58 which followed had a solid radar nose housing Oriol-D radar and variable intakes on the fuselage sides. The 'Flagon A' entered IA-PVO Strany service in 1967, and some 1500 Sukhoi 15s in all versions are estimated to have been built. All these aircraft served with Soviet air arms, since the aircraft was never made available for export. The aircraft were often armed with the huge AA-3 'Anab' AAM.

Country of origin:	USSR
Type:	single-seat all-weather interceptor
Powerplant:	two 6205kg (13,668lb) Tumanskil R-11F2S-300 turbojets
Performance:	maximum speed above 11,000m (36,090ft) approximately 2230km/h (1386mph); service celling 20,000m (65,615ft); combat radius 725km (450 miles)
Weights:	empty (estimated) 11,000kg (24,250lb); maximum take-off 18,000kg (39,680lb)
Dimensions:	wingspan 8.61m (28ft 3in); length 21.33m (70ft); height 5.1m (16ft 8.5in); wing area 36sq m (387.5sq ft)
Armament:	four external pylons for two R8M medium-range air-to-air missiles ouboard and two AA-8 'Aphid' short-range AAMs inboard, plus two under-fuselage pylons for 23mm UPK-23 cannon pods or drop tanks

Sukhoi Su-15TM 'Flagon-F'

A number of versions of the Su-15 were produced; the definitive Su-15TM 'Flagon-F' was designed in 1971 and introduced a low-drag ogival nose radome to cover the scanner for an uprated Typhoon M search radar for limited look-down/shoot-down capability, and more powerful engines. The Su-15TM entered service in 1975. By the mid-1990s only two PVO (Soviet home defence) units continued to operated the aircraft, and it has now been completely replaced in service by the Sukhoi Su-27 and Mikoyan-Gurevich MiG-31 from service. The aircraft achieved a degree of notoriety in 1983 when it was involved in the downing of a Korean Air Lines 747 passenger aircraft in the Sea of Japan, although it was for some time erroneously reported that this aircraft was an Su-21 – in fact this aircraft never even existed!

Country of origin:	USSR
Type:	single-seat all-weather interceptor
Powerplant:	two 7200kg (15,873lb) Tumanskii R-13F2-300 turbojets
Performance:	maximum speed above 11,000m (36,090ft) approximately 2230km/h (1386mph); service ceiling 20,000m (65,615ft); combat radius 725km (450 miles)
Weights:	empty (estimated) 11,000kg (24,250lb); maximum take-off 18,000kg (39,680lb)
Dimensions:	wingspan 9.15m (30ft); length 21.33m (70ft); height 5.1m (16ft 8.5in); wing area 36sq m (387.5sq ft)
Armament:	four external pylons for two AA-3 'Anab' medium-range air-to-air missiles ouboard and two AA-8 'Aphid' short-range AAMs inboard, plus two under-fuselage pylons for 23mm GSh-23L two-barrell cannon pods or drop tanks

Sukhoi Su-24MR 'Fencer-E'

The 'Fencer E' is a version of the Su-24 strike and attack aircraft, designed for tactical reconnaissance and intended as a replacement for the venerable Tupolev Tu-16. Approximately 65 Su-24MRs have been constructed with internal and external podded sensors of various types. Some of these sensors can transmit data to ground-based receivers for real-time surveillance. Externally, the aircraft are almost indistinguishable from the 'Fencer-D', and retain the ability to carry air-to-surface missiles. One obvious difference is the introduction of a larger heat exchanger on the dorsal spine to provide increased cooling for the surveillance equipment. Service deliveries began in 1985. The aircraft pictured was operated by the 11th Independent Reconnaissance Regiment of the Soviet air force. It has now passed to the air force of the Ukraine.

Country of origin:	USSR
Type:	two-seat maritime reconnaissance aircraft
Powerplant:	two 11,250kg (24,802lb) Lyul'ka AL-21F-3A turbojets
Performance:	maximum speed above 11,000m (36,090ft) approximately 2316km/h (1,439mph); service ceiling 17,500m (57,415ft); combat radius on hi-lo-hi mission with 3000kg (6614lb) load 1050km (650 miles)
Weights:	empty 19,00kg (41,888lb); maximum take-off 39,700kg (87,520lb)
Dimensions:	wingspan 17.63m (57ft 10in) spread and 10.36m (34ft) swept; length 24.53m (80ft 5.75in); height 4.97m (16ft 0.75in); wing area 42sq m (452.1 q ft)
Armament:	(in secondary strike role) nine external pylons with provision for up to 8000kg (17,635lb) of stores, which may include air-to-air missiles, air-to-surface missiles such as the AS-14 'Kedge' , or drop tanks and/or ECM pods

Sukhoi Su-24M 'Fencer-D'

In 1965, the Soviet government prompted Sukhoi to begin designing a new Soviet variable geometry attack aircraft comparable in performance to the F-111 due to enter service in the US. One of the primary requirements for the new aircraft was the ability to penetrate increasingly efficient radar defences by flying at very low-level and at supersonic speeds. It was also specified that the aircraft should be able to operate from short, unpaved airstrips. Initial development of a VTOL aircraft to meet these criteria was halted, and work began to develop the swing-wing aircraft, designated Su-24, which emerged to make its first flight in 1970. Service deliveries of the 'Fencer A' began in 1974. The 'Fencer D' (Su-24M), which entered service in 1986, is an improved version with inflight refuelling equipment, upgraded nav/attack systems, Kaira laser and TV designator and improved defensive aids.

Country of origin:	USSR
Type:	two-seat strike and attack aircraft
Powerplant:	two 11,250kg (24,802lb) Lyul'ka AL-21F-3A turbojets
Performance:	maximum speed above 11,000m (36,090ft) approximately 2316km/h (1,439mph); service ceiling 17,500m (57,415ft); combat radius on hi-lo-hi mission with 3000kg (6614lb) load 1050km (650 miles)
Weights:	empty 19,000kg (41,888lb); maximum take-off 39,700kg (87,520lb)
Dimensions:	wingspan 17.63m (57ft 10in) spread and 10.36m (34ft) swept; length 24.53m (80ft 5in); height 4.97m (16ft 0.75in); wing area 42sq m (452.1sq ft)
Armament:	one 23mm GSh-23-6 six-barrelled cannon; nine external pylons with provision for up to 8000kg (17,635lb) of stores, including nuclear weapons, air-to-air missiles, air-to-surface missiles such as the AS-14 'Kedge', guided bombs, cluster bombs, dispenser weapons, large-calibre rockets, rocket-launcher pods, drop tanks and ECM pods

Sukhoi Su-25 'Frogfoot-A'

Western intelligence sources first identified the 'Frogfoot' at Ramenskoye test centre in 1977 and gave it the provisional US designation 'Ram-J'. The prototype first flew in 1975, and production of the single-seat close-support Su-25K (often compared to the Fairchild A-10 Thunderbolt II) began in 1978. The pilot sits in an armoured cockpit, and on the Su-25K had a Sirena-3 radar-warning system and tailcone mounted chaff/decoy flare dispenser to protect his aircraft. A nose-mounted laser range finder and marked target seeker reportedly allows bombing accuracy to within 5 meters over a stand-off range of 20km (12.5 miles). A trial unit was deployed to Afghanistan as early as 1980, followed by a full squadron, to support Soviet troops fighting In the mountainous country. The squadron worked closely with Mi-24 'Hind' gunships and the aircraft became fully operational in 1984.

Country of origin:	USSR
Type:	single-seat close-support aircraft
Powerplant:	two 4500kg (9921lb) Tumanskii R-195 turbojets
Performance:	maximum speed at sea level 975km/h (606mph); service celllng 7,000m (22,965ft); combat radius on lo-lo-lo mission with 4400kg (9700lb) load 750km (466 miles)
Weights:	empty 9,500kg (20,950lb); maximum take-off 17,600kg (38,800lb)
Dimensions:	wingspan 14.36m (47ft 1.5in); length 15.53m (50ft 11.5in); height 4.8m (15ft 9in); wing area 33.7sq m (362.75sq ft)
Armament:	one 30mm GSh-30-2 cannon with 250 rds; eight external pylons with provision for up to 4400kg (9700lb) of stores, including AAMs, ASMs, ARMs, anti-tank missiles, guided bombs, cluster bombs, dispenser weapons, large-calibre rockets, rocket-launcher pods, drop tanks and ECM pods

Sukhoi Su-25UTG 'Frogfoot-B'

The adaptability of the Su-25 is demonstrated by the diversity of versions in which it has been produced. Among the first of these versions was the Su-25UB 'Frogfoot-B' two-seat trainer, which has a longer forward fuselage to accommodate a second cockpit. The aircraft retains the full operational capability of the close-support aircraft. A two-seat variant produced for export to Bulgaria, Czechoslovakia, Iraq and North Korea is designated Su-25UBK. At least one of the Iraqi aircraft was shot down during the 1991 Gulf War. Production of a navalised version, the Su-25UTG, began in the late 1980s with strengthened undercarriage and arrestor gear. The aircraft pictured passed to the Ukrainian air force after the dissolution of the USSR, but has since been superseded by the improved Su-25UBP. Note the unit insignia on the tail.

Country of origin:	USSR
Type:	two-seat carrier-training aircraft
Powerplant:	two 4,500kg (9,921lb) Tumanskii R-195 turbojets
Performance:	maximum speed at sea level 950km/h (590mph); service ceiling 10,000m (32,810ft); combat radius on lo-lo-lo mission with 4400kg (9700lb) load 4000km (248 miles)
Weights:	empty 9500kg (20,950lb); maximum take-off 17,600kg (38,800lb)
Dimensions:	wingspan 14.36m (47ft 1.5in); length 15.53m (50ft 11.5in); height 4.8m (15ft 9in); wing area 33.7sq m (362.75sq ft)
Armament:	one 30mm GSh-30-2 cannon with 250 rds; eight external pylons with provision for up to 4400kg (9700lb) of stores, including AAMs, ASMs, ARMs, anti-tank missiles, guided bombs, cluster bombs, dispenser weapons, large-calibre rockets, rocket-launcher pods, drop tanks and ECM pods

Sukhoi Su-27UB 'Flanker-C'

Development of the Su-27 began in the mid-1970s, with the aim of producing a combat aircraft for Soviet forces comparable to the McDonnell Douglas F-15 Eagle. Given this seemingly daunting design brief, Sukhoi proceeded with impressive haste, and by the end of May 1977 the prototype Su-27 had flown. Development from prototype stage was somewhat longer and involved some fundamental design changes., necessitated by poor structural strength, excessive drag, flutter and excess weight. It was not until 1980 that full-scale production began and service entry started in 1984. The aircraft represents a significant advance over previous generations of Soviet aircraft and presented an outstanding potential for development. Advanced avionics make it a formidable fighter. The first variant was the Su-27UB 'Flanker-C' tandem-seat trainer, which retains full combat capability.

Country of origin:	USSR
Type:	tandem-seat operational conversion trainer
Powerplant:	two 12,500kg (27,557lb) Lyul'ka AL-31F turbofans
Performance:	maximum speed at high altitude 2500km/h (1500mph); service ceiling 18,000m (59,055ft); combat radius 1500km (930 miles)
Weights:	maximum tak-off 30,000kg (66,138lb)
Dimensions:	wingspan 14.70m (48ft 2.75in); length 21.94m (71ft 11.5in); height 6.36m (20ft 10.25in); wing area 46.5sq m (500sq ft)
Armament:	one 30mm GSh-3101 cannon with 149 rds; 10 external hardpoints with provision for 6000kg (13,228kg) of stores, including AA-10A ('Alamo-A'), AA-10B ('Alamo-B'), AA-10C ('Alamo-C'), AA-11 ('Archer') or AA-8 ('Aphid') air-to-air missiles

Sukhoi Su-35

One of the ongoing developments of the Su-27 is the single-seat Su-35 all-weather air-superiority fighter (derived from the 'Flanker-B'). This aircraft, which has similar powerplant and configuration to the Su-27, is an attempt to provide a second-generation Su-27 with improved agility and operational capability. The program was severely delayed by problems with the radar and digital quadruplex fly-by-wire control systems, which replace the analogue system in the earlier aircraft. A new fire control system was incorporated, with air-to-ground and air-to-air modes, to improve the ground attack capability of the aircraft. This is linked to a new electro-optical complex incorporating laser and TV designation for air-to-surface missiles, as well as laser ranging. Inflight refuelling equipment is also fitted. The first of six Su-27M prototypes (as it was then known) made its maiden flight in1988.

Country of origin:	USSR
Type:	single-seat all-weather air superiority fighter
Powerplant:	two 12,500kg (27,557lb) Lyul'ka AL-31M turbofans
Performance:	maximum speed at high altitude 2500km/h (1500mph); service ceiling 18,000m (59,055ft); combat radius 1500km (930 miles)
Weights:	maximum take-off 30,000kg (66,138lb)
Dimensions:	wingspan 14.70m (48ft 2.75in); length 21.94m (71ft 11.5in); height 6.36m (20ft 10.25in); wing area 46.5sq m (500sq ft)
Armament:	one 30mm GSh-3101 cannon with 149 rounds; 10 external hardpoints with provision for 6,000kg (13,228kg) of stores, including AA-10A ('Alamo-A'), AA-10B ('Alamo-B'), AA-10C ('Alamo-C'), AA-11 ('Archer') or AA-8 ('Aphid') air-to-air missiles

Supermarine Swift FR.Mk 5

Designed by a Supermarine team that had cut its teeth on the Spitfire and the Attacker, the Swift had a problematic development which was matched by an unfulfilled service life. The prototype 541 Swift was deficient in many respects and spring-tab ailerons prohibited supersonic dives. Later geared-tab surfaces made transonic flight possible, but control was poor about all axes and dangerous above 25,000ft. The unsuitability of the Mk 1 and 2 as interceptor aircraft led to a decision to concentrate on development of the Swift as a a tactical reconnaissance aircraft. Sixty-two FR.Mk 5 were subsequently produced with lengthened nose to accommodate three cameras, a frameless canopy, and modified wing. The aircraft equipped both No.2 and No.79 Squadrons of the 2nd Allied Tactical Air Force in Germany.

Country of origin:	UK
Type:	single-seat tactical reconnaissance aircraft
Powerplant:	one 4287kg (9450lb) Rolls-Royce Avon 114 turbojet
Performance:	maximum speed 1100km/h (685mph); service ceiling 13,690m (45,800ft); range 1014km (630 miles)
Weights:	empty 5800kg (12,800lb); maximum take-off 9,706kg (21,400lb)
Dimensions:	wingspan 9.85m (32ft 4in); length 12.88m (42ft 3in); height 3.8m (12ft 6in); wing area 45.06sq m (485sq ft)
Armament:	two 30mm Aden cannon plus provision for underwing rockets and bombs

Supermarine Scimitar F.Mk 1

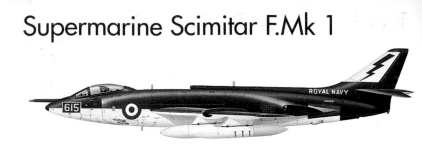

The Scimitar had an extremely protracted gestation period, explained in part by the muddled procurement programme, which in 1945 asked for naval fighters without normal landing gear to land on a flexible deck. The first prototype, the Supermarine 508, was a thin straight-winged design with a butterfly tail. This was changed to a conventional swept layout with cruciform tail on the 525, and finalised in the 544 with blown flaps, slab tail, and area-ruled body. Three prototype Type 544 aircraft were constructed, the first of which flew in January 1956. Production aircraft were delivered from August 1957, and the type became operational in June 1958 with newly-formed No. 803 Squadron. A total of 76 were built, providing the Fleet Air Arm with a capable low-level supersonic attacker until the Scimitar was superseded by the Buccaneer from 1969.

Country of origin:	UK
Type:	single-seat carrier-based multi-role aircraft
Powerplant:	two 5105kg (11,250lb) Rolls-Royce Avon 202 turbojets
Performance:	maximum speed 1143km/h (710mph); service ceiling 15,240m (50,000ft); range, clean at height 966km (600 miles)
Weights:	empty 9525kg (21,000lb); maximum take-off 15,513kg (34,200lb)
Dimensions:	wingspan 11.33m (37ft 2in); length 16.87m (55ft 4in); height 4.65m (15ft 3in); wing area 45.06sq m (485sq ft)
Armament:	four 30mm Aden cannon, four 454kg (1000lb) bombs or four Bullpup air-to-ground missiles, or four sidewinder air-to-air missiles, or drop tanks

Tupolev Tu-16 'Badger-A'

The 'Badger-A' was the first operational version of the Tu-16 medium bomber, which was designated Tu-88 in prototype form. The Tu-88 was first flown in the winter of 1952, and full-scale production commenced in 1953. Operational service with Soviet Long Range Aviation units commenced in 1955, making this perhaps the Soviet equivalent of the Boeing B-52. Technology throughout was derived directly from the Boeing B-29, which the Tupolev bureau had built in large numbers as the Tu-4. The new aircraft combined a swept wing, tricycle landing gear and indigenously produced Mikulin turbojets. The first 'Badger-A' version had a glazed nose, and is identifiable by a large radome under the nose covering the blind-bombing radar. The aircraft was supplied to Iraq, and license-built in China as the Xian H-6.

Country of origin:	USSR
Type:	medium bomber
Powerplant:	two 9500kg (20,944lb) Mikulin RD-3M turbojets
Performance:	maximum speed at 6000m (19,685ft) 960km/h (597mph); service ceiling 15,000m (49,200ft); combat range with maximum weapon load 4800km (2983 miles)
Weights:	empty 40,300kg (88,846lb); maximum take-off 75,800kg (167,110lb)
Dimensions:	wingspan 32.99m (108ft 3in); length 34.80m (114ft 2in); height 10.36m (34ft 2in); wing area 164.65sq m (1772.3sq ft)
Armament:	one forward and one rear ventral barbette each with two 23mm NR-23 cannon; two 23mm NR-23 cannon in radar-controlled tail position; internal bomb bay for up to 9000kg (19,842lb) of free-fall bombs

Tupolev Tu-16 'Badger-B'

The Tu-16 'Badger-B' was a development of the 'Badger-A', configured to carry the KS-1 Komet III (AS-1 'Kennel') air-to-surface missile on a pylon under each wing. Like the 'Badger-A' the aircraft has a fixed forward-firing cannon in the starboard side of the nose to complement the ventral, dorsal and tail turrets. A large fully retractable radar guidance radome is fitted under the central fuselage. The aircraft in service with the Soviet air armies retained their free-fall bombing capability and used on medium level area bombing in Afghanistan. Two squadrons of the aircraft were supplied to the Indonesian air force, with KS-1 Komet III (AS-1 'Kennel') ASMs for anti-ship attack. All the Indonesian aircraft, including that pictured, have been placed into long-term storage. Note the size of the AS-1 in comparison with the Tu-16.

Country of origin:	USSR
Type:	medium bomber and missile-launch platform
Powerplant:	two 9500kg (20,944lb) Mikulin RD-3M turbojets
Performance:	maximum speed 960km/h (597mph); service ceiling 15,000m (49,200ft); range with maximum load 4800km (2983 miles)
Weights:	empty 40,300kg (88,846lb); maximum take-off 75,800lb (167,110lb)
Dimensions:	wingspan 32.93m (108ft 0.5in); length 34.80m (114ft 2in); height 10.82m (35ft 6in); wing area 164.65sq m (1772.34sq ft)
Armament:	seven 23mm NR-23 cannon; internal bomb bay with provision for up to 9000kg (19,842lb) of conventional or nuclear bombs; wing pylons for two KS-1 Komet III (AS-1 'Kennel') air-to-surface missiles

Tupolev Tu-16 'Badger-G'

Soviet Naval Aviation was one of the most important elements in the defensive strategy of the former USSR, and the AVMF continues to remain a highly significant today. Although the Tu-26 'Backfire-B' is the most important maritime strike and reconnaissance aircraft in current service, a version of the long-serving Tu-16 'Badger' previously formed a very important part of the fleet. AV-MF (Aviatsiya Voyenno-Morskoi Flot) operated almost every variant of the Tu-16, in ECM, surveillance/electronic intelligence, airborne tanker, and anti-shipping roles. The aircraft pictured here is a 'Badger-G' (modified), similar to the standard 'Badger-G' and thus the 'Badger-A', but optimised to carry two AS-6 'Kingfish' air-to-surface missiles on the two underwing pylons. This aircraft is in Egyptian colours and carries two AS-5 'Kelt' missiles.

Country of origin:	USSR
Type:	maritime strike/missile launch platform
Powerplant:	two 9500kg (20.944lb) Mikulin RD-3M turbojets
Performance:	maximum speed at 6000m (19,685ft) 992km/h (616mph); service ceiling 12,300m (40,350ft); combat range with 3790kg (8360lb) weapon load 5925km (3680 miles)
Weights:	empty 37,200kg (82,000lb); maximum take-off 75,000kg (165,350lb)
Dimensions:	wingspan 32.99m (108ft 3in); length 34.80m (114ft 2in); height 10.36m (34ft 2in); wing area 164.65sq m (1772.3sq ft)
Armament:	one forward and one rear ventral barbette each with two 23mm NR-23 cannon; two 23mm NR-23 cannon in radar-controlled tail position; two wing pylons with provision for two AS-6 'Kingfish' air-to-surface missiles

Tupolev Tu-16R 'Badger-D'

The Tu-16R is a maritime/electronic reconnaissance version of the Tupolev medium bomber. Two distinct types were developed. The first was based on the 'Badger-C', which has the distinctive wide nose radome in place of the glazing (codenamed 'Puff Ball' by NATO) and was the first of the anti-shipping versions. The 'Badger-D' has a similar nose radome, an enlarged chin radome, and three radomes in tandem under the weapons bay. The other Tu-16R variants, 'Badger-E' and '-F', restored the glazed nose of the 'Badger-A' aircraft on which they were based. 'Badger-E' has provision for a photo-reconnaissance pallet in the weapons bay and passive Elint capability. 'Badger-F' is similar, but usually carries underwing ESM (Electronic Signal Monitoring) pods. These aircraft were regularly encountered over the Baltic by NATO interceptor squadrons.

Country of origin:	USSR
Type:	medium bomber
Powerplant:	two 9500kg (20.944lb) Mikulin RD-3M turbojets
Performance:	maximum speed at 6000m (19,685ft) 960km/h (597mph); service ceiling 15,000m (49,200ft); combat range with maximum weapon load 4800km (2983 miles)
Weights:	empty 40,300kg (88,846lb); maximum take-off 75,800kg (167,110lb)
Dimensions:	wingspan 32.99m (108ft 3in); length 36.5m (120ft); height 10.36m (34ft 2in); wing area 164.65sq m (1772.3sq ft)
Armament:	one forward and one rear ventral barbette each with two 23mm NR-23 cannon; two 23mm NR-23 cannon in radar-controlled tail position

Tupolev Tu-22 'Blinder-A'

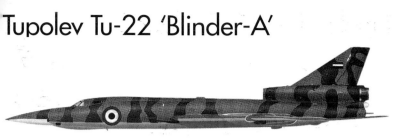

The 'Blinder-A' was produced in response to the growing capability of Western manned interceptors and surface-to-air missile systems in the early 1950s. The planners in the Soviet aviation industry were convinced that the days of the Tupolev Tu-16 as a viable strategic bomber were numbered. The result was the Tu-22, the prototype of which is believed to have flown in 1959. Western analysts were completely unaware of this aircraft until 10 took part in the 1961 air display at Tushino in 1961. This ignorance is not really surprising, as at first glance the Tu-22 appears to be of similar basic configuration to the Tu-16 with a mid-set swept wing, all-swept tail surfaces and the main units of its tricycle landing gear retracting into wing pods. However, the wing differs considerably from that of the Tu-16 in having compound sweep on the leading edge and less anhedral.

Country of origin:	USSR
Type:	medium bomber and missile-launch platform
Powerplant:	two 16,000kg (35,273lb) Koliesov VD-7M turbojets
Performance:	maximum speed 1487km/h (924mph); service ceiling 18,300m (60,040ft); range with maximum fuel 3100km (1926 miles)
Weights:	empty 40,000kg (88,185lb); maximum take-off 84,000lb (185,188lb)
Dimensions:	wingspan 23.75m (77ft 11in); length 40.53m (132ft 11.75in); height 10.67m (35ft); wing area 162sq m (1,722.28sq ft)
Armament:	one 23mm NR-23 cannon in tail turret; internal bomb bay with provision for up to 12,000kg (26,455lb) of conventional or nuclear bombs; or one AS-4 'Kitchen' air-to-surface missile semi-recessed under fuselage

Tupolev Tu-22K 'Blinder-B'

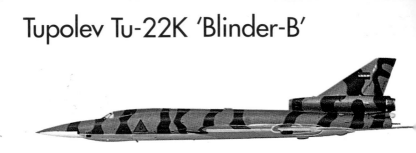

Iraq also took delivery of 12 Tu-22Ks in 1974, and subsequently used them in operations against Iran during the first Gulf War. Iran shot one down during an attack on the capital, Tehran, in 1981. The aircraft has also been used to bomb Kurdish villages accused of harbouring insurgents opposed to Saddam Hussein. The avionics fit on these aircraft was probably of a far reduced standard in comparison to the missile-carrying Soviet aircraft, and Soviet technical support was gradually withdrawn during the 1980s. In the wake of the almost wholesale destruction of the Iraqi air force during Operation Desert Storm it seems unlikely that any of the Iraqi aircraft remain operational. Note the row of windows for the navigator/systems operator in the bottom of the fuselage aft of the radome.

Country of origin:	USSR
Type:	medium bomber and missile-launch platform
Powerplant:	two 16,000kg (35,273lb) Koliesov VD-7M turbojets
Performance:	maximum speed 1487km/h (924mph); service ceiling 18,300m (60,040ft); range with maximum fuel 3100km (1926 miles)
Weights:	empty 40,000kg (88,185lb); maximum take-off 84,000lb (185,188lb)
Dimensions:	wingspan 23.75m (77ft 11in); length 40.53m (132ft 11.75in); height 10.67m (35ft); wing area 162sq m (1722.28sq ft)
Armament:	one 23mm NR-23 cannon in tail turret; internal bomb bay with provision for up to 12,000kg (26,455lb) of bombs

Tupolev Tu-22K 'Blinder-B'

The 'Blinder-B' is outwardly similar to the first production model, the 'Blinder-A', but is a more capable aircraft. The Tu-22 was originally conceived as a free-fall bomber but in 'Blinder-B' form was optimised to carry the giant AS-4 'Kitchen' missile. The missile-carrying Tu-22K also had an enlarged radome housing a 'Down Beat' missile guidance radar, and an overnose fairing housing a semi-retractable inflight refuelling probe. The weapons bay doors were cut away to allow the missile to be recessed on the centreline, and improved defensive equipment and avionics were fitted. Libya was supplied with 24 Tu-22Ks in the 1970s with no missile capability or inflight refuelling. These were used to bomb Tanzania in support of Ugandan forces, and in 1986 a single aircraft bombed N'Djamena airport in Chad in retaliation for the French raid on Ouadi Doum.

Country of origin:	USSR
Type:	medium bomber and missile-launch platform
Powerplant:	two 16,000kg (35,273lb) Koliesov VD-7M turbojets
Performance:	maximum speed 1487km/h (924mph); service ceiling 18,300m (60,040ft); range with maximum fuel 3100km (1926 miles)
Weights:	empty 40,000kg (88,185lb); maximum take-off 84,000kg (185,188lb)
Dimensions:	wingspan 23.75m (77ft 11in); length 40.53m (132ft 11.75in); height 10.67m (35ft); wing area 162 sq m (1,722.28 sq ft)
Armament:	one 23mm NR-23 cannon in tail turret; internal bomb bay with provision for up to 12,000kg (26,455lb) of conventional or nuclear bombs; or one AS-4 'Kitchen' air-to-surface missile semi-recessed under fuselage

Tupolev Tu-22R 'Blinder-C'

First identified at the 1961 Aviation Day at Tushino, as mentioned above, the Tu-22 was designed in the late 1950s to a Soviet air force requirement for a replacement for the Tu-16, which was effectively rendered obsolete by a new generation of Western interceptors and missile systems. The Tu-22 'Blinder' was designed to penetrate hostile airspace at high speed and high altitude. The rear-mounted engines reduce the aerodynamic drag penalties imposed by long inlet ducts. The aircraft entered service as the Tu-22, with the NATO reporting name 'Blinder-A', in the early 1960s. The Tu22R 'Blinder-C' was a dedicated maritime reconnaissance version of similar configuration to the 'A' with cameras and sensors in the weapons bay, inflight refuelling capability. Approximately 60 were built, but fewer than 20 now remain in service with naval aviation units.

Country of origin:	USSR
Type:	long-range maritime reconnaissance/patrol aircraft
Powerplant:	two (estimated) 14,028kg (26,455lb) Koliesov VD-7 turbojets
Performance:	maximum speed 1487km/h (924mph); service ceiling 18,300m (60,040ft); combat radius with internal fuel 3100km (1926 miles)
Weights:	empty 40,000kg (88,185lb); maximum take-off 84,000kg (185,188lb)
Dimensions:	wingspan 23.75m (77ft 11in); length 40.53m (132ft 11.75in); height 10.67m (35ft); wing area 162sq m (1722.28sq ft)
Armament:	one 23mm NR-23 two-barrell cannon in radar-controlled tail barbette; internal weapons bay with provision for 12,000kg (26,455lb) of stores, including nuclear weapons and free-fall bombs, or one AS-4 carried semi-recessed under the fuselage

Tupolev Tu-22M 'Backfire-A'

The Tu-22M 'Backfire' began life as a swing-wing derivative of the Tu-22 'Blinder' supersonic bomber and maritime patrol aircraft. The inability of this aircraft to fly strategic missions to the US (because of short range) led the Tupolev bureau to produce the 'Backfire-A' prototype (designated Tu-22M). Evaluation of this aircraft revealed that the aircraft fell far short of expectations, both in terms of speed and range, leading to the major design revisions incorporated on the Tu-22M-2. This aircraft entered service in 1975 and has the NATO reporting name 'Backfire-B'. Some 360 were produced in M-2 and M-3 configuration for Long Range Aviation and Naval Aviation units and are expected to remain in service well into the next decade. The light-blue two-tone colour scheme has been retained since the disbandment of the Soviet Union.

Country of origin:	USSR
Type:	medium strategic bomber and maritime reconnaissance/patrol aircraft
Powerplant:	two (estimated) 20,000kg (44,092lb) Kuznetsov NK-144 turbofans
Performance:	maximum speed 2125km/h (1321mph); service ceiling 18,000m (59,055ft); combat radius with internal fuel 4000km (2485 miles)
Weights:	maximum take-off 130,000kg (286,596lb)
Dimensions:	wingspan 34.3m (112ft 6.5in) spread and 23.4m (76ft 9.25in) swept; length 36.9m (129ft 11in); height 10.8m (35ft 5.25in); unswept wing area 183.58sq m (1892 q ft)
Armament:	two 23mm GSh-23 two-barrell cannon in radar-controlled tail barbette; internal weapons bay with provision for 12,000kg (26,455lb) of stores, including nuclear weapons and free-fall bombs, or two AS-4 'Kitchen' missiles carried under the wings, or one AS-4 carried semi-recessed under the fuselage, or up to three AS-16 missiles

Tupolev Tu-22M-3 'Backfire C'

The latest version of the Tu-22 in service with Long Range Aviation and Naval Aviation is the M-3. This aircraft differs externally by having wedge-type air inlets, and an upturned nosecone that carries a small pod on the tip. It also has a new radar (codenamed 'Down Beat') a new tail turret and a rotary launcher in the bomb bay. The aircraft entered service with the Soviet air forces in 1985 and remains in service in large number with former Soviet states. Defensive armament is reduced to a single twin-barrel cannon, and most aircraft do not have the inflight refuelling probe of the 'Backfire-B'. About 350 entered service, 240 of them with the Dal'naya Aviatsiya (long-range aviation) and the remainder with naval aviation units. The aircraft in Soviet service were noticeably short of any markings.

Country of origin:	USSR
Type:	medium strategic bomber and maritime reconnaissance/patrol aircraft
Powerplant:	two (estimated) 20,000kg (44,092lb) Kuznetsov NK-144 turbofans
Performance:	maximum speed 2125km/h (1321mph); service ceiling 18,000m (59,055ft); combat radius with internal fuel 4000km (2485 miles)
Weights:	maximum take-off 130,000kg (286,596lb)
Dimensions:	wingspan 34.3m (112ft 6.5in) spread and 23.4m (76ft 9.25in) swept; length 36.9m (129ft 11in); height 10.8m (35ft 5.25in); unswept wing area 183.58sq m (1,892 q ft)
Armament:	one 23mm GSh-23 two-barrell cannon in radar-controlled tail barbette; internal weapons bay with provision for 12,000kg (26,455lb) of stores, including nuclear weapons and free-fall bombs, or two AS-4 'Kitchen' missiles carried under the wings, or one AS-4 carried semi-recessed under the fuselage, or up to three AS-16 missiles

Tupolev Tu-28P 'Fiddler-B'

One of family of supersonic aircraft produced by Tupolev with technology explored with the 'Backfin' aircraft, the Tu-22 was designed as a long-range all-weather interceptor for the Soviet Air Force to counter the specific threat from Western long-range missile-carrying aircraft. The two prototype aircraft were first seen publicly in 1961 with the designation Tu-102 and identified by the NATO reporting name 'Fiddler-A'. These aircraft formed the basis for the Tu-128 which entered production in the early 1960s with the designation Tu-28P. These aircraft were not revealed until the 1967 Aviation Day, after which they were allocated the NATO name 'Fiddler-B'. The crew of two are accommodated in tandem cockpits, in what is still the largest interceptor aircraft ever built. All aircraft were replaced in service by 1992.

Country of origin:	USSR
Type:	long-range all-weather interceptor
Powerplant:	two 11,200kg (24,690lb) Lyul'ka AL-21F turbojets
Performance:	maximum speed at 11,000m (36,090ft) 1850km/h (1,150mph); service ceiling 20,000m (65,615ft); combat range with internal fuel 5000km (3105 miles)
Weights:	empty 25,000kg (55,125lb); maximum take-off 40,000kg (88,185lb)
Dimensions:	wingspan 18.10m (59ft 4.5in); length 27.20m (89ft 3in); height 7m (23ft)
Armament:	four wing pylons for four AA-5 'Ash' long-range air-to-air missiles

Tupolev Tu-160 'Blackjack-A'

The most recent and undoubtedly formidable aircraft to have emerged from the Tupolev Design Bureau is the Tu-160 long-range strategic bomber. Comparable too although much larger than the Rockwell B1-B Lancer, the aircraft has variable-geometry outer wings and two pairs of afterburning turbofans in underwing nacelles. It is optimised for high-level penetration but also has a low-level terrain-following capability, and has a higher maximum speed and greater unrefuelled range than the B-1. Production of the aircraft, which entered service in 1988, has been curtailed by arms limitation agreements. Those in service have suffered from serviceability problems and flight control system difficulties. With the change in strategic emphasis for the CIS, the Tu-160 is likely to have a short service life.

Country of origin:	USSR
Type:	long-range stategic penetration bomber and missile platform
Powerplant:	four 25,000kg (55,115lb) Kuznetsov NK-321 turbofans
Performance:	maximum speed at 11,000m (36,090ft) 2000km/h (1243mph); service ceiling 18,300m (60,040ft); combat range with internal fuel 14,000km (8699 miles)
Weights:	empty 118,000kg (260,140lb); maximum take-off 275,000kg (606,261lb)
Dimensions:	wingspan 55.70m (182ft 9in) spread and 35.60m (116ft 9.75in) swept; length 54.10m (177ft 6in); height 13.10m (43ft); wing area 360sq m (3875sq ft)
Armament:	provision for up to 16,500kg (36,376lb) of stores in two internal weapons bays and on hardpoints under wings; including nuclear and/or free-fall bombs, and/or missiles including up to 12 RK-55 (AS-15 'Kent') cruise missiles or 24 RKV-500B (AS-16 'Kickback') short-range attack missiles

VFW-Fokker Vak 191B

In the late 1960s the West German company Flugtechnische Werke GmBh went into partnership with the Dutch Fokker company. One of the first aircraft they planned to produce was the VAK 191B V/STOL reconnaissance/strike aircraft, which bears interesting comparison to both the Yak-38 'Forger' and BAe (HS) Harrier. The 191B was one of the most ambitious programmes undertaken by the post-war German aviation industry. The design was a fairly conventional swept-wing monoplane configuration, with a high-seat wing , bicycle-type undercarriage with retracting outriggers in the wingtips. Power was provided by two Rolls-Royce lift jets and a Rolls-Royce/MTU vectored/thrust turbofan for forward propulsion. The first of three prototype aircraft flew in 1971, but the small wing proved a hindrance to Short Take-Off and Landing performance and the project was terminated in the mid-1970s.

Country of origin:	Germany/Holland
Type:	experimental V/STOL aircraft
Powerplant:	two Rolls-Royce R.B 162-81 lift jets and one Rolls-Royce/MTU R.B 193-12 vectored/thrust turbofan for forward propulsion.
Performance:	maximum speed (est) 1046km/h (650 mph); service ceiling (est) 15,250m (50,000ft); range with maximum fuel after vertical take-off 500km (311 miles)
Weights:	maximum vertical take-off 8000kg (17,625lb)
Dimensions:	wingspan 6.16m (20ft); length 13m (42ft 0.5in); height 4m (13ft)

Vickers Valiant B.Mk 1

Although designed to the same B.35/46 specification as the Avro Vulcan and Handley Page Victor, the prototype Vickers 660 did not fully meet the detailed requirements of that document. However, the fact that it could be rapidly put into production and represented a lower risk than the radical Vulcan or Victor encouraged the government to order it under the reduced specification B.9/48. The prototype 660 first flew in May 1951; the first pre- production aircraft flew in December 1953, and service deliveries commenced in August the following year. Most aircraft were finished in white anti-flash paint and had an extended tailcone housing avionics. The aircraft were active during the Suez campaign. They conducted all live trails with British air-dropped nuclear weapons, but were assigned to low-level missions in 1963. The whole fleet was scrapped a year later.

Country of origin:	United Kingdom
Type:	strategic bomber
Powerplant:	four 4559kg (10,050lb) Rolls-Royce Avon 204 turbojets
Performance:	maximum speed at high altitude 912km/h (567mph); service ceiling 16,460m (54,000ft); maximum range 7242km (4,500 miles)
Weights:	empty 34,4191kg (75,881lb); maximum loaded with drop tanks 79,378kg (175,000lb)
Dimensions:	wingspan 34.85m (114ft 4in); length 33m (108ft 3in); height 9.8m (32ft 2in); wing area 219.43sq m (2,362sq ft)
Armament:	internal weapons bay with provision for up to 9525kg (21,000lb) of conventional or nuclear weapons

Vought A-7D Corsair II

Though derived from the Vought F-8 Crusader, the Corsair is a totally different aircraft. By restricting performance to high subsonic speed it was possible to reduce structural weight dramatically, and correspondingly the range increased dramatically and weapon load multiplied by nearly four times. Development was impressively rapid; the first flight was made in September 1965 and just over two years later the first A-7A aircraft were used in action in the Gulf of Tonkin. During the Vietnam War the 27 squadrons equipped with the A-7 flew more than 90,000 combat missions. Although predominantly a naval aircraft, the USAF also decided to adopt the A-7. The A-7D was a version with a Rolls-Royce Spey derived Allison engine, M61 cannon armament, inflight refuelling capability, advanced nav/attack systems and (from 1978) laser tracker. The aircraft retired in 1993.

Country of origin:	USA
Type:	single-seat attack aircraft
Powerplant:	one 6465kg (14,250lb) Allison TF41-1 (Rolls-Royce Spey) turbofan
Performance:	maximum speed at low-level 1123km/h (698mph); combat range with typical weapon load 1150km (4100 miles)
Weights:	empty 8972kg (19,781lb); maximum take-off 19,050kg (42,000lb)
Dimensions:	wingspan 11.8m (38ft 9in); length 14.06m (46ft 1.5in); height 4.9m (16ft 0.75in); wing area 34.84sq m (375sq ft)
Armament:	one 20mm M61 Vulcan with 1000 rounds, external pylons with provision for up to 6804kg (15,000lb) of stores, including guided and conventional bombs, cluster bombs, napalm tanks, air-to-surface missiles, and drop tanks

Vought A-7H Corsair II

A number of nations expressed interest in the Vought A-7 at an early stage in the programme but the first foreign nation to take delivery of the fighter was Greece. Sixty single-seat versions of the A-7E, designated A-7H, were delivered from new in the early 1970s. These deliveries were completed by 1977. The Greek air force has three A-7 squadrons, serving with two wings. The 115 Pterix Mahis is based at Souda Bay in Crete with two squadrons, 340 and 345 Mire Diesos. The A-7H aircraft are used in both ground attack and air-defence roles, and may be equipped with AIM-9L Sidewinder. The remaining squadron is 347 Mira Dioseos based at Larissa as part of 110 Pterix. These aircraft are used for the tactical air support of maritime operations. The Corsairs in Greek service will remain on duty well into the next century.

Country of origin:	USA
Type:	single-seat tactical fighter
Powerplant:	one 6804kg (15,000lb) Allison TF-41-A-400 turbofan
Performance:	maximum speed at sea level 1112km/h (691mph); service ceiling 15,545m (51,000ft); range with typical load 1127km (700 miles)
Weights:	empty 8,841kg (19,490lb); maximum take-off 19,051kg (42,000lb)
Dimensions:	wingspan 11.81m (38ft 9in); length 14.06m (46ft 1in); height 4.90m (16ft); wing area 34.84 sq m (375 sq ft)
Armament:	one 20-mm M61A1 multi-barrelled cannon; eight external pylons with provision for up to 6804kg (15,000lb) of stores, including bombs, cluster bombs, rocket pods and/or air-to-air missiles

Vought F-8D Crusader

In 1955, Vought began the development of a totally new Crusader. Designated XF8U-3 Crusader III, the three prototypes of this aircraft were powered with various J75 engines developing up to 13,064kg (28,800lb) of thrust. The aircraft were able to fly at 2543km/h (1580mph) at a height of up to 21,335m (70,000ft), but to the eternal regret of many US Navy aviators, the potentially world-beating aircraft was rejected in favour of the Phantom II. Vought continued to take the F-8 through various stages of development, hardly altering the airframe at each stage, but steadily improved the aircraft so that it remained competitive. The most potent of all these versions was the F-8D, with J57-P-20 turbojet, extra fuel in place of the underfuselage Zuni rocket pack and new radar for a specially produced radar-homing AIM-9C Sidewinder air-to-air missile. A total of 152 F-8Ds were produced.

Country of origin:	USA
Type:	single-seat carrier-based fighter
Powerplant:	one 8165kg (18,000lb) Pratt & Whitney J57-P-20 turbojet
Performance:	maximum speed at 12,192m (40,000ft) 1975km/h (1227mph); service ceiling about 17,983m (59,000ft); combat radius at high altitude 966km (600 miles)
Weights:	empty 9038kg (19,925lb); maximum take-off 15,422g (34,000lb)
Dimensions:	wingspan 10.72m (35ft 2in); length 16.61m (54ft 6in); height 4.8m (15ft 9in);
Armament:	four 20mm Colt Mk 12 cannon with 144 rpg, up to four Motorola AIM-9C Sidewinder air-to-air missiles; or two AGM-12A or AGM-12B Bullpup air-to-surface missiles

Vought F-8E Crusader

The final version in the highly successful Crusader family was introduced at a high when the McDonnell F-4 Phantom II was the yardstick against which all other fighter aircraft were measured. Nonetheless, Vought managed to secure a contract for 286 F-8Es, mainly due to the enhanced air combat capability that was afforded by the Magnavox APQ-94 radar (also fitted to the F-8D). Just above the enlarged radome to cover this unit was an AAS-15 heat- seeker pod slaved to the IR heads of the missiles, ensuring a high kill ratio. Fairly early in the production run two large underwing pylons were added for air-to-surface weapons, together with guidance electronics in a shallow dorsal blister. In total, Vought delivered 1,261 Crusaders, which remained in production for eight years. The final series of 48 F-8E (FN) were delivered in 1965 for use on board the carriers *Foch* and *Clemenceau*.

Country of origin:	USA
Type:	single-seat carrier-based fighter
Powerplant:	one 8165kg (18,000lb) Pratt & Whitney J57-P-20 turbojet
Performance:	maximum speed at 12,192m (40,000ft) 1800km/h (1120mph); service ceiling about 17,983m (59,000ft); combat radius at high altitude 966km (600 miles)
Weights:	empty 9038kg (19,925lb); maximum take-off 15,422g (34,000lb)
Dimensions:	wingspan 10.72m (35ft 2in); length 16.61m (54ft 6in); height 4.8m (15ft 9in);
Armament:	four 20mm Colt Mk 12 cannon with 144 rpg, up to four AIM-9 Sidewinder air-to-air missiles; or 12 250lb bombs or eight 500lb bombs; or eight Zuni rockets; or two AGM-12A or AGM-12B Bullpup air-to-surface missiles

Vought F-8E (FN) Crusader

Despite failing to win export contracts for the F-8 Crusader from the Royal Navy, or for a two-seat version for the US Navy, Vought did manage to clinch a deal with the French Aéronavale for a version of the F-8E, even though her carrier's *Foch* and *Clemenceau* were thought to be too small for such aircraft. To create the F-8E (FN) Vought redesigned the wing and tail to provide greater lift and to improve low-speed handling. The first FN flew on June 26, 1964, and all 42 had been delivered by the following January. Nearly 25 years after entering service, *Clemenceau*'s aircraft were involved in the Gulf War. The aircraft were slightly modified during the mid-1990s to maintain their combat-capability until the Dassault Rafale-M entered service. The aircraft pictured was operated by Flottille 12F of the Aéronavale.

Country of origin:	USA
Type:	single-seat carrier-borne interceptor and attack aircraft
Powerplant:	one 8165kg (18,000lb) Pratt & Whitney J57-P-20A turbojet
Performance:	maximum speed at 10,975m (36,000ft) 1827km/h (1135mph); service ceiling 17,680m (58,000ft); combat radius 966km (600 miles)
Weights:	empty 9038kg (19,925lb); maximum take-off 15,420kg (34,000lb)
Dimensions:	wingspan 10.87m (35ft 8in); length 16.61m (54ft 6in); height 4.80m (15ft 9in); wing area 32.51sq m (350sq ft)
Armament:	four 20-mm M39 cannon with 144 rpg; external pylons with provision for up to 2268kg (5000lb) of stores, including two Matra R530 air-to-air missiles or eight 5in rockets

Vought F-8H Crusader

Most F-8s underwent considerable alterations and improvement programs during their service lives. Total Crusader flight time passed 3,000,000 hours in the late-1970s, making this one of the most cost-effective post-war fighter series. The French Navy operated the type well into the 1990s, until its much upgraded F-8E (FN) aircraft were replaced by the Dassault Rafale. From 1966 to 1970 Vought actually remanufactured no fewer than 551 Crusaders to a wide number of configurations. One of the most numerous of these 'new' aircraft was the F-8H, of which 89 were remanufactured. These were F-8D models with reinforced airframe, blown flaps, and a host of new avionics. These aircraft actually scored more air-to-air combat victories over North Vietnamese MiGs than the F-4, but achieved less fame. In 1975 the Philippines Air Force received a squadron of fully refurbished F-8Hs.

Country of origin:	USA
Type:	single-seat carrier-based fighter
Powerplant:	one 8165kg (18,000lb) Pratt & Whitney J57-P-20 turbojet
Performance:	maximum speed at 12,192m (40,000ft) 1800km/h (1120mph); service ceiling about 17,983m (59,000ft); combat radius at high altitude 966km (600 miles)
Weights:	empty 9038kg (19,925lb); maximum take-off 15,422g (34,000lb)
Dimensions:	wingspan 10.72m (35ft 2in); length 16.61m (54ft 6in); height 4.8m (15ft 9in);
Armament:	four 20mm Colt Mk 12 cannon with 144 rpg, up to four AIM-9 Sidewinder air-to-air missiles; or 12 250lb bombs or eight 500lb bombs; or two AGM-12A or AGM-12B Bullpup air-to-surface missiles

Xian H-6IV

The Xian H-6 is a direct copy of the Tu-16 'Badger-A', and forms the backbone of the Chinese bomber fleet. Plans were were well underway to license-build the aircraft in China until the political break with Moscow in 1960. The programme restarted in 1962 without Soviet assistance, but nevertheless deliveries of the Xian H-6 began in 1963 to the Chinese air force. The aircraft is powered by a copied version of the Mikulin RD-3M engine, built at Xian as the Wopen-8. The aircraft are configured primarily for air-dropping nuclear weapons, and were heavily involved in the Chinese nuclear test programme at Lop Nur. Avionics fit is different to Soviet aircraft, a large drum type chin radar is fitted and the fixed forward gun is deleted. The aircraft pictured is one of approximately 150 in service, painted in anti-flash white paint and carrying a pair of C-601 air-to-surface missiles.

Country of origin:	China
Type:	medium bomber and missile-launch platform
Powerplant:	two 9500kg (20,944lb) Wopen-8 turbojets
Performance:	maximum speed 960km/h (597mph); service ceiling 15,000m (49,200ft); range with maximum load 4800km (2983 miles)
Weights:	empty 40,300kg (88,846lb); maximum take-off 75,800kg (167,110lb)
Dimensions:	wingspan 32.93m (108ft 0.5in); length 34.80m (114ft 2in); height 10.82m (35ft 6in); wing area 164.65sq m (1,772.34sq ft)
Armament:	six cannon; internal bomb bay with provision for up to 9000kg (19,842lb) of conventional or nuclear bombs; wing pylons for two C-601 air-to-surface missiles

Yakovlev Yak-26 'Mandrake'

Few details of this secretive aircraft, the Soviet equivalent of the Lockheed U-2, have emerged despite the end of Cold War hostilities. Stemming directly from the Yak-25R reconnaissance aircraft, the two aircraft share a similar fuselage and radome. The tandem seat cockpit on the Yak-25 'Flashlight' was reconfigured to a single-seat and the 'Mandrake' has a completely new long, unswept wing that was obviously designed for high-altitude operations. Bicycle type undercarriage is employed with twin outriggers mounted in wing-tip pods. Service entry was around 1957, and the aircraft was involved in operations over Eastern Asia, the Middle East and along the borders of communist territory before being retired in the early 1970s. Its replacement was the MiG-25 'Foxbat'. The aircraft pictured is preserved at the Monino Museum outside Moscow.

Country of origin:	USSR
Type:	single-seat high-altitude reconnaissance aircraft
Powerplant:	two 2803kg (6173lb) Tumanskii RD-9 turbojets
Performance:	maximum speed at altitude 755km/h (470mph); service ceiling about 19,000m (62,000ft); range 4000km (2500 miles)
Weights:	empty 8165kg (18,000lb); maximum take-off 13,600kg (30,000lb)
Dimensions:	wingspan 22m (71ft); length 15.5m (51ft); height 4m (13ft)

Yakovlev Yak-28P 'Firebar'

The Yak-28P two-seat all-weather interceptor has a generally similar configuration to the earlier Yak-25/26 family, but has a high shoulder-set wing with the leading edge extended further forward, a taller fin and rudder, revised powerplant in different underwing nacelles and different nosecone. The Yak-28 was designed in the late 1950s as a multi-role aircraft and was produced in tactical attack, ('Brewer-A, -B and -C), reconnaissance (Yak-28R 'Brewer-D'), electronic counter-measures (Yak-28E 'Brewer-E'), and trainer versions (Yak-28U 'Maestro') alongside the Yak-28P 'Firebar'. The suffix 'P' indicates that the design was adapted to the interceptor role, rather than designed only for it from the outset. After introduction of the type in 1962, approximately 60 remained in service in 1990 and all have now been withdrawn.

Country of origin:	USSR
Type:	two-seat all-weather interceptor
Powerplant:	two 6206kg (13,669lb) Tumanskli R-11 turbojets
Performance:	maximum speed 1180km/h (733mph); service ceiling 16,000m (52,495ft); maximum combat radius 925km (575 miles)
Weights:	maximum take-off 19,000kg (41,890lb)
Dimensions:	wingspan 12.95m (42ft 6in); length (long-nose late production) 23m (75ft 7.5in); height 3.95m (12ft 11.5in); wing area 37.6 q m (404.74sq ft)
Armament:	four underwing pylons for two AA-2 'Atoll', AA-2-2 ('Advanced Atoll') or AA-3 ('Anab') air-to-air missiles

Yakovlev Yak-38 'Forger-A'

Apart from the Harrier family of aircraft, the Yak-38 is the only other operationa jet VTOL aircraft in the world, albeit a far less capable one. Development of th Yak-36MP prototype began in the late 1960s and operational service began in 1976 Unlike the Harrier, the Yak-38 uses two fixed turbojets mounted in tandem behind the cockpit for lift, which have auxiliary inlets on the top of the fuselage. These ar augmented by a third vectoring thrust unit in the rear fuselage which is used for level flight. The wing folds at mid-span for carrier stowage, and at the tips there ar reaction control jets. A small tailcone at the rear has a reaction control nozzle on either side. Although VTOL operations are possible, a short take-off run with both lift jets operative for the carriage of a useful weapon load. Production has been limited to about 90 aircraft, and as many as 37 of these have been lost in accidents

Country of origin:	USSR (CIS)
Type:	V/STOL carrier-based fighter-bomber
Powerplant:	two 3050kg (6724lb) Rybinsk RD-36-35VFR lift turbojets; one 6950kg (15,322lb) Tumanskii R-27V-300 vectored-thrust turbojet
Performance:	maximum speed at high altitude 1009km/h (627mph); service ceiling 12,000m (39,370ft); combat range on hi-lo-hi mission with maximum weapon load 370km (230 miles)
Weights:	empty 7485kg (16,502lb); maximum take-off 11,700kg (25,795lb)
Dimensions:	wingspan 7.32m (24ft); length 15.5m (50ft 10in); height 4.37m (14ft 4in); wing area 18.5sq m (199.14sq ft)
Armament:	four external hardpoints with provision for 2000kg (4409lb) of stores, including air-to-air missiles, air-to-surface missiles, bombs, rocket-launcher pods, cannon pods, and drop tanks

Yakovlev Yak-41 'Freestyle'

As is so often the case with modern combat aircraft, the replacement for the Yak-38 was in the planning stage before the aircraft had even entered service. The first of two prototype aircraft flew in March 1989, with the bureau designation Yak-141. Yakovlev experienced severe funding difficulties with the project despite the fact that by 1991 the aircraft had taken almost all the FIA V/STOL records from the Harrier. The problems worsened when the second prototype was badly damaged while landing on the carrier Gorshkov in 1991 The first prototype is still being developed. It has a single vectoring thrust engine, augmented by a pair of lift jets mounted in tandem. Control is via a triplex digital fly-by-wire system, which it is claimed gives a degree of manoeuvrability comparable to the MiG 29. The aircraft boasts other advanced avionics, including the sighting system of the Su-27.

Country of origin:	USSR (CIS)
Type:	V/STOL carrier-based fighter-bomber
Powerplant:	two 4264kg (9392lb) RKBM RD-41 lift turbojets; one 10,989kg (24,206lb) MNPK 'Soyuz' R-79V-300 vectored-thrust turbojet
Performance:	maximum speed at 11,000m (36,090ft) 1800km/h (1,118mph); service ceiling 15,000m (49,215ft); combat range after STO 1400km (870 miles)
Weights:	maximum take-off 19,500kg (42,989lb)
Dimensions:	wingspan 10.1m (33ft 1.75in); length 18.3m (60ft); height 5m (16ft 5in)
Armament:	one 30mm GSh-30-1 cannon with 120rds; four wing hardpoints with provision for up to 2600kg (5732lb) of stores, including air-to-air missiles such as AA-10 'Alamo', AA-11 'Archer', or Vympel AAM-AE, plus air-to-surface missiles, bombs, rocket-launcher pods, cannon pods; 5th under-fuselage point for a drop tank

Glossary

AAM: Air-to-Air Missile

ADV: Air Defence Variant

AEW: Airborne Early Warning

AFB: Air Force Base

AGM: Air-to-Ground Missile

ASM: Anti-Ship Missile

AMRAAM: Advanced Medium-Range Air-to-Air Missile

ANG: Air National Guard

Avionics: any electronic system used to control the working of an aircraft

Cluster bomb: an air-delivered, free-fall weapon that contains numerous small submunitions or bomblets

Conventional weapons: non-nuclear weapons

Doppler radar: radar that utilises the Doppler effect (the frequency shift in propagated electromagnetic energy caused by the relative motion of the source of the energy and of a reflecting object, i.e. the target)

Drop tank: additional fuel tank that can be jettisoned when empty

ECM: Electronic Countermeasures

Elint: Electronic intelligence

EW: Electronic Warfare

Hardpoint: a reinforced position in the wings or fuselage of an aircraft, to which external loads can be attached

HUD: Head-Up Display

IDF: Israeli Defence Forces

IFF: Identification, Friend or Foe

IR: Infra-Red

JASDF: Japanese Air Self Defence Force

Luftwaffe: German Air Force

MAC: Military Airlift Command

n/a: not available

Napalm: Napthenic Acid and Palmitate, a jellied incendiary used as a filler for bombs

NATO: North Atlantic Treaty Organisation

RAF: Royal Air Force

rpg: rounds per gun

SAAF: South African Air Force

SAC: Strategic Air Command

SRAM: Short Range Attack Missile

STOL: Short Take-Off and Landing

USAF: United States Air Force

USMC: United States Marine Corps

V/STOL: Vertical/Short Take-Off and Landing

Index